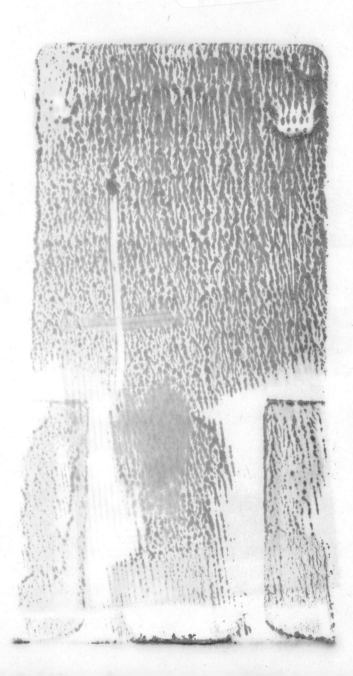

LECTURES ON THE
PHILOSOPHY OF RELIGION

LECTURES

ON THE

PHILOSOPHY OF RELIGION

TOGETHER WITH A WORK ON THE PROOFS
OF THE EXISTENCE OF GOD

By GEORG WILHELM FRIEDRICH HEGEL

TRANSLATED FROM THE SECOND GERMAN EDITION

By THE REV. E. B. SPEIRS, B.D., AND
J. BURDON SANDERSON

THE TRANSLATION EDITED

By THE REV. E. B. SPEIRS, B.D.

IN THREE VOLUMES
VOL. III

NEW YORK
HUMANITIES PRESS INC.

This edition first published in the U.S.A. 1962
Reprinted 1968

Printed in Great Britain

CONTENTS

PART III

LECTURES ON THE PROOFS OF THE EXISTENCE OF GOD

THE PHILOSOPHY OF RELIGION

PART III

THE ABSOLUTE RELIGION—(Continued)

C.

THE DIVISION OF THE SUBJECT.

I. The absolute, eternal Idea is, in its essential existence, in and for itself, God in His eternity before the creation of the world, and outside of the world.

II. *The Creation of the World.*—What is thus created, this otherness or other-Being, divides up within itself into two sides, physical Nature and finite Spirit. What is thus created is therefore an Other, and is placed at first outside of God. It belongs to God's essential nature, however, to reconcile to Himself this something which is foreign to Him, this special or particular element which comes into existence as something separated from Him, just as it is the nature of the Idea which has separated itself from itself and fallen away from itself, to bring itself back from this lapse to its truth or true state.

III. It is the way or process of reconciliation whereby Spirit unites and brings into harmony with itself what it distinguished from itself in the state of diremption and differentiation, and thus Spirit is the ˙Holy Spirit, the Spirit is present in its Church.

Thus the distinctions we make are not made in an

external fashion; but, on the contrary, the action, the developed life-force of the Absolute Spirit, is itself an eternal life; it is a development and a carrying back of this development into itself.

Put more definitely, what is involved in this idea is that the universal Spirit, the Whole which this Spirit is, posits itself together with its three characteristics or determinations, develops itself, realises itself, and that only at the end we have in a completed form what constitutes at the same time its presupposition. It exists at first as a Whole, it pre-posits or presupposes itself, and exists likewise only at the end. Spirit has thus to be considered in the three forms or elements in which it posits itself.

The three forms indicated are: eternal Being in and with itself, the form of Universality; the form of manifestation or appearance, that of Particularisation, Being for another; the form of the return from appearance into itself, absolute Singleness or individuality.

The divine Idea unfolds itself in these three forms. Spirit is divine history, the process of self-differentiation, of separation or diremption, and of the resumption of this; it is divine history, and this history is to be considered in each of these three forms.

Considered in relation to the subjective consciousness, they may further be defined as follows. The first form is the element of thought. In pure thought God is as He is in-and-for-Himself, is revealed, but He has not yet reached the stage of manifestation or appearance, He is God in His eternal essence, God abiding with Himself and yet revealed. According to the second form He exists in the element of the popular or figurative idea, in the element of particularisation. Consciousness here takes up an attitude of reserve in reference to the "Other," and this represents the stage of appearance or manifestation. The third element is that of subjectivity as such. This subjectivity is partly immediate, and takes the form of feeling, idea, sentiment; but it is also partly subjectivity which represents the Notion, thinking reason, the thought of free Spirit, which is free only when it returns into itself.

As regards place or space, the three forms, since they appear as development and history in different places, so to speak, are to be explained as follows. The divine history in its first form takes place outside of the world, outside of finitude where there is no space, representing God as He is in His essential being or in-and-for-Himself. The second form is represented by the divine history in a real shape in the world, God in definite completed existence. The third stage is represented by the inner place, the Spiritual Community, existing at first in the world, but at the same time raising itself up to heaven, and which as a Church already has Him in itself here on earth, full of grace, active and present in the world.

It is also possible to characterise the three elements, and to distinguish them in accordance with the note of Time. In the first element God is beyond time, as the eternal Idea, existing in the element of eternity in so far as eternity is contrasted with time. Thus time in this complete and independent form, time in-and-for-self, unfolds itself and breaks up into past, present, and future. Thus the divine history in its second stage as appearance is regarded as the past, it is, it has Being, but it is Being which is degraded to a mere semblance. In taking on the form of appearance it is immediate existence, which is at the same time negated, and this is the past. The divine history is thus regarded as something past, as representing the Historical properly so called. The third element is the present, yet it is only the limited present, not the eternal present, but rather the present which distinguishes itself from the past and future, and represents the element of feeling, of the immediate subjectivity of spiritual Being which is now. The present must, however, also represent the third element; the Church raises itself to Heaven too, and thus this Present is one which raises itself as well and is essentially reconciled, and is brought by means of the negation of its immediacy to a perfected form as universality, a perfection or completion which, however, does not yet exist, and which is therefore to be conceived of as future.   It is a Now of the present whose perfect stage is before it, but this perfect stage is distinguished from the particular Now which is still immediacy, and it is thought of as future.

We have, speaking generally, to consider the Idea as divine self-revelation, and this revelation is to be taken in the sense indicated by the three categories just mentioned.

According to the first of these, God exists in a pure form for the finite spirit only as thought.   This is the theoretical consciousness in which the thinking subject exists in a condition of absolute composure, and is not yet posited in this relation, not yet posited in the form of a process, but exists in the absolutely unmoved calm of the thinking spirit.   Here God is for it *thought* of, exists for thought, and Spirit thus rests in the simple conclusion that He brings Himself into harmony with Himself by means of His difference—which, however, here exists only in the form of pure ideality, and has not yet reached the form of externality—and is in immediate unity with Himself.   This is the first of these relations, and it exists solely for the thinking subject which is occupied with the pure content only.   This is the Kingdom of the Father.

The second characteristic is the Kingdom of the Son, in which God exists, in a general way, for idea or figurative thought in the element of mental pictures or representation by ideas.   This is the moment of separation or particularisation in general.   Looked at from this second standpoint, what in the first stage represented God's Other or object, without, however, being defined as such, now receives the character or determination of an

Other. Considered from the first standpoint, God as the Son is not distinguished from the Father, but what is stated of Him is expressed merely in terms of feeling. In connection with the second element, however, the Son is characterised as an Other or object, and thus we pass out of the pure ideality of Thought into the region of ordinary thought or idea. If, according to the first characterisation, God begets only one Son, here He produces Nature. Here the Other is Nature, and the element of difference thus receives its justification. What is thus differentiated is Nature, the world in general, and Spirit which is related to it, the natural Spirit. Here the element which we have already designated Subject comes in, and itself constitutes the content. Man is here involved in the content. Since Man is here related to Nature, and is himself natural, he has this character only within the sphere of religion, and consequently we have here to consider Nature and Man from the point of view of religion. The Son comes into the world, and this is the beginning of faith. When we speak of the coming of the Son into the world we are already using the language of faith. God cannot really exist for the finite spirit as such, for in the very fact that God exists for it it is directly involved that the finite spirit does not maintain its finitude as something having Being, but that it stands in a certain relation to Spirit and is reconciled to God. In its character as the finite spirit it is represented as in a state of revolt and separation with regard to God. It is thus in contradiction with what is its own object and content, and in this contradiction lies the necessity for its abolition and elevation to a higher form. The necessity for this supplies the starting-point, and the next step in advance is that God exists for Spirit, that the divine content presents itself in a pictorial form to Spirit. Here, however, Spirit exists at the same time in an empirical and finite form, and thus what God is appears to Spirit in an empirical way. Since, however, the Divine comes into view, and exists for Spirit in history of this kind, this history has no longer the character of outward history; it becomes divine history, the history of the manifestation of God Himself. This constitutes the transition to the Kingdom of the Spirit, in which we have the consciousness that Man is implicitly reconciled to God, and that this reconciliation exists for Man. The process of reconciliation itself is contained in Worship.

It has to be noted further that we do not, as we did previously, draw a distinction between Notion, Form, and Worship. It will become evident, as we go on to treat of the subject, that worship enters in directly everywhere. The following general remarks may here be made on this point. The element with which we have got to do is Spirit, and Spirit is what manifests itself, what essentially exists for self, or has actual existence, and as thus conceived of it never exists alone, but always possesses the character of something revealed, something which exists for an Other, for *its own* Other, *i.e.*, for that side of Being which is represented by the finite spirit. Worship thus is the relation of the finite spirit to the absolute Spirit, and for this reason we find that this idea of worship is present in each of these elements.

In this connection a distinction has to be drawn between the Idea as it exists in the various elements for the Notion, and the Idea as it appears in the form of ordinary conception. Religion is universal, not only for thought which is marked by culture and intellectual grasp, for the philosophical consciousness; but the truth of the Idea of God is manifest also to the ordinary consciousness which represents things pictorially by ideas, and is marked by those necessary characteristics which are inseparable from the ordinary or popular ideas of things.

I.

GOD IN HIS ETERNAL IDEA IN-AND-FOR-SELF.

Thus, regarded in the element of thought, God is, so to speak, outside of or before the creation of the world. In so far as He is thus in Himself, He represents the eternal Idea which is not yet posited in its reality, but is itself as yet merely the abstract Idea.

Thus. God in His eternal Idea still exists in the abstract element of thought, and not in that of notional comprehension. It is this pure Idea with which we are already acquainted. This is the element of thought, the Idea in its eternal presence, as it exists for free thought, whose fundamental characteristic is the untroubled light, self-identity, an element which is as yet unaffected by the presence of Being other than itself.

Within this sphere or element (1.) Determination is necessary, inasmuch as thought in general is different from thought which comprehends or grasps the process of Spirit. The eternal Idea in its essential existence, in-and-for-self, is present in thought, the Idea in its absolute truth. Religion has thus a content, and the content is an object; religion is the religion of men, and Man, besides his other qualities, is a thinking consciousness, and therefore the Idea must exist for thinking consciousness. But this is not all that Man is, for it is in the sphere of thought that he first finds his true nature, and it is only for thought that a universal object exists, only to thought can the essence of the object show itself; and since in religion God is the object, He is essentially an object for thought. He is object inasmuch as Spirit is consciousness, and He exists for thought because it is God who is the object.

For sensuous or reflective consciousness God cannot exist as God, *i.e.*, in His eternal and absolute essentiality. His manifestation of Himself is something different from this, and is made to sensuous consciousness.   If God were present only in feeling, then men would be no higher than the beasts.   It is true that He does exist for feeling too, but only in the region of appearance or manifestation.   Nor does He exist for consciousness of the rationalistic type.   Reflection is certainly thought too ; but it has at the same time an accidental character, and because of this its content is something chosen at random, and is limited.   God is certainly not a content of this kind.   He thus exists essentially for thought.   It is necessary to put the matter thus when we start from what is subjective, from Man.   But this is the very truth we reach, too, when we start from God.   Spirit exists for the spirit for which it does exist, only in so far as it reveals and differentiates itself, and this is the eternal Idea, thinking Spirit, Spirit in the element of its freedom. In this region God is the self-revealer, just because He is Spirit ; but He is not yet present as outward manifestation. That God exists for Spirit is thus an essential principle.

Spirit is what thinks.   Within this pure thought the relation is of an immediate kind, and there exists no difference between the two elements to differentiate them. Nothing comes between them.   Thought is pure unity with itself, from which all that is obscure and dark has disappeared.   This kind of thought may also be called pure intuition, as being the simple form of the activity of thought, so that there is nothing between the subject and the object, as these two do not yet really exist.   This kind of thought has no limitation, it is universal activity, and its content is no other than the Universal itself ; it is pure pulsation within itself.

2. It, however, passes further into the stage of absolute Diremption.   How does this differentiation come about ?   Thought is *actu*, unlimited.   The element of difference in its most immediate form consists in this that the two sides which we have seen to be the two sorts of modes in which the principle appears, show their dif-

ference in their differing starting-points. The one side, subjective thought, is the movement of thought in so far as it starts from immediate individual Being, and, while within this, raises itself to what is Universal and Infinite, as is the case with the first proof of the existence of God. In so far as it has arrived at the stage of the Universal, thought is unlimited ; its end is infinitely pure thought, so that all the mist of finitude has disappeared, and it here thinks God ; every trace of separation has vanished, and thus religion, thinking upon God, begins. The second side is that which has for its starting-point the Universal, the result of that first movement, thought, the Notion. The Universal is, however, in its turn again an inner movement, and its nature is to differentiate itself within itself, and thus to preserve within itself the element of difference, but yet to do this in such a way as not to disturb the universality which is also there. Here universality is something which has this element of difference within itself, and is in harmony with itself. This represents the abstract content of thought, and this abstract thought is the result which has followed from what has taken place.

The two sides are thus mutually opposed or contrasted. Subjective Thought, the thought of the finite spirit, is a Process too, inner mediation ; but this process goes on outside of it, or behind it. It is only in so far as subjective thought has raised itself to something higher that religion begins, and thus what we have in religion is pure motionless abstract thought. The concrete, on the other hand, is found in its Object, for this is the kind of thought which starts from the Universal, which differentiates itself, and consequently is in harmony with itself. It is this concrete element which is the object for thought, taking thought in a general sense. This kind of thought is thus abstract thought, and consequently the finite, for the abstract is finite ; the concrete is the truth, the infinite object.

3. God is Spirit ; in His abstract character He is

characterised as universal Spirit which particularises itself. This represents the absolute truth, and that religion is the true one which possesses this content.

Spirit is the process referred to; it is movement, life; its nature is to differentiate itself, to give itself a definite character, to determine itself; and the first form of the differentiation consists in this, that Spirit appears as the universal Idea itself. This Universal contains the entire Idea, but it only *contains* it, it is the Idea potentially only.

In the act of judgment or separation, the Other, what is put in contrast with the Universal, the Particular, is God as that which is distinguished from the Universal, but as implying that what is thus distinguished represents His entire Idea in-and-for-itself. Thus these two characteristics mean the same thing in reference to each other—mean that there is an identity between them, that they are one, that this difference is not merely done away with implicitly and that we are merely aware of this, but that the fact of their being the same has been brought forward into actuality or posited, and that these differences are done away with in so far as this differentiation just means that the difference is actually shown to be no difference, and thus the One is at home with itself in the Other.

The fact that this is so is just what is meant by Spirit, or, expressed in terms of feeling, by eternal Love. The Holy Spirit is eternal love. When we say God is love, we are expressing a very great and true thought; but it would be unreasonable merely to take this in such a simple way as a simple characterisation of God without analysing the meaning of love.

For love implies a distinguishing between two, and yet these two are, as a matter of fact, not distinguished from one another. Love, this sense of being outside of myself, is the feeling and consciousness of this identity. My self-consciousness is not in myself, but in another; but this Other in whom alone I find satisfaction and am at peace with myself—and I exist only in so far as I am at peace with myself, for if I had not this inner peace I would be the contradiction which breaks itself up into parts—this Other, just because it is outside of me, has its self-consciousness only in me. Thus the two are represented simply by this consciousness of their being outside of themselves and of their identity, and this perception, this feeling, this knowledge of the unity, is love.

God is love; *i.e.*, He represents the distinction referred to, and the nullity of this distinction, the sort of play of this act of distinction which is not to be taken seriously, and which is therefore posited as something abolished, *i.e.*, as the eternal, simple Idea.

This eternal Idea, accordingly, finds expression in the Christian religion under the name of the Holy Trinity, and this is God Himself, the eternal Triune God.

Here God exists only for the man who thinks, who keeps within the quiet of his own mind. The ancients called this enthusiasm; it is pure theoretic contemplation, the supreme repose of thought, but at the same time its highest activity manifested in grasping the pure Idea of God and becoming conscious of this Idea. The mystery of the dogma of God's nature is disclosed to men; they believe in it, and have already vouchsafed to them the highest truth, although they apprehend it only in the form of a popular or figurative idea, without being conscious of the necessary nature of this truth, and without grasping it in its entirety or comprehending it. Truth is the unveiling of what Spirit is in-and-for-itself. Man is himself Spirit, and therefore the truth exists for him. To begin with, however, the truth which comes to him does not yet possess for him the form of freedom; it is for him merely something given and received, which, however, he can receive only because he is Spirit. This truth, this Idea, has been called the dogma of the Trinity. God is Spirit, the activity of pure thought, the activity which is not outside of itself, which is within the sphere

of its own being. It was Aristotle chiefly who conceived
of God under the abstract determination of activity.
Pure activity is knowledge (in the scholastic period *actus
purus*); but in order that it may actually appear as
activity, it has to be posited in its moments or stages.
Knowledge implies the existence of an Other or object
which is consciously known, and since it is knowledge
which knows it, it is reckoned as belonging to it. This
explains how God, who represents Being in-and-for-self,
eternally produces Himself in the form of His Son, distinguishes Himself from Himself, and is the absolute act
of judgment or differentiation. What He thus distinguishes from Himself does not take on the form of something which is other than Himself; but, on the contrary,
what is thus distinguished is nothing more nor less than
that from which it has been distinguished. God is
Spirit; and no darkness, no colouring or mixture enters
into this pure light. The relation between Father and
Son is expressed in terms of organic life, and is used in
the popular or figurative sense. This natural relation is
merely pictorial, and, accordingly, never entirely corresponds to the truth that is sought to be expressed. We
say that God eternally begets His Son, that God distinguishes Himself from Himself, and thus we begin to
say of God that He does this, and that in being in the
Other whom He has brought into definite existence, or
posited, He is simply with Himself, has not gone outside
of Himself, and this is the form of love; but, at the same
time, we ought to know that God is Himself just this
entire act. God is the beginning; He does this definite
thing; but He is equally the end only, the totality, and
it is as totality that God is Spirit. God thought of
simply as the Father is not yet the True. (Thus in the
Jewish religion He is conceived of without the Son.)
He is, on the contrary, Beginning and End; He is His
own presupposition, He constitutes Himself His presupposition—this is simply another form of the fact of

differentiation—He is the eternal Process. The fact that this is the truth, and the absolute truth, appears rather in the form of something given or taken for granted. That this should be consciously known as the entire and absolute truth, the truth in-and-for-itself, is, however, just the work of philosophy, and is the entire content of philosophy. In it it is seen how all that constitutes Nature and Spirit presses forward in a dialectic form to this central point as to its absolute truth. Here we are not concerned to prove that the dogma, this silent mystery, is the eternal Truth. That is done, as has been said, in the whole of philosophy.

By way of giving a more definite explanation of these characteristics, we may further call attention to the following points :—

(*a*.) When the intention is to express what God is, the attributes are what is first thought of. These attributes are God ; He is defined by means of predicates, and this is a mode of expressing the truth which is characteristic of the ordinary thought, of the understanding. Predicates are definite characteristics, particularisations, such as goodness, almighty power, &c.

The predicates certainly do not represent natural immediacy, but have got a permanence by means of reflection, and in this way the definite content which they represent has become immovably fixed in itself, exactly as is the natural content by means of which God is represented in the religion of Nature. Natural objects, such as the sun, the sea, &c., *are*, they exist ; but the determinations of reflection are as much self-identical as is natural immediacy.

As Orientals have a feeling that this is not the true mode of expressing the nature of God, they say that He is πολυώνυμος, that His nature cannot be exhausted by predicates, for names are in this connection the same as predicates.

What is really defective in this way of defining God

by means of predicates is that these predicates are only
particular characterisations, and that there are many such
particular characterisations, and that it is the subject as
essentially undifferentiated to which they are attached ;
and this explains, too, how there comes to be such an
infinite number of predicates.   Since there are particular determinations, and since these particularisations are
viewed in accordance with their determinateness, and are
made the subject of thought, they come to be in opposition
or contradiction with each other, and these contradictions
accordingly are not harmonised.

This is further seen when these predicates are taken
as expressing the relation of God to the world, and when
the world is thought of as something different from God.
Being particularisations, they cannot adequately express
His nature, and this explains that other way of considering them as expressing certain relations between God and
the world, such as the omnipresence, the infinite wisdom
of God in the world.

They do not contain the true relation of God to Himself, but to an Other, the world namely, and thus they
are limited, and in this way get to be contradictory.   We
have the feeling that God is not represented in this way
as living when so many particular features are counted
up one after the other.   Nor is the contradiction which
they involve truly harmonised by taking away their determinateness when the Understanding demands that they
should be taken merely *sensu eminentiori.*   The true
harmony or solution of the contradiction is contained in
the Idea, which is the self-determination of God to the
act of distinguishing Himself from Himself, but is at the
same time the eternal abolition of the distinction.

If the element of difference were left remaining, there
would be contradiction, and if this difference were permanent, then finitude would arise.   Both are independent
in reference to each other, and they are in relation to each
other as well.   It is not the nature of the Idea to allow

the difference to remain; but, on the contrary, its nature is just to resolve or cancel the difference. God posits Himself in this element of difference, but He also abolishes it as well.

When accordingly we attach predicates to God in such a way as to make them particular, our first concern is to harmonise this contradiction. This is an external act, the act of our reflection, and consequently, owing to the fact that it is external and takes place *in us*, and is not the content of the Divine Idea, it follows that the contradictions cannot be harmonised. The Idea in its very nature implies the abolition of the contradiction. Its essential content and nature consists in the very fact that it posits this difference and cancels it absolutely, and this represents the living nature of the Idea itself.

(*b.*) In the metaphysical proofs of the existence of God, we can see that, in passing from Notion to Being, the Notion is not thought of merely as Notion, but as *existing* also, as having reality. It is in connection with the standpoint with which we are now dealing, that the necessity arises of making the transition from the Notion to Being.

The divine Notion is the pure Notion, the Notion without any limitation whatsoever. The Idea implies that the Notion determines itself, and consequently posits itself as something different from itself. This is a moment or stage of the divine Idea itself, and just because the thinking, reflecting spirit has this content before it, there arises the necessity for this transition, this forward movement.

The logical element of this transition is contained in those so-called proofs. It is within the Notion itself, and with the Notion as the starting-point, and, in fact, by means of the Notion, that the transition must be made to objectivity, to Being, and this in the element of thought. This which appears in the form of a subjective necessity is content, is the *one* moment of the divine Idea itself.

When we say, God has created a world, we imply
that there has been a transition from the Notion to
objectivity, only the world is here characterised as
essentially God's Other, and as being the negation of
God, outside of God, without God, godless.   In so far as
the world is defined as this Other, the difference does
not present itself to us as being in the Notion itself or
as contained in the Notion; *i.e.*, Being, Objectivity must
be shown to be in the Notion, must be shown to exist
in the form of activity, consequence, determination of
the Notion itself.

It is thus shown, at the same time, that this is implicitly the same content, that the necessity for transition is seen in the form of the proof of the existence of
God referred to.   In the absolute Idea, in the element of
thought, God is this purely concrete Universal, *i.e.*, He
is thought of as positing Himself as an Other, but in
such a way that this Other is immediately and directly
characterised as God Himself, and the difference as being
merely ideal is directly done away with, and does not
attain to the form of externality, and this just means
that what has thus been posited as difference has been
shown to exist in and to be involved in the Notion.

It is characteristic of the logical sphere in which this
shows itself that it is the nature of every definite conception or notion to annul itself, to be its own contradiction,
and consequently to appear as its own difference, and
to posit itself as such.   Thus the Notion itself is still
affected by this element of one-sidedness and finitude,
and is something subjective; and the characteristics of the
Notion, its differences, are posited as ideal merely, and
do not actually appear in a definite form as differences.
Such is the Notion which gives itself an objective form.

When we say *God*, we speak of Him merely as
abstract; or when we say God the Father, the Universal,
we speak of Him in terms of finite existence merely.
His infinitude consists just in this, that He does away

with this form of abstract universality, of immediacy,
and in this way difference is posited; but it is just
His very nature to abolish this difference. It is consequently then only that He is truly reality, truth,
infinitude.

This Idea is the speculative or philosophical Idea,
i.e., the rational element, and inasmuch as it is reached by
thinking, it is the act of thinking upon what is rational.
Thought which is not speculative, thought which is the
product of the Understanding, is the thought which does
not get beyond difference as difference, nor beyond the
finite and the infinite. Both have an absoluteness attributed to them, and yet they are thought of as being in
relation to each other, and as so far constituting a unity,
and consequently as having in them the element of contradiction.

(*c.*) This speculative Idea stands opposed to the sense
element in thought and also to the Understanding. It is
consequently a secret or mystery to the senses and their
way of looking at things, and to the Understanding also.
For both it is a μυστήριον, *i.e.*, so far as regards what
is rational in it. The nature of God is indeed not a
mystery in the ordinary sense of the term, and least
of all in the Christian religion, for in it God has communicated the knowledge of Himself, He has shown
what He is, He has revealed Himself; but it is a mystery for sense-perception, for idea or ordinary thought,
for the senses and their way of looking at things, and
for the Understanding.

Speaking generally, the fundamental characteristic of
the sensuous is externality, the idea of things as being
outside of one another. In space the differences are
contiguous, in time they are successive. Space and
Time represent the externality in which they exist.
Thus it is characteristic of the mode of regarding things
which belongs to the senses, that differences should present themselves as lying outside of one another.

Thus, sense-knowledge is based on the idea that the differences have an independent existence and remain external to one another.

Thus, for the senses, what is in the Idea is a mystery; for in the region of the Idea, the way in which things are looked at, the relations ascribed to things, and the categories employed, are entirely different from what we have in the region of sense. The Idea is just this act of distinguishing or differentiation which at the same time gives no difference and does not hold to this difference as permanent. God beholds Himself in what is differentiated; and when in His Other He is united merely with Himself, He is there with no other but Himself, He is in close union only with Himself, He beholds *Himself* in His Other.

In connection with the senses we have something quite the reverse of this. In sense-knowledge one thing is here and another there, each passes for something independent, it does not pass for being something which is what it is because it finds itself in an Other. In the region of sense-knowledge two things cannot be in one and the same place; they are mutually exclusive.

In the Idea the differences are posited, not as exclusive, but as existing only in this mutual inclusion of the one by the other. This is the true supersensuous, not the ordinary supersensuous, which is regarded as something above; for this latter equally belongs to the region of the sensuous, in which things are outside of one another and indifferent to one another. In so far as God is characterised as Spirit, externality is done away with and absorbed, and therefore this is a mystery for sense.

This Idea is equally something beyond the grasp of the Understanding and is for it a secret, for it is the very nature of the Understanding to hold fast by and keep unchangeably to the idea that the categories of thought are absolutely exclusive and different, and that they

remain unalterably independent in relation to each other.
The Positive is not the same as the Negative, as, for
example, cause-effect.

But, so far as the Notion is concerned, it is equally
true that these differences cancel themselves. It is just
because they are differences that they remain finite, and
it is the nature of the Understanding to stick to the
finite, and even when it is dealing with the Infinite
itself it has the Infinite on the one side and the finite
on the other.

The real truth is that the finite, and the Infinite which
is put in contrast with the finite, have no true existence,
but are themselves merely transitory. So far this is a
secret for the sensuous way of conceiving of things and for
the Understanding, and they struggle against the element
of rationality in the Idea. Those who oppose the doctrine of the Trinity are men who are guided merely by
their senses and understanding.

The Understanding is equally powerless to grasp the
meaning of anything else whatever, or to get at the truth
regarding anything. Animal life also exists as Idea, as
a unity of the notion or conception of the soul and bodily
form. For the Understanding each of these exists for
itself. They are undoubtedly different, but it is equally
their nature to abolish this difference. Life is simply
this perennial process. What has life exists; it has
impulses, needs, and consequently it has within itself
difference, and this originates within it. There thus
comes to be a contradiction, and the Understanding takes
these differences as implying that the contradiction does
not cancel itself; when they are brought into relation
with each other nothing exists but just the contradiction,
which cannot be cancelled.

The contradiction is there; it cannot cease to exist if
the elements of difference are held to be perennial elements
of difference, just because it is the fact of this difference
that is insisted upon. What has life has certain needs,

and thus involves a contradiction, but the satisfaction of these is the removal of the contradiction.

In the case of impulse, in the presence of any need, I am distinguished from myself, and this within myself. But life just means the harmonising of the contradiction, the satisfying of the need, the attainment of peace, in such a way, however, that a contradiction springs up again. What we have is the alternation of the act of differentiation or contradiction, and of the removal of the contradiction.

The two are different in point of time, the element of succession is present in connection with them, and they are on that account finite. Here, too, the Understanding, in considering impulse and the satisfaction of impulse by themselves, fails to grasp the truth that in the very act of affirmation, in the very feeling of self, there is at the same time contained the negation of the feeling of self, limitation, defect, and yet I as having this feeling of self at once pass beyond this element of defect.

This is the ordinary definite idea of a μυστήριον. A mystery is also described as the incomprehensible; but it is just the Notion itself, the speculative element in thought, which is described as incomprehensible, the fact that what is rational is stated in terms of thought. It is just by means of thought that the element of difference is definitely developed.

The thinking of the impulse is merely the analysis of what the impulse is; the affirmation and the negation involved in it, the feeling of self, the satisfaction of the impulse and the impulse. To think it is just to recognise the element of difference which is in it. When, accordingly, the Understanding gets so far, it says : this is a contradiction, and it remains at this point, it holds by the contradiction in face of experience, which teaches that life itself just means the removal of the contradiction.

Thus, when the impulse is analysed, the contradiction comes to light, and then it can be said : impulse is some-

thing incomprehensible. The nature of God is equally
something incomprehensible. This Incomprehensible is
really nothing but the Notion itself, which involves the
power of differentiation, and the Understanding does not
get beyond the fact of the existence of the difference.

Thus it says : this cannot be comprehended ; for the
principle of the Understanding is abstract self-identity,
and not concrete identity, according to which these differences exist in something which is one. For the Understanding God is the One, the Essence of Essences. This
empty identity without difference is the false representation of God given by the Understanding and by modern
theology. God is Spirit, what gives itself an objective
form and knows itself in that. This is concrete identity,
and thus the Idea is also an essential moment. According
to the idea of abstract identity, on the other hand, the
One and the Other exist independently, each for itself,
and are at the same time related to each other, and
therefore we get a contradiction.

This, then, is what is called the incomprehensible.
The cancelling or resolution of the contradiction is the
Notion ; the Understanding does not get the length of
the cancelling of the contradiction, because it starts with
the presupposition of its existence ; for it the two sides
which form the contradiction are and remain in a state
of mutual independence.

One reason why it is said that the Divine Idea is
incomprehensible is that, since religion, the truth, exists
for all men, the content of the Idea appears in a sensuous form, or in the form of something which can be
grasped by the Understanding. It appears, we repeat,
in a sensuous form, and so we have the expressions
Father and Son descriptive of a relation which exists in
the sphere of life, a designation which has been adopted
from what is seen in the sense-life.

In religion the truth is revealed in accordance with
the content ; but it is something different for it to appear

in the form of the Notion, of thought, or as the Notion in a speculative form. However happily expressed those naïve forms, such as begetting, son, &c., given to faith, may be, whenever the Understanding takes them in hand and applies its categories to them, they are at once perverted, and whenever it is in the mood it does not cease to point out the contradictions involved in them. It gets the power and the right to do this from the differentiation and reflection into themselves which exist in these forms. But it is just God or Spirit who Himself abolishes these contradictions. He does not require to wait for the Understanding to remove those characteristics which contain contradiction. It is just the very nature of Spirit to remove them; and so, too, it belongs essentially to Spirit to posit these characteristics, to make distinctions within itself, to bring about this separation or diremption.

When, again, we say that the idea of God in His eternal universality implies that He differentiates Himself, determines Himself, posits something that is His Other or object, and at the same time abolishes the difference, is not outside of Himself in the difference, and is Spirit only through what He thus accomplishes, then we get another example of how the Understanding treats the question. It takes up this thought, brings its categories of finitude to bear upon it, counts one, two, three, and introduces into it the unfortunate category of number. Here, however, we have nothing to do with number; numeration is something which implies utter absence of thought, and if we introduce this category here we introduce the element of incomprehensibility.

It is possible in the exercise of Reason to make use of all the categories of the Understanding which imply relation. Reason, however, does not only use them, it destroys them, and so, too, here. This is indeed hard for the Understanding, since it imagines that because they have been made use of they have won some kind of *right* to exist. They are, however, misused when, as here, they are used in connection with the expression, three are one. It is accordingly easy to point out that there are contradictions in such ideas, differences which get the length of being opposites, and the sterile Understanding prides itself on amassing these. In all that is concrete, in all that has life, this contradiction is involved, as has been already shown. It is only the dead Understanding that is self-identical. In the Idea, on the other hand, we see the contradiction cancelled as well, and it is just this cancelling or harmonising which is spiritual unity.

To enumerate the moments of the Idea as three units appears to be something quite ingenuous and natural, and which does not require to be explained. Only, in accordance with the nature of number, which is here introduced into the matter, each characteristic gets a fixed form as one, and we are required to conceive of three units as only one unit, a demand which it is extremely hard to entertain, and which is, as is sometimes said, an utterly irrational demand.

It is the Understanding alone that is always haunted by this idea of the absolute independence of the unit or One, this idea of absolute separation and rupture. If, on the contrary, we regard the matter from the point of view of logic, we see that the One has an inner *dialectic* movement, and is not truly independent. It is only necessary to think of matter which is the true One or unity that offers resistance, but which is subject to the law of gravitation, *i.e.*, it makes an effort not to be one, and rather to do away with its state of independence, and thus confesses that this is a nullity. In fact, just because it is only matter, and continues to be the most external externality, it remains in the condition merely of something which ought to be. Matter as such is the poorest, most external, most unspiritual mode of existence; but it is gravitation, or the abolition of the oneness, which constitutes the fundamental characteristic of matter.

The idea of a unit or a One is, to begin with, something wholly abstract; these units get a still deeper meaning when they are expressed in terms of Spirit since they are characterised as persons. Personality is something which is essentially based on freedom, freedom in its first, deepest, most inward form, but also in its most abstract form as the freedom which proclaims its presence in the subject by saying, I am a person, I exist for myself. This is isolation pure and simple, a condition of pure reserve.

When, therefore, these differences are defined thus, and each is taken as a unit, or in fact as a person, owing to the infinite form according to which each moment is regarded as a subject, the difficulty of satisfying the demand of the Idea that these differences should be regarded as differences which are not different, but are purely one, and that this difference should be abolished, appears to be still more insurmountable.

Two cannot be one; each person has a rigid, reserved, independent, self-centred existence. Logic shows that the category of the unit is a poor category, a wholly abstract unit. But when we are dealing with personality, the contradiction seems to be pushed so far as to be incapable of any solution; still the solution is contained in the fact that there is only one person, and this three-fold personality, this personality which is consequently posited merely as a vanishing moment, expresses the truth that the antithesis is an absolute one, and is not to be taken as an inferior antithesis, and that it is just exactly when it has got to this point it abolishes itself. It is, in short, the nature or character of what we mean by person or subject to abolish its isolation, its separateness.

Morality, love, just mean the giving up of particularity or of the particular personality and its extension to universality, and so, too, is it with the family and friendship, for there you have the identity of the one with the other. Inasmuch as I act rightly towards another, I consider him as identical with myself. In friendship and love I give up my abstract personality, and in this way win it back as concrete personality.

It is just this winning back of personality by the act of absorption, by the being absorbed into the other, which constitutes the true nature of personality. Such forms of the Understanding directly prove themselves in experience to be of those which annul themselves.

In love, in friendship, it is the person or individual who maintains himself, and by means of love gets the subjectivity which is his personality. If here, in connection with religion, the idea of personality is clung to in an abstract way, then we get three Gods, and the infinite form, absolute negativity is forgotten, or if personality is regarded as not cancelled, then we have evil, for personality which does not yield itself up to the absolute Idea is evil. In the divine unity personality is held to be cancelled, and it is only in appearance that the negativity of personality is distinguished from that whereby it is done away with.

The Trinity has been reduced to a relation of Father, Son, and Spirit, and this is a childlike relation, a childlike natural form. The Understanding has no category, no relation which in point of suitability for expressing the truth can be compared with this. At the same time it must be understood that it is merely pictorial, and that Spirit does not actually enter into a relation of this kind. Love would be a still more suitable expression, but Spirit is the really true one.

The abstract God, the Father, is the Universal, the eternal, all - embracing, total particularity. We have reached the stage of Spirit; here the Universal includes everything within itself; the Other, the Son, is infinite particularity, manifestation; the third, the Spirit, is individuality as such. The Universal, however, as totality is itself Spirit; all three are Spirit. In the third, God is Spirit, we say, but He is presupposed to be this as well, and the third is also the first. This is a truth which

must be held to as essential. When, for instance, we
say that God, in accordance with His conception or
notion, is potentially the immediate Power which differentiates itself and returns to itself, it is implied that He
is this only as being negativity which is immediately
related to itself, *i.e.*, as absolute reflection into self, which
is just the characteristic of Spirit. Should we, accordingly, wish to speak of God as presented in His first
determination, in accordance with His Notion, and should
we wish to go on from this to the other determinations,
we are already speaking of the third ; *the last is the first.*
When, in order to avoid this, and if we begin in an
abstract way, we speak of the first only in accordance
with its own determination, or when the imperfection
of the notion renders it necessary to do this, then the
first is the Universal, and that activity, that begetting or
creating, is already a principle distinct from the abstract-
Universal, which thus appears and can appear as a second
principle, as something which manifests itself, externalises
itself (*Logos, Sophia*), just as the first exists as the abyss
of Being. This is made clear by the nature of the
Notion itself. It comes to the front in connection with
every end and with every manifestation of life. Life
maintains itself ; to maintain or preserve means to pass
into difference, into the struggle with particularity, means
that something finds itself to be distinct from inorganic
nature. Life is thus only a resultant inasmuch as it
has brought itself into being, is a product which in turn
produces ; what is thus produced is itself living, *i.e.*, it is
its own presupposition, it passes through its process, and
nothing new comes out of this ; what is produced was
already there from the beginning. The same holds true
of love and reciprocal love. In so far as love exists, it is
the beginning, and all action is merely its confirmation by
which it is at once produced and nourished. But what is
produced already exists, it is confirmation of the presence
of love, since nothing comes out of it but what is already

there. In the same way Spirit presupposes itself, it is
what begins.

The differentiation through which the Divine Life
passes is not of an external kind, but must be defined
as an inward differentiation in such a way that the First,
or the Father, is to be conceived of as the Last. The
process is thus nothing but the play of self-preservation
or self-confirmation. This characteristic is of importance
in this respect that it constitutes the criterion by which
to estimate the value of many of the popular conceptions
of God, and by which what is defective in them can be
detected and criticised, and it is specially owing to the
presence of that defective element that this characteristic
is often overlooked or misunderstood.

We are considering the Idea in its universality, as it
exists in pure thought, and as defined by means of pure
thought. This Idea is all truth and the one truth, and
consequently everything particular which is to be conceived of as true must be conceived of in accordance with
the Form of this Idea.

Nature and the finite spirit are a product of God, and
therefore possess rationality. The fact that they have
been made by God involves their having truth in themselves, divine truth in general, *i.e.*, the characteristic of
this Idea considered generally.

The Form of this Idea exists in God only as Spirit; if
the Divine Idea exists in those forms which belong to
finitude, it is not in that case posited in its true and
entire nature, in-and-for-self; it is only in Spirit that it
is so posited. In these finite forms it exists in a finite
way; but the world is something which has been produced
by God, and therefore the Divine Idea always constitutes
its basis if we consider it in a general aspect. To know
the truth regarding anything just means to know it and
define it in accordance with the form of this Idea.

In the earlier religions, particularly in the religion of
India, we have ideas which are in accord with that of the

Trinity as the true determination. This idea of threefold-
ness was actually consciously reached, the idea that the
One cannot continue to exist as One and has not the
true form it ought to have, that the One does not represent the truth except as it appears in the form of movement, of difference in general, and as standing in relation
to some other. *Trimurti* is the rudest form in which
this determination appears.

The third is not, however, Spirit, is not true reconciliation, but origination and decay, change in fact, a category
which is a unity of these differences, but represents a
union of a very subordinate kind.

It is not in immediate Appearance or manifestation,
but only when Spirit has taken up its abode in the
Church, when it is immediate, believing Spirit, and raises
itself to the stage of thought, that the Idea reaches perfection. We are interested in considering the workings
or ferment of this Idea, and in learning to recognise what
lies at the basis of the marvellous manifestations which
occur. The definition of God as the Three-in-One is one
which, so far as philosophy is concerned, has quite ceased
to be used, and in theology it is no longer seriously
adopted. In fact, in certain quarters an attempt has
been made to belittle the Christian religion by maintaining that this definition which it employs is already older
than Christianity, and that it has got it from somewhere
or other. But, to begin with, any such historical statement does not for that matter of it decide anything
whatsoever with regard to the inner truth. It must,
moreover, be understood, too, that those peoples and
individuals of former ages were not themselves conscious
of the truth which was in the idea, and did not perceive
that it contained the absolute consciousness of the truth;
they regarded it as merely one amongst other characteristics, and as different from the others. But it is a point
of the greatest importance to determine whether such a
characteristic is the first and absolute characteristic which

underlies all others, or whether it is just one form which appears amongst others, as, for instance, in the case of Brahmā, who is the One, but is not at the same time an object of worship. This form has certainly the least chance of appearing in the Religion of Beauty and in that of External Utility. In the multiplicity and particularisation which are characteristic of these religions, it is not possible to meet with the element of measure which limits itself and returns to itself. Still they are not devoid of traces of this unity. Aristotle, speaking of the Pythagorean numbers, of the triad, says : We believe that we have really called on the gods only when we have called on them three times. Amongst the Pythagoreans and in Plato we come upon the abstract basis of the Idea, but the characteristics do not in any way get beyond this condition of abstraction, and partly continue in the abstract state represented by one, two, three ; though in Plato they get a rather more concrete form, where we have described the nature of the One and the Other, that which is different in itself, θάτερον, and the third which is the unity of both.

The thought here is not of the fanciful kind which we have in the Indian religions, but is rather a mere abstraction. We have actual categories of thought which are better than numbers, better than the category of number, but which, all the same, are entirely abstract categories of thought.

It is, however, chiefly about the time of Christ's birth, and during several centuries after, that we come upon a philosophical representation of this truth in a figurative form, and which has for its basis the popular idea expressed by the Trinity. It is found partly in philosophical systems pure and simple, such as that of Philo, who had carefully studied Pythagorean and Platonic philosophy, and then in the later writers of the Alexandrian School, but more especially in a blending of the Christian religion with philosophical ideas of the kind referred to, and it is this blending of the two which constitutes in a large measure the various heresies, particularly the Gnostic heresy. Speaking generally, we see in these attempts to grasp the Idea of the Three-in-One, the reality which characterises Western thought refined away into an intellectual world through the influence of Eastern idealism. These are, to be sure, only first attempts resulting in what were merely paltry and fantastic conceptions. Still we can see in them at least the struggle of Spirit to reach truth, and this deserves recognition.

An almost countless number of forms of stating the truth may be observed here ; the First is, the Father, the Ὄν, terms which express something which is the abyss or depths of Being, *i.e.*, something, in fact, which is as yet empty, which cannot be grasped by thought, but is incomprehensible and beyond the power of any conception to express.

For what is empty, indeterminate, is undoubtedly the Incomprehensible, the negative of the Notion, and it is the nature of its notion to be this negative since it is merely one-sided abstraction, and constitutes what is merely a moment of the Notion. The One for itself, is not yet the Notion, the True.

If the First is defined as the merely Universal, and if the definitions or determinations are simply referred to the Universal, to the ὄν, then we certainly get the incomprehensible, for it is without content ; anything comprehensible is concrete, and can be comprehended only in so far as it is determined as a moment. And it is in this that the defect lies, namely, that the First is not conceived of as being by its very nature totality.

Another idea of the same kind is expressed when it is said that the First is the βυθός, the Abyss, the depths, αἰών, the Eternal, whose dwelling is in the inexpressible heights, who is raised above all contact with finite things, out of whom nothing is evolved, the First Principle, the Father of all existence, the Propator, who is a Father only mediately, the προαρχη, He who was before the beginning. The revelation of this abyss of Being, of this hidden God, is defined as self-contemplation, reflection into self, concrete determination in general; self-contemplation begets, it is, in fact, the begetting of the Only-begotten; this represents the fact that the Eternal is in process of being comprehended, because here we get the length of determination.

This Second, Other-Being or object, determination, action in short as shown in self-determination, is the most general determination, as it appears in the form of the λόγος, the activity which determines itself after the manner of reason, known also as the Word. The Word is this simple self-expression which does not make any hard and fast distinction, and does not become a hard and fast distinction, but is taken in an immediate sense, and which being thus immediate is taken up into the inner life of the Eternal, and returns to its original source. It is further expressed by the word σοφία, Wisdom, the original Man in the absolute purity of his Being, something which actually exists, and is other than that first universality—in short, a particular something with a definite character. God is the Creator, and He is this in His specific character as the Logos, as the self-externalising, self-expressing Word, as the ὅρασις, the vision of God.

This Second came to be further defined as the archetype of Man, Adam Kadmon, the Only-begotten. This does not describe some accidental characteristic, but, on the contrary, eternal action, which is not confined simply to one time. In God there is only one birth, activity in the form of eternal activity, a characteristic which essentially belongs to the Universal itself.

Here we have the true differentiation or distinction which has reference to the quality of both, but this quality is only one and the same Substance, and the difference is accordingly merely superficial as yet even when defined as a person.

The essential point is that this σοφία, the Only-begotten, remains likewise in the bosom of God, and the distinction is no real distinction.

It was in forms such as these that the Idea showed its workings. The most important point of view from which to regard the matter is that which will enable us to see that, however rude were the shapes taken by these thoughts, they are to be considered as rational, and from which we shall perceive that they are based on reason, and discover what amount of reason is in them. Still it is necessary at the same time to be able to distinguish the form of rationality which is present, and which is not yet adequate to express content.

This Idea is usually put somewhere beyond Man, beyond thought and reason, and forms an antithesis to these, so that this characteristic, which is all truth, and alone is truth, comes to be regarded as something peculiar to God only, something which remains in a region beyond human life, and does not reflect itself into its Other, which appears in the form of the world, Nature, Man. So far this fundamental idea is not regarded as the Universal Idea.

To Jacob Böhme this mystery of the threefold nature became clear in another fashion. His way of conceiving of the truth, and his style of thought, are certainly of a rather wild and fantastic sort. He did not attain to the use of the pure forms of thought, but the ruling and fundamental principle of all the ideas which fermented in his mind, and of all his struggles to reach the truth, was the recognition of the presence of Trinity everywhere and in everything, as, *e.g.*, when he says, " It must be born in the heart of Man."

It forms the universal basis of everything which is looked at in a true way, it may indeed be as finite, but still as something which even in its finitude has the truth in it. Thus Jacob Böhme attempted to represent under this category Nature and the heart or spirit of Man.

In more recent times the conception of Trinity has,

through the influence of the Kantian philosophy, been brought into notice again in an outward way as a type, and, as it were, as a ground-plan of thought, and this in very definite forms of thought. When this Idea is thus known to represent what is the one and essential nature of God, the next step is to cease to regard it as something belonging to a region above human thought and beyond this world, and to feel that the goal of knowledge is the recognition of the truth in the Particular as well, and if it is thus recognised as present in it, then all that is true in the Particular involves this determination.

To know in the philosophical sense, means to know anything in its determinateness. Its nature, however, is just the nature of the determinateness itself, and it is unfolded in the Idea. Logical exposition and logical necessity mean that this Idea represents truth in general, and that all thought-determinations can be reduced to this movement of determination.

II.

THE ETERNAL IDEA OF GOD IN THE ELEMENT OF CONSCIOUSNESS AND ORDINARY THOUGHT (*VORSTELLEN*), OR, DIFFERENCE; THE KINGDOM OF THE SON.

We have here to consider how this Idea passes out of its condition of universality and infinity into the determination or specific form of finitude. God is everywhere present, and the presence of God is just the element of truth which is in everything.

To begin with, the Idea was found in the element of thought. This forms the basis, and we started with it. The Universal, and what is consequently the more abstract, must precede all else in scientific knowledge. Looking at the matter from a scientific point of view, it is what comes first, though actually it is what comes later, so far as its existence in a definite form is concerned. It is what is potential and essential, but it is what appears later in knowledge, and reaches the stage of consciousness and knowledge later.

The Form of the Idea actually appears as a *result* which, however, is essentially *potentiality ;* and just as the content of the Idea means that the last is the first and the first is the last, so what appears as a result is the presupposition, potentiality, basis. This Idea is now to be considered as it appears in the second element, in the element of manifestation in general. In its form as objectivity, or as potential, the absolute Idea is complete; but this is not the case with the Idea in its subjective aspect, either in itself as such, or when subjectivity actually appears in the Divine Idea. The progress of the Idea here referred to may be looked at from two sides.

Looking at it from the first of these, we see that the subject for which this Idea exists is the thinking subject. Even the forms used by ordinary conception do not take anything from the nature of the fundamental form, nor hinder this fundamental form from being for man a form characterised by thought. The subject, speaking generally, exists as something which thinks, it thinks this Idea, and yet it is concrete self-consciousness. This Idea must exist for the subject as concrete self-consciousness, as an actual subject.

Or it may be put thus—the Idea in its first form is the absolute truth, while in its subjective form it exists for thought ; but not only must the Idea be truth for the subject, the subject on its part must have the certainty of the Idea, *i.e.,* the certainty which belongs to this subject as such, as finite, as a subject which is empirical, concrete, and belonging to the sphere of sense.

The Idea possesses certainty for the subject, and the subject has this certainty only in so far as the Idea is actually perceived, in so far as it exists for the subject. If I can say of anything, "that is," then it possesses certainty for me, this is immediate knowledge, this is certainty. The next form of mediation consists in proving that what is is likewise necessary, that it is true, that it is something certain. This accordingly is the transition to the Universal.

By starting from the form of truth, we have reached the definite thought that this form possesses certainty, that it exists for me.

The other mode of viewing the advance of the Idea to manifestation is to regard it from the side of the Idea itself.

1. Eternal Being, in-and-for-itself, is something which unfolds itself, determines itself, differentiates itself, posits itself as its own difference, but the difference, again, is at the same time eternally done away with and absorbed ; what has essential Being, Being in-and-for-itself, eternally returns to itself in this, and only in so far as it does this is it Spirit.

What is differentiated is determined in such a way that the difference directly disappears, and so, that this is seen to be a relation of God merely to Himself, of the Idea merely to itself. This act of differentiation is merely a movement, a playing of love with itself, in which it does not get to be otherness or Other-Being in any serious sense, nor actually reach a condition of separation and division.

The Other is defined as the Son, as love regarded from the side of feeling, or, defined from a higher point of view, as Spirit which is not outside of itself, which is with itself, which is free. In this determination, the determination of difference is not yet complete so far as the Idea is concerned. What we have here is merely abstract difference in general, we have not yet got to difference in the form which peculiarly belongs to it ; difference here is only one characteristic or determination amongst others.

In this respect we can say that we have not yet got the length of difference. The things differentiated are considered to be the same ; we have not yet reached that determination according to which the things differentiated should have a different determination. Regarded from this side, we have to think of the judgment or differentiating act of the Idea as implying that the Son gets the determination of the Other as such, that He exists as a free personality, independently or for Himself, that He appears as something real outside of and apart from God, as something, in fact, which actually is.

His ideality, His eternal return into essential Being, is posited in the Idea in its first form as immediate and identical. In order that there may be difference, and in order that it may be properly recognised, it is necessary to have the element of Otherness, necessary that what is thus distinguished should appear as Otherness which is possessed of Being.

It is only the absolute Idea which determines itself, and which, in determining itself, is inwardly certain that it is absolutely free in itself ; and in thus determining itself it implies that what is thus determined is allowed to exist as something which is free, as something independent, as an independent object. The Free exists only for the Free, and it is only for free men that an other is free too.

The absolute freedom of the Idea means that in determining itself, in the act of judgment, or differentiation, it grants the free independent existence of the Other. This Other, as something thus allowed to have an independent existence, is represented by the World taken in a general sense. The absolute act of judgment which gives independence to that aspect of Being called Other-Being might also be called Goodness, which bestows upon this side of Being in its state of estrangement the whole Idea, in so far as and in the way in which it is able to receive and represent the Idea.

2. The truth of the world is its ideality only, and does not imply that it possesses true reality ; it is involved in its

nature that it should *be*, but only in an *ideal* sense ; it is not something implicitly eternal, but, on the contrary, it is something created, its Being is something which has been merely posited, or is dependent on something else.

The Being of the world means that it has a moment of Being, but that it annuls this separation and estrangement from God, and that it is its true nature to return to its source, to get into a relationship of Spirit or Love.

We thus get the Process of the world which implies a passing from the state of revolt and separation to that of reconciliation. What first appears in the Idea is merely the relation of Father and Son ; but the Other also comes to have the characteristic of Other-Being or otherness, of something which *is*.

It is in the Son, in the determination or specifying of the difference, that an advance is made to further specification in the form of more differences, and that difference gets its rights, the right of being different. Jacob Böhme described this transition in the stage represented by the Son as follows : The first and Only-begotten was Lucifer, the light-bearer, clearness, brightness, but he imaged himself in himself, *i.e.*, posited an independent existence for himself, advanced to a condition of Being, and so to a state of revolt, and that then the eternal and Only-begotten was immediately put in his place.

Regarded from the first of the two standpoints, the relation is that God exists in His eternal truth, and this is thought of as the state of things which existed before time was, as the state in which God was when the blessed spirits and the morning stars, the angels, His children, sang His praises. The relation thus existing is described as a state, but it is an eternal relation of thought to its object. Later on a revolt occurred, as it is expressed, and this is the positing of the second standpoint, the one side of the truth represented by the analysis of the Son, the keeping apart of the two

moments which are contained in Him.   The other side,
again, is represented by subjective consciousness, the finite
spirit, and this as pure thought is regarded as implicitly
the Process which found its starting-point in the Immediate, and raised itself to the condition of truth.   This is
the second form.

We thus enter the sphere of determination, enter space
and the world of finite Spirit.   This may be more definitely expressed as a positing or bringing into view of
the determinations or specific qualities, as a difference
which is momentarily maintained ; it is an act of going
out on the part of God into finitude, an act of manifestation in finitude, for finitude taken in its proper meaning,
implies simply the separation of what is implicitly
identical, but which maintains itself in the act of
separation.   Regarded from the other side, that of subjective Spirit, this is posited as pure thought, though it
is implicitly a result, and this has to be posited as it is
potentially in its character as the movement of thought,
or, to put it otherwise, pure thought has to go into itself,
and it is in this way that it first posits itself as finite.

Regarding the matter from this standpoint, this Other
is not represented by the Son, but by the external world,
the finite world, which is outside of truth, the world of
finitude, in which the Other has the form of Being, and
is yet in its nature merely the ἕτερον, the definite, the
differentiated, the limited, the negative.

The relation of these two spheres to the first may thus
be defined by saying that it is the same Idea potentially
which is present, though with this different specific form.
The absolute act involved in that first judgment or act of
differentiation is implicitly the same as the second here
referred to ; it is only in ordinary thought that the two
are regarded as separate, as two absolutely distinct spheres
and acts.

And, as a matter of fact, they have to be distinguished and
kept separate ; and when it is said that they are implicitly

the same, we must carefully define the sense in which
this is to be understood, else we may get a false meaning
and an incorrect conception, implying that the eternal
Son of the Father, the Godhead who exists objectively
for Himself, is the same as the world, and that we are
to understand by the former nothing more than what we
mean by the latter.

It has been already remarked, and is, indeed, self-
evident, that it is only the Idea of God as previously
unfolded in what was called the first sphere which is the
true and eternal God, while His higher realisation and
manifestation in the detailed process of Spirit is what
is treated of in the third sphere.

When the world in its immediate form is taken as
something which has an essential existence of its own,
and when the sensuous and the temporal are regarded as
having Being, then either the false meaning before referred to is attached to what is thus predicated of them, or
else we are, at the very outset, forced to think of there
being two eternal acts on the part of God. God's active
working, however, is emphatically one and the same, and
does not show itself in manifold forms of varying activity, such as is expressed by the terms now, after,
separate, &c.

Thus this differentiation when it takes the form of
independence is merely the negative moment of Other-
Being in an independent form or for itself, or of Being
external to itself, which as such has no truth, but is
merely a stage, and regarded from the point of time is
merely a moment, and not even a moment, but something which possesses this kind of independence only as
contrasted with finite Spirit, inasmuch as it itself as
actually existing represents this kind and mode of independence. In God Himself this Now, this independent
existence or Being-for-self, is the vanishing moment of
manifestation.

This moment certainly now has the extension, breadth,

and depth which belong to a world; it is heaven and
earth, with all their infinite organisation, internal and
external. When, accordingly, we say that the Other is
a vanishing moment; that it is merely the gleam of the
lightning-flash, which, in appearing, directly disappears;
that it is the sound of a word, which, in being spoken
and heard, disappears so far as its outward existence is
concerned—we are very apt, when we think of things
of this transitory sort, to have always before our minds
the idea of the momentary in time, with its before and
after, and yet it *is* in neither of the two. What we have
really got to do is to get rid of that time-determination,
whether it be of duration or of the present, and merely
to keep to the simple thought of the Other, the *simple*
thought, for the Other is an abstraction. That this
abstraction has actually taken an extended form in the
world of space and time is explained by the fact that it
is the simple moment of the Idea itself, and accordingly
receives the Idea wholly into itself; but because it is the
moment of otherness or Other-Being it takes the form
of immediate, material extension.

Questions as to whether the world or matter is eternal,
and has existed from all eternity, or has begun in time,
belong to the empty metaphysics of the Understanding.
In the phrase " from all eternity," eternity itself is represented in a figurative way as infinite time, in accordance
with a false kind of infinitude, the infinitude and the
determination being those of Reflection merely. It is
the world which is really the region of contradiction ;
in it the Idea appears in a specialised form which is
inadequate to express it. As soon as the world enters
into the region of ordinary thought or figurative idea,
the element of time comes in, and next, by means of reflection, the infinitude or eternity referred to. We must,
however, understand that this characteristic in no way
applies to the Notion itself.

Another question, or what is partly the same question

with a broader meaning, is raised when it is said that
the world or matter, inasmuch as it is regarded as having
existed from all eternity, is uncreated and exists immediately for itself. The separation made by the Understanding between form and matter lies at the basis
of this statement; while the real truth is that matter
and the world, regarded according to their fundamental
characteristics, are this Other, the negative, which is
itself simply a moment or element of posited Being.
This is the opposite of something independent, and the
meaning of its existence is simply that it annuls itself
and is a moment in the Process. The natural world
is relative, it is Appearance, *i.e.*, it is this not only for us,
but implicitly, and it belongs to its quality or character
to pass over and return into the ultimate Idea. It is in
the determination of the independence of Other-Being
that all the various metaphysical determinations given
to the ὕλη amongst the ancients, and also amongst those
Christians who indulged in philosophical speculations,
the Gnostics particularly, have their root.

It is owing to the otherness or Other-Being of the
world that this latter is simply something created and
has not a complete and independent Being, Being in-and-
for-itself, and when a distinction is drawn between the
beginning as creation and the preservation of what
actually exists, this is done in accordance with the
ordinary conception which implies that such a material
world is actually present and is possessed of real Being.
It has always been correctly held that since the world
does not possess Being, an independence belonging to it
in virtue of its own nature, preservation is a kind of
creation. But if we can say that creation is also
preservation, we would express ourselves thus merely in
virtue of the fact that the moment of Other-Being is
itself a moment of the Idea, or else it would be
presupposed, as was done previously, that something
possessed of Being preceded the act of creation.

Thus inasmuch as Other-Being has been characterised as the totality of appearance or manifestation, it expresses in itself the Idea, and it is this which is really designated by the term, the wisdom of God.   Wisdom is, however, so far a general expression, and it is the business of philosophical knowledge to understand this conception in Nature, to conceive of it as a system in which the Divine Idea is mirrored.   This Idea is manifested, but its content is just the manifestation, and consists in its distinguishing itself as an Other, and then taking back this Other into itself, so that the expression taking back applies equally to what is done outside and inside. In Nature these stages break up into a system of king-doms of Nature, of which that of living things is the highest.

Life, however, the highest form in which the Idea exhibits itself in Nature, is simply something which sacrifices itself and whose essence is to become Spirit, and this act of sacrifice is the negativity of the Idea as against its existence in this form.   Spirit is just this act of advance into reality by means of Nature, *i.e.*, Spirit finds its antithesis, or opposite, in Nature, and it is by the annulling of this opposition that it exists for itself and is Spirit.

The finite world is the side of the difference which is put in contrast with the side which remains in its unity ; and thus it breaks up into the natural world and into the world of finite Spirit.   Nature enters into a relation with Man only, and not on its own account into a re-lation with God, for Nature is not knowledge ; God is Spirit, but Nature knows nothing of Spirit.

Nature has been created by God, but she does not of herself enter into a relation with God, by which is meant that she is not possessed of knowledge.   She stands in a relation to Man only, and in this relation to Man she represents what is called the side of his dependence.

In so far as she is known by thought to have been created by God, and to have understanding and reason in her, she is consciously known by Man as a thinking being; and she is put in relation with the Divine to the extent to which her truth or true nature is recognised. The discussion of the manifold forms expressive of the relation of the finite spirit to Nature does not belong to the philosophy of religion. Their scientific treatment forms part of the Phenomenology of Spirit, or the Doctrine of Spirit. Here this relation has to be considered in so far as it comes within the sphere of religion, and in such a way as to show that Nature is for Man not only the actual immediate external world, but a world in which Man knows God; Nature is thus for Man a revelation of God. We have already seen how this relation of Spirit to Nature is present in the ethnic religions in which we encountered those forms which belong to the advance of Spirit from what is immediate to what is necessary and to the thought of something which acts wisely and in accordance with an end, Nature meanwhile being regarded as contingent. Thus the consciousness of God on the part of the finite spirit is reached through Nature, mediated by it. Man sees God by means of Nature; Nature is so far merely a veiling and imperfect embodiment of God.

What is distinguished from God is here really an Other, and has the form of an Other or object; it is Nature which exists for Spirit and for Man. It is through this that the unity of the two is to be brought about, and the consciousness attained that the end and the essential character of religion is reconciliation. The first thing is the abstract act of becoming conscious of God, that Man raises himself in Nature to God. This stage we saw represented in the proofs of the existence of God, and connected with it, too, are those pious reflections as to how gloriously God has made everything how wisely He has arranged all things. This elevation

of the soul takes it straight to God, and may start from
any set of facts. The pious mind makes edifying reflections upon what it sees, and beginning with what
is most insignificant and most special, recognises in it
something which is essentially higher. Very often you
find mixed up with these reflections the perverted
notion that what goes on in the world of Nature is to
be regarded as belonging to a higher order of things
than what is found in the human sphere. This way of
looking at things, however, is inadequate, from the very
fact that it starts from what is individual or particular.
We may look at things in another way which will be
the opposite of this. The cause, it may be argued, must
correspond to the phenomenon, and must itself contain the element of limitation which belongs to the
phenomenon; we desire a particular ground or basis
upon which this particular phenomenon is based. This
element of inadequacy always attaches to the consideration of any particular phenomenon. Further, these particular phenomena belong to the realm of the natural;
God, however, must be conceived of as Spirit, and the
element in which we recognise His presence must also
be spiritual. "God thunders with His thunder," it is
said, "and is yet not known." The spiritual man, however, demands something higher than what is merely
natural. If God is to be known as Spirit, He must do
more than thunder.

The truth is that we reach a higher mode of viewing
Nature, and perceive the deeper relation in which it must
be placed in regard to God, when it is itself conceived of
as spiritual, *i.e.*, as something which is the natural side
of Man's nature. It is only when the subject ceases to
be classed as belonging to the immediate Being of the
Natural, and is made to appear what it implicitly is,
namely, movement, and when it has gone *into itself*, that
we get finitude as such, and finitude, in fact, as shown
in the process of the relation in which the need of the

absolute Idea and its manifestation come to exist for it. What comes first here is the necessity or need of truth, while the kind and manner of the manifestation of the truth is what is second.

As regards the first point, the necessity for truth, it is presupposed that there exists in subjective Spirit a demand to know the absolute truth. This necessity directly involves the supposition that the subject exists in a state of untruth; as Spirit, however, the subject is at the same time implicitly raised above this state of untruth, and for this reason its condition of untruth is one which has to be surmounted.

Untruth more strictly defined means that the subject is in a state of alienation from itself, and the need for truth so far expresses itself in the fact that this division or alienation is in the subject, and is just because of this also annulled by truth, that it is thus changed into reconciliation, and that this reconciliation which is within itself can only be a reconciliation with the truth.

This is the necessity or need of truth in its more strictly defined form. Its essential character implies that the alienation is really in the subject, that the subject is evil, that it is inner division or alienation, inherent contradiction, not, however, contradiction of the mutually exclusive kind, but is something which at the same time keeps itself together, and that the alienation takes place only when it is an inner contradiction in the subject.

3. This reminds us that we are called on to define the nature or essential character of Man, and to show how it is to be regarded, how Man ought to regard it, and what he has got to know of it.

And here we (1) at once meet with characteristics which are mutually opposed: Man is *by nature good*, he is not divided against himself, but, on the contrary, his essence, his Notion, consists in this, that he is by nature good, that he represents what is harmony with itself, inner peace; and—Man is *by nature evil*.

The first of these characteristics thus means that Man is by nature good, that his universal substantial essence is good ; the second characteristic is the opposite of this. This, then, to begin with, is the nature of these contrary propositions, so far as we are concerned, and so far as the outward way of looking at things is concerned. The next step is to perceive that we do not merely thus reflect upon things, but that Man has an independent knowledge of himself, and knows how he is constituted and what is his essential character.

We have, to start with, the one proposition: Man is by nature good, what has no element of division ; thus he has no need of reconciliation, and if reconciliation is not at all necessary, then the course of development we are considering here and this whole part of the subject are superfluous.

To say that Man is by nature good amounts substantially to saying that he is potentially Spirit, rationality, that he has been created in the image of God ; God is·the Good, and Man as Spirit is the reflection of God, he is the Good potentially. It is just on this very proposition and on it alone that the possibility of his reconciliation rests ; the difficulty, the ambiguity is, however, in the potentiality.

Man is potentially good—but when that is said everything is not said ; it is just in this potentiality that the element of one-sidedness lies. Man is good potentially, *i.e.*, he is good only in an inward way, good so far as his notion or conception is concerned, and for this very reason not good so far as his actual nature is concerned.

Man, inasmuch as he is Spirit, must actually be, be for himself, what he truly is ; physical Nature remains in the condition of potentiality, it is potentially the Notion, but the Notion does not in it attain to independent Being, to Being-for-self. It is just in the very fact that Man is only potentially good that the defect of his nature lies.

The potentiality of Nature is represented by the laws

of Nature; Nature remains true to its laws, and does not go beyond them; it is this which constitutes its substantiality, and just in consequence of this it is in the sphere of necessity. But in contrast to this, Man must be actually, for himself, what he potentially is, his potential being must come to be for him actual.

What is good by nature is good in an immediate way, and it is just the very nature of Spirit not to be something natural and immediate; rather, it is involved in the very idea of Man as Spirit that he should pass out of this natural state into a state in which there is a separation between his notion or conception and his immediate existence. In the case of physical Nature this separation of an individual thing from its law, from its substantial essence, does not occur, just because it is not free.

What is meant by Man is, a being who sets himself in opposition to his immediate nature, to his state of being in himself, and reaches a state of separation.

The other assertion made regarding Man springs directly from the statement that Man must not remain what he is immediately; he must pass beyond the state of immediacy; that is the notion or conception of Spirit. It is this passing beyond his natural state, his potential Being, which first of all forms the basis of the division or disunion, and in connection with which the disunion directly arises.

This disunion is a passing out of this natural cóndition or immediacy; but we must not take this to mean that it is the act of passing out of this condition which first constitutes evil, for, on the contrary, this passing out of immediacy is already involved in the state of nature. Potentiality and the natural state constitute the Immediate; but because it is Spirit it is in its immediacy the passing out of its immediacy, the revolt or falling away from its immediacy, from its potential Being.

This involves the second proposition : Man is by nature evil; his potential Being, his natural Being, is evil. It is just in this his condition as one of natural Being that his defect is found; because he is Spirit he is separated from this natural Being, and is disunion. One-sidedness is directly involved in this natural condition. When Man is only as he is according to Nature, he is evil.

The natural man is Man as potentially good, good according to his conception or notion; but in the concrete sense that man is natural who follows his passions and impulses, and remains within the circle of his desires, and whose natural immediacy is his law.

He is natural, but in this his natural state he is at the same time a being possessed of will, and since the content of his will is merely impulse and inclination, he is evil. So far as form is concerned, the fact that he is will implies that he is no longer an animal, but the content, the ends towards which his acts of will are directed, are still natural. This is the standpoint we are concerned with here, the higher standpoint according to which Man is by nature evil, and is evil just because he is something natural.

The primary condition of Man, which is superficially represented as a state of innocence, is the state of nature, the animal state. Man must be culpable; in so far as he is good, he must not be good as any natural thing is good, but his guilt, his will, must come into play, it must be possible to impute moral acts to him. Guilt really means the possibility of imputation.

The good man is good along with and by means of his will, and to that extent because of his guilt. Innocence implies the absence of will, the absence of evil, and consequently the absence of goodness. Natural things and the animals are all good, but this is a kind of goodness which cannot be attributed to Man; in so far as he is good, it must be by the action and consent of his will.

What is absolutely required is that Man should not continue to be a natural being, to be natural will. Man, it is true, is possessed of consciousness, but he can still

be a natural being although he is Man, in so far as
what is natural constitutes the end, the content, and the
essential character of his acts of will.

It is necessary to view this characteristic in a stricter
way. Man is Man as being a subject or person, and as
a natural subject he is a definite single subject, and his
will is a definite single will; particularity constitutes the
content of his will, *i.e.*, the natural man is selfish.

We demand of the man who is called good that he
should at least regulate his conduct in accordance with
general principles and laws. The naturalness of will is,
strictly speaking, the selfishness of will as distinguished
from the universality of will, and as contrasted with the
rationality of the will which has been trained to guide
itself by universality. This Evil personified in a general
way is the Devil. This latter, as representing the Negative which wills itself, is because of this, self-identity,
and must accordingly have the element of affirmation
also in him, as he has in Milton, where his energy, which
is full of character, makes him better than many an
angel.

But the fact that Man in so far as he represents the
natural will is evil, does not imply that we can no longer
regard him from the other point of view, according to
which he is potentially good. He always remains good,
viewed in accordance with his notion or conception; but
Man is consciousness, and is consequently essentially
differentiation, and therefore a real, definite subject as
distinguished from his notion; and since this subject is,
to begin with, merely distinguished from its notion, and
has not yet returned into the unity of its subjectivity
with the notion, into the rational state, this reality which
it has is natural reality, and that is selfishness.

The fact of evil directly presupposes a relation between
reality and the Notion, and consequently we thus get
simply the contradiction which is in potential Being, the
contradiction of the Notion and particularity, of Good and

Evil. It is to put a false question to ask, Is Man good by nature, or is he not? That is a false position, and so, too, it is superficial to say, He is as much good as evil.

In reference particularly to the statement that the will is caprice or arbitrary will, and can will good or evil, it may be remarked that, as a matter of fact, this arbitrary will is not will. It is will only in so far as it comes to a resolution, for in so far as it wills this or that it is not will. The natural will is the will of the desires, of inclination which wills the immediate, and does not as yet will anything definite, for in order to do that it would have to be rational will and be able to perceive that law is rational. What is demanded of Man is that he should not be natural will, that he should not be as he is merely by nature. The conception of volition is something different from this; so long as Man continues to exist ideally as will, he is only potentially will, he is not yet actual will, he does not yet exist as Spirit. This is the truth in its universal aspect; the special aspect of it must here be left out of consideration. We can speak of what belongs to the definite sphere of morality only when we are dealing with some particular condition in which Man is placed; it has nothing to do with the nature of Spirit.

As opposed to the view that the will is evil, we have the fact that when we regard Man in a concrete way we speak of volition, and this concrete, this actual element cannot be simply something negative; the evil will, however, is thought of as purely negative volition, and this is a mere abstraction. If Man is not by nature what he should be, then he is implicitly rational, implicitly Spirit. This represents the affirmative element in him, and the fact that in the state of nature he is not what he ought to be, has reference accordingly only to the form of volition, the essential point being that Man is potentially Spirit. This potentiality persists when the natural will is being yielded up; it is the Notion, the persistent element, the self-producing element. When, on the other hand, we speak of the will being evil by nature, we are thinking of the will in its negative aspect merely. We thus have in our minds at the same time this particular concrete element with which the abstraction referred to is in contradiction. We carry this so far that when we set up a Devil we have to show that there is something affirmative in him, strength of character, energy, consistency. When we come to the concrete we at once find that affirmative characteristics must show themselves present in it. In all this it is forgotten that when we speak of men they are thought of as men who have been educated and trained by customs, laws, &c. People say, Men are, after all, not so bad—just look round you; but then the men round about us are men who are already educated ethically and morally, men already reconstructed and brought into a certain state of reconciliation.

The main thing is, that in connection with religion we should not think of a moral condition, such as that of the child; on the contrary, in any description of the truth, what is essentially presented to us is the logical unfolding of the history of what Man is. It is the speculative way of regarding things which rules here; the abstract differences of the Notion are presented in successive order. If it is the trained and cultured man who has to be studied, then the change and reconstruction and discipline through which he has passed must necessarily appear in him as representing the transition from natural volition to true volition, and his immediate natural will must necessarily appear in this case as something which has been absorbed in what is higher.

(2.) If, therefore, the first characteristic means that Man in his immediate state is not what he is intended to be, then we have to remember that Man has also to reflect upon himself as he thus is; the fact of his being evil is thus brought into relation with reflection. This is readily taken to mean that it is only in accordance with this knowledge he comes to be regarded as evil, so that this reflection is a sort of external demand or condition implying that if he were not to reflect upon himself in this way the other characteristic, namely, that he is evil, would drop away.

When this act of reflection is made a duty, then it may be so represented as to suggest that it only is what is essential, and that there can be no content without it. Further, the relation of reflection is stated also in such a way as to imply that it is reflection or knowledge which makes man evil, so that it is evil, and it is this knowledge which ought not to exist, and which is the source of evil. In this way of representing it, we have the connection which exists between the fact of being evil and knowledge.   This is a point of essential importance.

In its more definite form this idea of evil implies that Man becomes evil through knowledge, or, as the Bible represents it, that he ate of the tree of knowledge.   In this way, knowledge, intelligence, the theoretic element, and will enter into a more definite relation, and the nature of evil gets to be discussed in a more definite way. In this connection it may accordingly be remarked that as a matter of fact it is knowledge which is the source of all evil, for knowledge or consciousness is just the act by which separation, the negative element, judgment, division in the more definite specific form of independent existence or Being-for-self in general, comes into existence.   Man's nature is not as it ought to be; it is knowledge which reveals this to him, and brings to light that condition of Being in which he ought not to be. This obligation which lies on him is his Notion, and the fact that he is not what he should be originates first of all in the sense of separation or alienation, and from a comparison between what he is and what he is in his essential nature, in-and-for-himself.   It is knowledge which first brings out the contrast or antithesis in which evil is found.   The animal, the stone, the plant is not evil; evil is first present within the sphere of knowledge; it is the consciousness of independent Being, or Being-for-self relatively to an Other, but also relatively to an Object which is inherently universal in the sense that it is the Notion, or rational will. It is only by means of this separation that I exist independently, for myself, and it is in this that evil lies. To be evil means in an abstract sense to isolate myself; the isolation which separates me from the Universal represents the element of rationality, the laws, the essential characteristics of Spirit. But it is along with this separation that Being-for-self originates, and it is only when it appears that we have the Spiritual as something universal, as Law, what ought to be.

It is therefore not the case that reflection stands in an external relation to evil, but, on the contrary, reflection itself is evil. This is the condition of contrast to which Man, because he is Spirit, must advance ; he has, in fact, to be independent or for himself in such a way that he has as his object something which is his' own object confronting him, which exists for him, the Good, the Universal, his essential or ideal character. Spirit is free, and freedom has within itself the essential element of the disunion referred to. It is in this disunion that independent Being or Being-for-self originates, and it is in it that evil has its seat; here is the source of the evil, but here also the point which is the ultimate source of reconciliation. It is at once what produces the disease, and the source of health. We cannot, however, better illustrate the character and mode of this movement of Spirit than by referring to the form it takes in the story of the Fall.

Sin is described by saying that Man ate of the tree of knowledge, &c. This implies the presence of knowledge, division, disunion in which good as existing for Man first shows itself, but, as a consequence, evil too. According to the story it is forbidden to eat of the tree, and thus evil is represented in a formal way as the transgression of a divine command, which might have had any kind of content. Here, however, it is just the knowledge referred to which essentially constitutes the command. It is upon this that the rise of consciousness depends, but it is at the same time to be thought of as a standpoint at which consciousness cannot rest, but which is to be absorbed in something higher, for consciousness must not remain at that point at which Being-for-self is in a state of disunion. The serpent further says that Man by the act of eating would become equal to God, and by speaking thus he made an appeal to Man's pride. God says to Himself, Adam is become as one of us. The serpent had thus not lied, for God confirms what it said. A great deal of trouble has been taken with the explanation of this passage, and some have gone the length of explaining it as irony. The truer explanation, however, is that the Adam referred to is to be understood as representing the second Adam, namely, Christ. Knowledge is the principle of spiritual life, but it is also, as was remarked, the principle of the healing of the injury caused by disunion. It is in fact this principle of knowledge which supplies also the principle of man's divineness, a principle which by a process of self-adjustment or elimination of difference must reach a condition of reconciliation or truth; or, in other words, it involves the promise and certainty of attaining once more the state in which Man is the image of God. We find such a prophecy expressed pictorially in what God says to the serpent, " I will put enmity, &c." Since the serpent represents the principle of knowledge as something existing independently outside of Adam, it is clearly perfectly logical that Man, as representing concrete knowledge, should have in himself the other side of the truth, that of conversion and reflection, and that this other side should bruise the head of the serpent as representing the opposite side.

This is what the first man is represented as having

actually done, but here again we are using the language
of sense ; the first man, considered from the point of
view of thought, signifies Man as Man, not any individual
accidental single man out of many, but the first man
absolutely, Man regarded in accordance with his conception or notion.   Man as such is consciousness, and
consequently he enters into this state of disunion—consciousness, namely, which when it gets a more· specific
character is knowledge.

In so far as the universal man is represented as the
first man, he is distinguished from other men, and so the
question arises : It is only this particular individual who
has done the evil deed, how, then, has it affected others ?
Here accordingly we have the popular conception of in-
heritance, and by means of it the defect which attaches
to the representation of Man as such, as an individual
first man, is corrected.

Division or disunion is essentially implied in the
conception of Man ; the one-sided view involved in the
representation of his act as the act of one individual is
thus changed into a complete view by the introduction
of the idea of communicated or inherited evil.

Work, &c., is declared to be the punishment of sin,
and this from a general point of view is a necessary
consequence.

The animal does not work, it works only when compelled, it does not work by nature, it does not eat its
bread in the sweat of its brow, it does not produce its
own bread ; it directly finds in Nature satisfaction for all
the needs it has.   Man, too, finds the material for doing
this ; but the material, we may say, is for Man the least
important part ; the infinite means whereby he satisfies
his needs come to him through work.

Work done in the sweat of his brow, both bodily
work, and the work of the spirit, which is the harder
of the two, is immediately connected with the knowledge
of good and evil.   That Man must make himself what

he is, that he must eat his bread in the sweat of his brow, that he must produce the nature which is his, belongs to what is essential to and most distinctive of Man, and is necessarily connected with the knowledge of good and evil.

The story further describes how the tree of life also stood in the garden ; and the representation of this fact is of a simple and childlike character. The Good to-wards which men direct their wishes is of two kinds. Man wishes, on the one hand, to live in undisturbed hap-piness, in harmony with himself and outward Nature ; the animal continues in this condition of unity, but Man has to pass beyond it ; his other wish practically is to live eternally—and it is in accordance with these wishes that this pictorial conception has been constructed.

When we consider this representation of primitive man more closely, it is at once seen to be of a merely childlike sort. Man as an individual living thing, his individual life, his natural life, must die. But when we look more narrowly at the narrative, this is seen to be the wonderful part of it, the self-contradictory element in it.

In this contradiction Man is characterised as having an existence of his own, as being for himself. Being-for-self, in its character as consciousness, self-conscious-ness, is infinite self-consciousness, abstractly infinite. The fact that he is conscious of his freedom, of his absolutely abstract freedom, constitutes his infinite Being-for-self, which did not thus come into consciousness in the earlier religions in which the contrast or opposition did not get to this absolute stage, nor attain to this depth. Owing to the fact that this has happened here, the worth or dignity of Man is directly put on a much higher level. The subject has hereby attained absolute importance ; it is essentially an object of interest to God, since it is self-consciousness which exists on its own account. It appears as the pure certainty of itself within itself, there exists in it a centre or point of infinite subjectivity; it is certainly abstract, but it is abstract essential Being, Being in-and-for-self. This takes the form of the assertion that Man as Spirit is immortal, is an object of God's interest, is raised above finitude and dependence, above external circumstances, that he has freedom to abstract himself from everything, and this implies that he can escape mortality. It is in religion that the immortality of the soul is the element of supreme importance, because the antithesis involved in religion is of an infinite kind.

What is mortal is what can die; what is immortal is what can reach a state in which death cannot enter. Combustible and incombustible are terms implying that combustion is a possibility merely, which attaches to the object in an external way. The essential character of Being is not, however, a possibility after this fashion, but, on the contrary, is an affirmative determinate quality which it already now possesses in itself.

Thus the immortality of the soul must not be represented as first entering the sphere of reality only at a later stage; it is the actual present quality of Spirit; Spirit is eternal, and for this reason is already present. Spirit, as possessed of freedom, does not belong to the sphere of things limited; it, as being what thinks and knows in an absolute way, has the Universal for its object; this is eternity, which is not simply duration, as duration can be predicated of mountains, but knowledge. The eternity of Spirit is here brought into consciousness, and is found in this reasoned knowledge, in this very separation, which has reached the infinitude of Being-for-self, and which is no longer entangled in what is natural, contingent, and external. This eternity of Spirit in itself means that Spirit is, to begin with, potential; but the next standpoint implies that Spirit ought not to continue to be merely natural Spirit, but that it ought to be what it is in its essential and complete nature, in-and-for-self.

Spirit must reflect upon itself, and in this way disunion arises, it must not remain at the point at which it is seen not to be what it is potentially, but must become adequate to its conception or notion, it must become universal Spirit. Regarded from the standpoint of division or disunion, its potential Being is for it an Other, and it itself is natural will; it is divided within itself, and this division is so far its feeling or consciousness of a contradiction, and there is thus given along with it the necessity for the abolition of the contradiction.

On the one hand, it is said that Man in Paradise without sin would have been immortal—immortality on earth and the immortality of the soul are not separated in this statement—and would have lived for ever. If this outward death is to be regarded as merely a consequence of sin, then he would be implicitly immortal; on the other hand, we have it also stated in the story that it was not till Man should eat of the tree of life that he was to become immortal.

The matter, in fact, stands thus. Man is immortal in consequence of knowledge, for it is only as a thinking being that he is not a mortal animal soul, and is a free, pure soul. Reasoned knowledge, thought, is the root of his life, of his immortality as a totality in himself. The animal soul is sunk in the life of the body, while Spirit, on the other hand, is a totality in itself.

The next thing is, that this idea which we have reached in the region of thought should take an actual shape in Man, i.e., that Man should come to see the infinite nature of the opposition, of the opposition, that is, between good and evil, that he should know himself to be evil in so far as he is something natural, and thus become conscious of the antithesis, not merely in general, but as actually existing in himself, and see that it is he who is evil, and realise that the demand that the Good should be attained, and consequently the consciousness of disunion and the feeling of pain because of the contradiction and opposition, have been awakened in him.

We have found the form of the opposition in all religions ; but the opposition between Man and the power of Nature, between Man and the moral law, the moral will, morality, fate, is an opposition of a subordinate kind, involving opposition merely in reference to some particular thing.

The man who transgresses a commandment is evil, but he is evil only in this particular case, he is in a condition of opposition only in reference to this special commandment. We saw that in the Persian religion good and evil stood to each other in a relation of general opposition ; there the opposition is *outside* of Man, who is himself outside of it. This abstract opposition is not present within himself.

It is accordingly required that Man should have this abstract opposition *within* himself and overcome it, not merely that he should not obey this or the other command, since the truth rather really is that he is implicitly evil, evil in his universal character, in his most inward nature, purely evil, evil in his inner being, and that this quality of evil represents the essential quality of his conception, and that he has to become conscious of this.

(3.) It is with this depth of Spirit that we are concerned. Depth means the abstraction of the opposition, the pure universalisation of the opposition, so that its two sides acquire this absolutely universal character in reference to each other.

This opposition has, speaking generally, two forms : on the one hand, it is the opposition of evil as such, implying that it is the opposition itself which is evil— this is the opposition viewed in reference to God ; on the other hand, it is opposition as against the world, implying that it is out of harmony with the world—this is misery, the condition of division or · disunion viewed from the other side.

In order that the need of universal reconciliation, and as a part of this divine reconciliation, absolute reconciliation in Man, should arise, it is necessary that the opposition should get this infinite character, and that it should be seen that this universality comprises Man's most inward nature, that there is nothing which is outside of this opposition, that the opposition is not of a particular kind. This is the deepest depth.

(a.) We have first to consider the relation in which the disunion stands to one of the extremes, namely, to God. Man is inwardly conscious that in the depths of his being he is a contradiction, and thus there arises an infinite feeling of sorrow in reference to himself. Sorrow is present only where there is opposition to what ought to be, to an affirmative. What is no longer in itself an affirmative has no contradiction, no sorrow in it either; sorrow is just negativity in the Affirmative, it means that the Affirmative is something self-contradictory, that it is wounded by its own act.

This sorrow is the one element of evil. Evil existing simply by itself is an abstraction, it exists only in opposition to good; and since it is present in the unity of the subject, the feeling of opposition in reference to this disunion constitutes infinite sorrow. If the consciousness of good did not thus exist in the subject itself, and if the infinite demand made by good was not present in the inmost being of the subject, then there would be no sorrow there, evil itself would be an empty nothing; it is present only in this antithesis or opposition.

Both evil and this sorrow can be infinite only when good, God, is known as one God, as a pure spiritual God, and it is only when good is this pure unity, when we have belief in one God, and only in connection with such a belief, that the negative can and must advance to this determination of evil, and that the negation also can advance to this condition of universality.

The one side of this disunion thus becomes apparent by the elevation of Man to the pure spiritual unity of God. This sorrow and this consciousness represent Man's descent into himself, and consequently into the negative moment of disunion or evil.

This is the negative, or inward, descent or absorption into evil; inward absorption of an affirmative kind is absorption into the pure unity of God. When this stage is reached, it is seen that I as a natural man do not correspond to what represents the truth, and that I am entangled in the multiplicity of natural particular things, and just as the truth of the one Good is present in me with an infinite certainty, so this want of correspondence gets a determinate character as something which ought not to be.

The problem, the demand, is of an infinite kind. It may be said that since I am a natural man I have from one point of view a consciousness of myself; but to be in a state of nature means that I am without consciousness in reference to myself, means the absence of will; I am a being of the kind which acts in accordance with Nature, and so far regarded from this side I am, as is often said, innocent, I have, so far, no consciousness of what I do, I am without any will of. my own, what I do I do without definite inclination, and allow myself to be surprised into doing it by impulse.

Here, however, in this state of opposition this innocence disappears. For it is just this natural, unconscious, and will-less Being of Man which ought not to be, and it is consequently determined to evil in presence of the pure unity, the perfect purity which I know as representing the True and the Absolute. In putting it thus we imply that when this point has been reached it is essentially this very unconsciousness and absence of will which is to be considered as evil.

The contradiction, however, still remains, turn it how you will. Since this so-called innocence characterises itself as evil, the want of correspondence between myself and the Absolute, my inadequacy to express my essence, remain, and thus, from whichever side I regard myself, I always know myself to be something which ought not to be.

This expresses the relation in reference to the one extreme, and the result, this sorrow in a more definite form, is my humility, the feeling of contrition, the fact that I experience sorrow because I as a natural being do not correspond to what I at the same time know myself to be in my knowledge and will.

(b.) As regards the relation to the other extreme, the separation appears in this case in the form of misery arising from the fact that Man does not find satisfaction in the world.   His desire for satisfaction, his natural wants have no longer any rights, any claims to be satisfied. As a natural being, Man stands related to an Other, and that Other is related to him in the form of forces, and his existence is to this extent contingent, just as that of other things is.

The demands of his nature, however, in reference to morality, the higher moral claims of his nature, are demands and determinations of freedom.   In so far as these demands, which are implicitly legitimate, and are grounded in his notion or conception—for he knows about the Good, and the Good is in him—do not find their satisfaction in the existing order of things, in the external world, he is in a state of misery.

It is misery which drives Man into himself, forces him back into himself, and because this fixed demand that the world should be rational exists in him, he gives up the world, and seeks happiness, satisfaction, in himself, as the harmony of the affirmative side of his nature with himself.   Because he seeks after this, he gives up the external world, transfers his happiness into himself, and finds satisfaction in himself.

We had this demand and this unhappiness in the

two following forms. We saw how the sorrow which comes from universality, from above, was found amongst the Jewish people; in connection with it there is ever present the infinite demand for absolute purity in my natural existence, in my empirical willing and knowing. The other form they took, the retreat from misery into self, represents the standpoint at which the Roman world arrived and where it ended, namely, the universal misery of the world.

We saw how this formal inwardness which finds satisfaction in the world, this dominion as being the aim or end of God, was represented, and known, and thought of as worldly dominion. Both of these aspects of the truth are one-sided; the first may be defined as the feeling of humiliation, the other is the abstract elevation of Man in himself, of Man as self-centred. Thus it is Stoicism or Scepticism.

According to the Stoical or Sceptical view, Man is driven back upon himself, he has to find satisfaction in himself, in this state of independence; in remaining inflexibly self-centred he has to find happiness, inner harmony of soul, he is to rest in this abstract, present, self-conscious inwardness of his.

It is in this separation or disunion, as we have said, that the subject thus takes on a definite character, and conceives of itself as the extreme of abstract Being-for-self, of abstract freedom; the soul plunges into its depths, into its absolute abyss. This soul is the undeveloped monad, the naked monad, the empty soul devoid of content; but since it is potentially the Notion, the concrete, this emptiness or abstraction stands in a relation of contradiction to its essential character, which is, to be concrete.

Thus the universal element is represented by the fact that in this separation which develops into an infinite antithesis, the abstraction is to be done away with and absorbed. This abstract " I " is also in itself, a will, it is

concrete, but the immediate element which is present in
it and gives it substance is the natural will. The soul
finds nothing in itself except desires, selfishness, &c. ; and
this is one of the forms of the opposition, that " I," as
representing the soul in the depth of its nature, and the
real side, are distinct from one another, and in such a way
that the real side is not something which has been made
adequate to express the Notion and is accordingly carried
back to it, but, on the contrary, finds in itself only the
natural will.

The sphere of opposition in which the real side is
further developed, is the world, and thus the unity of
the Notion has opposed to it the natural will as a whole,
the principle of which is selfishness, and the realisation
of which appears in the form of depravity, cruelty, &c.
The objectivity which this pure " I " has, and which
exists for it as something adequate to express it, is not
found in the natural will, nor in the world either; on the
contrary, the objectivity which adequately corresponds
to it is the universal Essence only, that One which does
not find its realisation or fulness in it, and which has all
that supplies realisation, or the world, confronting it.

Accordingly the consciousness of this opposition, of
this division between the " I " and the natural will, is that
of an infinite contradiction. This " I " exists in an immediate relation to the natural will and to the world,
and at the same time it is repelled by them. This is
infinite sorrow, the world's Passion. The reconciliation
which we have hitherto found to be connected with this
standpoint is only partial, and for that reason unsatisfactory. The harmony of the " I " within itself, which
it attains in the Stoic philosophy, is of a merely abstract kind ; it here knows itself as what thinks, and its
object is what is thought, the Universal, and this is for it
simply everything, the true essentiality, and thus this has
for it the value of something thought, and has value for the
subject as being what it itself has posited. This recon-

ciliation is merely abstract, for all determination lies outside of what is thus thought, and we have merely formal self-identity. Such an abstract kind of reconciliation cannot find, and ought not to find, a place in connection with this absolute standpoint, nor can the natural will find satisfaction within itself either, for neither it nor the world as it is can satisfy him who has become conscious of his infinity. The abstract depth of the opposition demands an infinite suffering on the part of the soul, and consequently a reconciliation which will be correspondingly complete.

These are the highest, most abstract moments, and the opposition or antithesis is the highest of all. The two sides represent the opposition in its most complete universality, in what is most inward, in the Universal itself, the two sides of the antithesis in the case in which the opposition goes deepest. Both sides are, however, one-sided; the first side contains the sorrow, the abstract humiliation referred to; what is highest here is simply this inadequacy of the subject to express the Universal, this division or disruption, which is not healed nor adjusted, representing the opposition between an infinite on the one side, and a fixed finitude on the other side. This finitude is abstract finitude; anything in this connection reckoned as belonging to me is, according to this way of looking at it, simply evil.

This abstraction finds its completion in the Other; this is thought in itself, it implies that I am adequate to myself, that I find satisfaction in myself and can be satisfied in myself. This second side is, however, actually just as one-sided, for it is merely the Affirmative, my self-affirmation in myself. The first side, the brokenness of heart, is merely negative, without affirmation in itself; the second is meant to represent this affirmation, this satisfaction of self within self. This satisfaction of myself in myself, however, is a merely abstract satisfaction reached by fleeing from the world, from reality, by passivity. Since this is a fleeing from reality, it is also a fleeing from *my* reality, not a fleeing from external reality, but from the reality of my own volition.

The reality of my volition, I as a definite subject, the will in a realised form, are no longer mine ; but what is left to me is the immediacy of my self-consciousness, the individual self - consciousness. This is certainly completely abstract, still this final point of the spirit's depth is contained in it, and I have preserved myself in it.

This abstraction from my abstract reality is not in me or in my immediate self-consciousness, in the immediacy of my self-consciousness. On this side, therefore, it is affirmation which is the predominant factor, affirmation without the negation of the one-sidedness of immediate Being. In the other case it is the negation which is one-sided.

These are the two moments which contain the necessity for transition. The conception or notion of the preceding religions has purified itself and thus reached this antithesis, and the fact that this antithesis or opposition has shown itself to be, and has taken the form of, an actually existing necessity, is expressed by the words, "When the time was fulfilled," *i.e.*, Spirit, the demand of Spirit, is actually present, Spirit which points the way to reconciliation.

(*c.*) *Reconciliation.*—The deepest need of Spirit consists in the fact that the opposition in the subject itself has attained its universal, *i.e.*, its most abstract extreme. This is the division, the sorrow referred to. That these two sides are not mutually exclusive, but constitute this contradiction in one, is what directly proves the subject to be an infinite force of unity ; it can bear this contradiction. This is the formal, abstract, but also infinite energy of the unity which it possesses.

What satisfies this need, we call the consciousness of reconcilement, the consciousness of the abolition, of the nullity of the opposition, the consciousness that this opposition is not the truth, but that, on the contrary, the truth consists in reaching unity by the negation of this opposition, *i.e.*, the peace, the reconciliation which this need demands. Reconciliation is the demand of the subject's sense of need, and is inherent in it as being what is infinitely one, what is self-identical.

This abolition of the opposition has two sides. The subject must come to be conscious that this opposition is not something implicit or essential, but that the truth, the inner nature of Spirit, implies the abolition and absorption of this opposition. Accordingly, just because it is implicitly, and, from the point of view of truth, done away with in something higher, the subject as such in its Being-for-self can reach and arrive at the abolition of this opposition, that is to say, can attain to peace or reconciliation.

1. The very fact that the opposition is implicitly done away with constitutes the condition, the presupposition, the possibility of the subject's ability to do away with it actually. In this respect it may be said that the subject does not attain reconciliation on its own account, that is, as a particular subject, and in virtue of its own activity, and what it itself does ; reconciliation is not brought about, nor can it be brought about, by the subject in its character as subject.

This is the nature of the need when the question is, By what means can it be satisfied ? Reconciliation can be brought about only when the annulling of the division has been arrived at ; when what seems to shun reconciliation, this opposition, namely, is non-existent; when the divine truth is seen to be for this, the resolved or cancelled contradiction, in which the two opposites lay aside their mutually abstract relation.

Here again, accordingly, the question above referred to once more arises. Can the subject not bring about this reconciliation by itself by means of its own action, by bringing its inner life to correspond with the divine Idea

through its own piety and devoutness, and by giving
expression to this in actions ? And, further, can the
individual subject not do this, or, at least, may not *all
men* do it who rightly will to adopt the divine Law as
theirs, so that heaven might exist on earth, and the Spirit
in its graciousness actually live here and have a real
existence ? The question is as to whether the subject
can or cannot effect this in virtue of its own powers as
subject. The ordinary idea is that it can do this. What
we have to notice here, and what must be carefully kept
in mind, is that we are dealing with the subject thought
of as standing at one of the two extremes, as existing for
itself. To subjectivity belongs, as a characteristic feature,
the power of positing, and this means that some particular thing exists owing to me. This positing or making
actual, this doing of actions, &c., takes place through
me, it matters not what the content is ; the act of producing is consequently a one-sided characteristic, and the
product is merely something posited, or dependent for its
existence on something else ; it remains as such merely
in a condition of abstract freedom. The question referred
to consequently comes to be a question as to whether it
can by its act of positing produce this. This positing
must essentially be a pre-positing, a presupposition, so that
what is posited is also something implicit. The unity of
subjectivity and objectivity, this divine unity, must be a
presupposition so far as my act of positing is concerned,
and it is only then that it has a content, a substantial
element in it, and the content is Spirit, otherwise it is
subjective and formal ; it is only then that it gets a true,
substantial content. When this presupposition thus gets
a definite character it loses its one-sidedness, and when a
definite signification is given to a presupposition of this
kind the one-sidedness is in this way removed and lost.
Kant and Fichte tell us that man can sow, can do good
only on the presupposition that there is a moral order in
the world ; he does not know whether what he does will

prosper and succeed; he can only act on the presupposition that the Good by its very nature involves growth and success, that it is not merely something posited, but, on the contrary, is in its own nature objective. Presupposition involves essential determination.

The harmony of this contradiction must accordingly be represented as something which is a presupposition for the subject. The Notion, in getting to know the divine unity, knows that God essentially exists in-and-for-Himself, and consequently what the subject thinks, and its activity, have no meaning in themselves, but are and exist only in virtue of that presupposition. The truth must therefore appear to the subject as a presupposition, and the question is as to how and in what form the truth can appear in connection with the standpoint we now occupy; it is infinite sorrow, the pure depth of the soul, and it is for this sorrow that the cancelling or solution of the contradiction has to exist. This cancelling has, to begin with, necessarily the form of a presupposition, because what we have here is a one-sided extreme.

What belongs to the subject, therefore, is simply this act of positing, action as representing merely one side; the other side is the substantial and fundamental one, which contains in it the possibility of reconciliation. This means that this opposition does not really exist implicitly. To put it more correctly, it means that the opposition springs up eternally, and at the same time eternally abolishes itself, is at the same time eternal reconciliation.

That this is the truth, we saw when dealing with the eternal divine Idea, which implies that God as living Spirit distinguishes Himself from Himself, posits an Other, and in this Other remains identical with Himself, and has in this other His self-identity with Himself.

This is the truth; it is this truth which must constitute the one side of what Man has to become conscious of, the potentially existing, substantial side.

We may express it in a more definite form by saying that the opposition is inadequacy in general. The opposition, Evil, represents the natural aspect of human existence and volition, or immediacy. This is just the mode of existence characteristic of the natural life; it is just when we have immediacy that we have finitude, and this finitude or natural life is inadequate to express the universality of God, of the absolutely free, self-existent, infinite, eternal Idea.

This inadequacy is the starting-point which constitutes the need of reconciliation. The stricter definition of it would not consist in saying that the inadequacy attaching to both sides disappears for consciousness. The inadequacy *exists;* it is involved in what is spiritual. Spirit means self-differentiation, the positing or making explicit of differences.

If these are different, then, by the very fact that according to this moment they are differences, they are not alike; they are· distinguished from each other, they do not correspond to each other. The inadequacy or want of correspondence cannot disappear; if it were to disappear then Spirit's power of judgment or differentiation, its life, would disappear, in which case it would cease to be Spirit.

2. A further determination is reached when we say that, spite of this want of correspondence, the identity of the two exists; that otherness or Other-Being, finitude, weakness, the frailty of human nature, cannot in any way impair the value of that unity which forms the substantial element in reconciliation.

This, too, we recognised as present in the divine Idea; for the Son is other than the Father, and this Other-Being is difference, for if it were not, it would not be Spirit. But the Other is God, and has the entire fulness of the Divine nature in Himself. The characteristic of Other-Being in no way detracts from the value of the fact that this Other is the Son of God, and is consequently God; and so, too, it does not detract from the divine character of the Other as it appears in human nature.

This otherness or Other-Being is Being which eternally annuls itself, which eternally posits itself and eternally annuls itself, and this self-positing and annulling of Other-Being is love or Spirit. Evil, as representing one side of Being, has been defined simply as the Other, the finite, the negative, and God has been placed on the other side as the Good, the True. But this Other, this negative, contains within itself affirmation as well, and in finite Being it must come to be consciously known that the principle of affirmation is contained in this Other, and that there lies in this principle of affirmation the principle of identity with the other side, just as God is not only the True, abstract self-identity, but has in the Other, in negation, in the self-positing of the Other, His peculiarly essential characteristic, which is indeed the peculiar characteristic of Spirit.

The possibility of reconciliation rests only on the conscious recognition of the implicit unity of divine and human nature; this is the necessary basis. Thus Man can know that he has been received into union with God in so far as God is not for him something foreign to his nature, in so far as he does not stand related to God as an external accident, but when he has been taken up into God in his essential character, in a way which is in accordance with his freedom and subjectivity ; this, however, is possible only in so far as this subjectivity which belongs to human nature exists in God Himself.

Infinite sorrow must come to be conscious of this implicit Being as the implicit unity of divine and human nature, but only in its character as implicit Being or substantiality, and in such a way that this finitude, this weakness, this Other-Being, in no way impairs the substantial unity of the two.

The unity of divine and human nature, Man in his

universality, is the Thought of Man, and the Idea of
absolute Spirit in-and-for-itself. In the process also
in which Other-Being annuls itself, this Idea and the
objectivity of God are implicitly real, and they are in
fact immediately present in *all* men; out of the cup of
the entire spirit-realm there foams for him infinitude.
The sorrow which the finite experiences in being thus
annulled and absorbed, does not give pain, since it is
by this means raised to the rank of a moment in the
process of the Divine.

> "Why should that trouble trouble us, since it makes our
> pleasure more ?"

Here, however, at the standpoint at which we now
are, it is not with the Thought of Man that we have
got to do. Nor can we stop short at the characteristic of
individuality in general, which is itself again universal,
and is present in abstract thinking as such.

3. On the contrary, if Man is to get a consciousness
of the unity of divine and human nature, and of this
characteristic of Man as belonging to Man in general;
or if this knowledge is to force its way wholly into the
consciousness of his finitude as the beam of eternal
light which reveals itself to him in the finite, then it
must reach him in his character as Man in general,
i.e., apart from any particular conditions of culture or
training; it must come to him as representing Man in
his immediate state, and it must be universal for immediate consciousness.

The consciousness of the absolute Idea, which we have
in thought, must therefore not be put forward as belonging to the standpoint of philosophical speculation, of
speculative thought, but must, on the contrary, appear
in the form of certainty for men in general. This does
not mean that they think this consciousness, or perceive
and recognise the necessity of this Idea; but what we are
concerned to show is rather that the Idea becomes for

them certain, *i.e.*, this Idea, namely, the unity of divine and human nature, attains the stage of certainty, that, so far as they are concerned, it receives the form of immediate sense-perception, of outward existence—in short, that this Idea appears as seen and experienced in the world. This unity must accordingly show itself to consciousness in a purely temporal, absolutely ordinary manifestation of reality, in one particular man, in a definite individual who is at the same time known to be the Divine Idea, not merely a Being of a higher kind in general, but rather the highest, the absolute Idea, the Son of God.

The expression, "the divine and human natures in One," is a harsh and awkward one; but we must forget the pictorial idea associated with it. What we have got to think of in connection with it is the spiritual substantiality which it suggests; in the unity of the divine and human natures everything belonging to outward particularisation has disappeared; the finite, in fact, has disappeared.

It is the substantial element in the unity of the divine and human natures of which Man attains the consciousness, and in such a way that to him Man appears as God and God as Man. This substantial unity is Man's potential nature; but while this implicit nature exists for Man, it is above and beyond immediate consciousness, ordinary consciousness and knowledge; consequently it must be regarded as existing in a region above that subjective consciousness which takes the form of ordinary consciousness and is characterised as such.

This explains why this unity must appear for others in the form of an individual man marked off from or excluding the rest of men, not as representing all individual men, but as One from whom they are shut off, though he no longer appears as representing the potentiality or true essence which is above, but as individuality in the region of certainty.

It is with this certainty and sensuous view that we
are concerned, and not merely with a divine teacher,
nor indeed simply with morality, nor even in any way
simply with a teacher of this Idea either. It is not
with ordinary thought or with conviction that we have
got to do, but with this immediate presence and certainty of the Divine; for the immediate certainty of
what is present represents the infinite form and mode
which the "Is" takes for the natural consciousness.
This Is destroys all trace of mediation; it is the final
point, the last touch of light which is laid on. This
Is is wanting in mediation of any kind such as is
given through feeling, pictorial ideas, reasons; and it
is only in philosophical knowledge, by means of the
Notion only in the element of universality, that it returns again.

The Divine is not to be conceived of merely as a
universal thought, or as something inward and having
potential existence only; the objectifying of the Divine
is not to be conceived of simply as the objective form it
takes in all men, for in that case it would be conceived
of simply as representing the manifold forms of the
Spiritual in general, and the development which the
Absolute Spirit has in itself and which has to advance
till it reaches the form of what is the form of immediacy, would not be contained in it.

The One we find in the Jewish religion exists in
thought, not in the form of sense-perception, and consequently has not reached the perfect form of Spirit. It
is just this attaining of a complete and perfect form
in Spirit which we call subjectivity, which endlessly
alienates or estranges itself, and then from this absolute opposition, from the furthest point of manifestation,
returns to itself.

The principle of individuality, it is true, was already
present in the Greek ideal, but there it was wanting just
in that universal essentially existing infinitude; the Uni-

versal *as* Universal is posited only in the subjectivity
of consciousness; it is this subjectivity only which is
infinite inner movement, in which all the determinateness of definite existence is cancelled, and which at
the same time is present in existence in its most finite
form.

This individual, accordingly, who represents for others
the manifestation of the Idea, is a particular Only One,
not some ones, for the Divine in some would become an
abstraction. The idea of some is a miserable superfluity
of reflection, a superfluity because opposed to the conception or notion of individual subjectivity. In the
Notion once is always, and the subject must turn exclusively to one subjectivity. In the eternal Idea there is
only one Son, and thus there is only One in whom the
absolute Idea appears, and this One excludes the others.
It is this perfect development of reality thus embodied
in immediate individuality or separateness which is the
finest feature of the Christian religion, and the absolute
transfiguration of the finite gets in it a form in which it
can be outwardly perceived.

This characteristic, namely, that God becomes Man,
and consequently that the finite spirit has the consciousness of God in the finite itself, represents what is the
most difficult moment of religion. According to a
common idea, which we find amongst the ancients
particularly, the spirit or soul has been forced into this
world as into an element which is foreign to it; this
indwelling of the soul in the body, and this particularisation in the form of individuality, are held to be a
degradation of Spirit. In this is involved the idea of
the untruth of the purely material side, of immediate
existence. On the other hand, however, the characteristic of immediate existence is at the same time an
essential characteristic, it is the final tapering point of
Spirit in its subjectivity. Man has spiritual interests
and is spiritually active; he can feel that he is hindered

in connection with these interests and activities; in so far as he feels himself to be in a condition of physical dependence, and has to provide for his own support, &c., his thoughts are taken away from his spiritual interests through his being bound to Nature. The stage of immediate existence is, however, contained in Spirit itself. The essential characteristic of Spirit is that it should advance to this stage. The natural life is not simply an external necessity; on the contrary, Spirit, as subject in its infinite reference to itself, has the characteristic of immediacy in it. In so far, accordingly, as the nature of Spirit happens to be revealed to Man, the nature of God in the entire development of the Idea must be revealed, and thus this form must also be present here, and that is just the form of finitude. The Divine must appear in the form of immediacy. This immediate presence is merely a presence of the Spiritual in that spiritual form which is the human form. This manifestation is not true when it takes any other form, certainly not when it is a manifestation of God in the burning bush, and the like. God appears as an individual person to whose immediacy all kinds of physical necessities are attached. In Indian pantheism a countless number of incarnations occur; there subjectivity, human existence, is only an accidental form; in God it is simply a mask which Substance adopts and changes in an accidental way. God as Spirit, however, contains in Himself the moment of subjectivity, of singleness; His manifestation, accordingly, can only be a single one, can take place only once.

In the Church Christ has been called the God-Man. This is the extraordinary combination which directly contradicts the Understanding; but the unity of the divine and human natures has here been brought into human consciousness and has become a certainty for it, implying that the otherness, or, as it is also expressed, the finitude, the weakness, the frailty of human nature is not

incompatible with this unity, just as in the eternal
Idea otherness in no way detracts from the unity which
God is.

This is the extraordinary combination the necessity of
which we have seen.   It involves the truth that the
divine and human natures are not implicitly different.
God in human form.   The truth is that there is only
one reason, one Spirit, that Spirit as finite has no true
existence.

The substantiality of the form of manifestation is unfolded or made explicit.   Because it is the manifestation
of God, it is essentially for the community of believers.
Manifestation means Being for an Other, and this other
is the community of believers.

This historical manifestation may, however, be looked at
in two different ways.   On the one hand, it may be held
to be Man as he is in his outward condition in the sense
of ordinary Man, the sense in which Man is taken in the
irreligious way of regarding this manifestation.   Then,
on the other hand, it may be looked at in spirit or in
a spiritual way, and with the spirit, which presses on
to reach its truth, and which, just because it has this
infinite division, this sorrow within itself, wills the truth,
wills to have, and must have, the need of truth and the
certainty of truth.   This is the true way of regarding
the manifestation so far as religion is concerned.   We
must distinguish between these two standpoints—the
immediate way of looking at the question, and the way
followed by faith.

By faith this individual is known to possess divine
nature, whereby God ceases to be a Being beyond this
world.   When Christ is looked at in the same way as
Socrates is, He is looked at as an ordinary man, just as
the Mohammedans consider Christ as God's ambassador
in the general sense in which all great men are God's
ambassadors or messengers.   If we say nothing more of
Christ than that He was a teacher of humanity, a martyr

for the truth, we do not occupy the Christian standpoint, the standpoint of the true religion.

The one side is this human side, this appearance of one who was a living man. As an immediate or natural man he is subject to the contingency which belongs to outward things, to all temporal relations and conditions; he is born, as Man he has the needs which all other men have except that he does not share in the corruption, the passions, the particular inclinations of men, in the special interests of the worldly life in connection with which uprightness and moral teaching may also find a place; on the contrary, he lives only for the truth and the proclamation of the truth, his activity consists simply in fulfilling the higher consciousness of men.

It is to this human side, therefore, that the doctrine of Christ chiefly belongs. The question is, How can such doctrine exist, and in what way is it formed? The doctrine in its first form cannot have been composed of the same elements as afterwards appeared in the doctrine of the Church. It must have certain peculiarities which in the Church of necessity partly receive another signification and are partly dropped. Christ's teaching in its immediate form cannot be Christian Dogmatics, cannot be Church-doctrine. When the Christian community has been set up, when the Kingdom of God has attained reality and a definite existence, this teaching can no longer have the same signification as before.

The principal contents of this teaching can only be general and abstract. If something new, a new world, a new religion, a new conception of God, is to be given to the world of ordinary thought, then the first thing needed is the general sphere of ideas in which this can show itself, and the second thing is the particular, the determinate, the concrete. The world of ordinary thought, in so far as it thinks, thinks merely abstractly, it thinks only what is general; it is reserved for Spirit, which comprehends things through the Notion, to recognise the particular in the general, and to see how this particular proceeds out of the Notion by its own power. For the world of ordinary or popular thought, the basis on which universal Thought rests, and particularisation, development, are separated. This general or universal basis may therefore be made use of for the true notion of God, by means of doctrine.

Since what we have got to do with is a new consciousness on the part of men, a new religion, it is for that reason the consciousness of absolute reconciliation ; this involves a new world, a new religion, a new reality, a world in a different condition, for it is religion which is the substantial element in external determinate Being or existence.

This is the negative or polemical side, as against continuance in this externality on the part of the consciousness or faith of Man. The new religion declares itself to be a new consciousness, a consciousness of the reconciliation of Man with God; this reconciliation as expressing a condition is the Kingdom of God, the Eternal as the home of Spirit, a real world in which God reigns ; the spirits, the hearts here are reconciled with Him, and thus it is God who has attained to authority over them. This so far represents the general sphere or basis.

This Kingdom of God, the new religion, thus contains within itself the characteristic of negation in reference to all that is actual. This is the revolutionary side of its teaching which partly throws aside all that actually exists, and partly destroys and overthrows it. All earthly and worldly things drop away as being without value, and are expressly declared to be valueless. What has hitherto existed is altered, the hitherto existing relations, the condition of religion and of the world, cannot remain as they have hitherto been. What, therefore, has to be done is to get Man—who must reach a consciousness of reconciliation—drawn out of his present condition, and to get him to seek after this abstraction or with-drawal from actual reality.

This new religion as yet concentrates itself, and does not actually exist as a church or community of believers, but shows itself rather in that energy which constitutes the sole interest of the man who has to fight and struggle in order to obtain this new condition, because it is not yet in harmony with the actual state of the world, and is not yet brought into connection with his world-consciousness.

This new religion, therefore, on its first appearance presents a polemical aspect, involves a demand that finite things should be abandoned ; it demands that Man should rise to the exercise of an infinite energy in which the Universal demands that it should be laid hold of for its own sake, and in which all other ties have to be treated as matters of indifference, and all that had hitherto been regarded as moral and right, all other ties, have to be put aside.

" Who is my mother and my brother ?" &c.   " Let the dead bury their dead," &c.   " Whoever puts his hand to the plough and looks back is not fit for the Kingdom of God."   " I am come to bring a sword," &c.   In these words we see how a polemic is directed against all ordinary moral relations—" Take no thought for the morrow," " Give your goods to the poor."

All those relations which have reference to property, disappear ; meanwhile they in turn cancel themselves, for if everything is given to the poor then there are no poor. All this represents doctrines and special characteristics which belong to the first appearance of the new religion when it constitutes man's sole interest, which he must believe he is as yet in danger of losing, and when its teaching is addressed to men with whom the world is done and who are done with the world. The one side is represented by this renunciation ; this giving up, this slighting of every substantial interest and of moral ties, is an essential characteristic of the concentrated manifestation of truth, a characteristic which subse-

quently, when truth has attained a sure existence, loses
some of its importance. In fact, if this religion at its
start as suffering, appears in relation to what is outside
of it as willing to endure, to yield, to submit to death,
in course of time, when it has grown strong, its inner
energy will act towards what is outside of it with a correspondingly violent display of force.

The next thing in the affirmative part of this religion
is the proclamation of the Kingdom of God; into this
Kingdom, as representing the Kingdom of love to God,
Man has to transport himself, and he does this by directly
devoting himself to the truth it embodies. This is expressed with the most absolute and startling frankness,
as, for instance, at the beginning of the so-called Sermon
on the Mount: " Blessed are the pure in heart, for they
shall see God." Words like these are amongst the grandest
that have ever been uttered. They represent a final central
point in which all superstition and all want of freedom on
Man's part are done away with. It is of infinite importance that, by Luther's translation of the Bible, a popular
book has been put into the hands of the people, in which
the heart, the spirit can find itself at home in the very
highest, in fact in an infinite way; in Catholic countries
there is in this respect a grave want. For Protestant
peoples the Bible supplies a means of deliverance from
all spiritual slavery.

There is no mention of any mediation in connection
with this elevating of the spirit whereby it may become
an accomplished fact in Man; but, on the contrary, the
mere statement of what is required implies this immediate Being, this immediate self-transference into Truth,
into the Kingdom of God. It is to the intellectual and
spiritual world, to the Kingdom of God, that Man ought
to belong, and in it it is feeling or moral disposition
alone which has value, but not abstract feeling, not mere
chance opinion, but that absolute feeling or disposition
which has its basis in the Kingdom of God. It is in

connection with this Kingdom of God that the infinite
worth of inwardness first comes into view. This is
proclaimed in the language of enthusiasm, in tones so
penetrating as to thrill the soul, and, as Hermes the
psychagogue did, to draw it out of the body and bear it
away beyond the temporal into its eternal home. " Seek
first the Kingdom of God and His righteousness."

Along with this elevation above, and complete abstraction from all that the world counts great, we everywhere
find in Christ's teaching a lament over the degradation of
His nation, and of men in general. Jesus appeared at a
time when the Jewish nation, owing to the dangers to
which its worship had been exposed and was still exposed,
was more obstinately absorbed in its observance than ever,
and was at the same time compelled to despair of seeing
its hopes actually realised since it had come in contact
with a universal humanity, the existence of which it could
no longer deny, and which nevertheless was completely
devoid of any spiritual element—He appeared, in short,
when the common people were in perplexity and helpless.

" I thank Thee, Father, Lord of heaven and earth,
that Thou hast hid these things from the wise and
prudent, and hast revealed them unto babes."

Accordingly, this substantial element, this universal
divine heaven of the inner life, leads, under the influence
of reflection of a more definite kind, to moral commands
which are the application of that universal element to
particular circumstances and situations. These commands,
however, themselves partly apply only to limited spheres
of action, and are partly intended for those stages in
which we are occupied with absolute truth ; they contain
nothing striking, or else they are already contained in
other religions and in the Jewish religion. These commands are comprised in the command of *Love* as their
central point, love which has for its aim, not the rights,
but the well-being of the other, and thus expresses a
relation to its particular object. " Love thy neighbour

as thyself." This command, thought of in the abstract and more extended sense as embracing the love of men in general, is a command to love *all* men. Taken in this sense, however, it is turned into an abstraction. The people whom one can love, and for whom our love is real, are a few particular individuals; the heart which seeks to embrace the whole of humanity within itself indulges in a vain attempt to spread out its love until it becomes a mere idea, the opposite of real love.

Love, in the sense in which Christ understood it, is primarily moral love of our neighbour in those particular relations in which we stand to him ; but, above all, it is meant to express the relation existing between His disciples and followers, the bond which makes them one. And here it is not to be understood as meaning that each is to have his particular occupation, interests, and relations in life, and is further to love in addition to all this, but that this love, as something apart which abstracts from all else, is to be the central point in which they live, and is to constitute their business.

They are to love one another, nothing more or less, and consequently are not to have any particular end in view whatever, ends connected with the family, political ends, nor are they to love because of these particular ends. Love, on the contrary, is abstract personality, and the identity of this in one consciousness in which it is not any longer possible for special ends to exist. Here, therefore, no other objective end exists unless this love. This love, which is independent, and which is thus made a centre, finally becomes the higher divine love itself.

At first, however, this love, as a love which as yet has no objective end, also takes up a polemical attitude to the existing order of things, especially to the Jewish existing order. All those actions commanded by the Law by the doing of which apart from love, men formerly estimated their moral worth, are declared to be dead works, and Christ Himself heals on the Sabbath.

The following moment or determinate element accordingly enters into these doctrines. While this command of love is directly expressed in the words, "Seek the Kingdom of God," abandon yourself to the truth; and while the demand is made in this immediate way, it appears as if in the form of a subjective statement, and so far the *person* speaking comes into view.

In accordance with this reference to a person, Christ does not speak as a teacher merely who states his own subjective view, and who is conscious of what he produces in the way of truth and of his own action in the matter, but as a prophet; He is one who, since this demand is direct, utters the command directly from God, and as one out of whom God thus speaks.

The fact that this possession of this life of the spirit in truth is attained without intermediate helps, is expressed in the prophetic manner, namely, that it is God who thus speaks. Here it is with absolute, divine truth, truth in-and-for-itself, that we are concerned; this utterance and willing of the truth in-and-for-itself, and the carrying out of what is thus expressed, is described as an act of God, it is the consciousness of the real unity of the divine will, of its harmony with the truth. It is as conscious of this elevation of His spirit, and in the assurance of His identity with God that Christ says, "Woman, thy sins are forgiven thee." Here there speaks in Him that overwhelming majesty which can undo everything, and actually declares that this has been done.

So far as the form of this utterance is concerned, what has mainly to be emphasised is that He who thus speaks is at the same time essentially Man, it is the Son of Man who thus speaks, in whom this utterance of the truth, this carrying into practice of what is absolute and essential, this activity on God's part, is essentially seen to exist as in one who is a man and not something superhuman, not something which appears in the form of an outward revelation—in short, the main stress is to be laid on the fact that this divine presence is essentially identical with what is human.

Christ calls Himself the Son of God and the Son of Man; these titles are to be taken in their strict meaning. The Arabs mutually describe themselves as the son of a certain tribe; Christ belongs to the human race; that is His tribe. Christ is also the Son of God; it is possible to explain away by exegesis the true sense of this expression, the truth of the Idea, what Christ has been for His Church, and the higher Idea of the truth which has been found in Him in His Church, and to say that all the children of men are children of God, or are meant to make themselves children of God, and so on.

Since, however, the teaching of Christ taken by itself belongs to the world of ordinary figurative ideas only, and takes to do with inner feeling and disposition, it is supplemented by the representation of the Divine Idea in His life and fate. That Kingdom of God, as constituting the content of Christ's teaching, is at first the Idea in a general form, represented as yet in a general conception; it is by means of this individual man that it enters into the region of reality, so that those who are to reach that Kingdom can do it through that one individual.

The primary point is, to start with, the abstract correspondence between the acts, deeds, and sufferings of this teacher, and His own teaching, the fact that His life was wholly devoted to carrying it out, that He did not shun death, and that He sealed His faith by His death. The fact that Christ became a martyr for the truth has an intimate connection with His appearing thus on the earth. Since the founding of the Kingdom of God is in direct contradiction with the actually existing State, which is based on a different view of religion, and which ascribes a different character to it, the fate of Christ, whereby—to put it in human language—He became a martyr for the truth, is in close connection with the manner of His appearing above referred to.

These are the principal elements in the manifestation
of Christ in a human form.   This teacher gathered friends
around Him.   Inasmuch as His doctrines were revolutionary Christ was accused and condemned, and so He sealed
the truth of His teaching by His death.   Even unbelief goes
this length in the view it takes of His history; it is exactly
similar to that of Socrates, only in different surroundings.
Socrates, too, made men conscious of the inwardness
of their nature.   His δαιμονιον is nothing else than this
inner life.   He, too, taught that Man must not stop
short with obedience to ordinary authority, but form
convictions for himself, and act in accordance with these
convictions.   These two individualities are similar, and
their fates are also similar.   The inwardness of Socrates
was in direct opposition to the religious belief of his
nation, and to the form of government, and consequently
he was condemned; he, too, died for the truth.

Christ lived merely amongst a different people, and
His teaching has so far a different complexion.   But the
Kingdom of God and the idea of purity of heart contain
an infinitely greater depth of truth than the inwardness of
Socrates.   This is the outward history of Christ, which is
for unbelief just what the history of Socrates is for us.

With the *death* of Christ, however, there begins the
conversion of consciousness.   The death of Christ is the
central point round which all else turns, and in the conception formed of it lies the difference between the outward way of conceiving of it and Faith, *i.e.*, regarding it
with the spirit, taking our start from the spirit of truth,
from the Holy Spirit.   According to the comparison above
referred to, Christ is a man just like Socrates, a teacher
who lived virtuously, and made men conscious of what
is essentially true, of what must constitute the basis of
human consciousness.   According to the higher way of
regarding the matter, however, the divine nature was
revealed in Christ.   This consciousness is reflected in those
passages which state that the Son knows the Father, &c.,

expressions which, to begin with, have in themselves a
certain generality, and which exegesis can transfer to the
region of general views, but which Faith by its explanation of the death of Christ lays hold of in their true
meaning; for Faith is essentially the consciousness of
absolute truth, of what God is in His true nature. But
we have already seen what God is in His true essential
nature; He is the life-process, the Trinity, in which the
Universal puts itself into antithesis with itself, and is in
this antithesis identical with itself. God in this element
of eternity represents what encloses itself in union with
itself, the enclosing of Himself with Himself. Faith
simply lays hold of the thought and has the consciousness
that in Christ this absolute essential truth is perceived
in the process of its development, and that it is through
Him that this truth has first been revealed.

This view represents, to begin with, the religious
attitude as such, in which the Divine is itself an essential moment. This anticipation, this imagining, this
willing of a new Kingdom, "a new heaven and a new
earth," of a new world, is found amongst those friends
and acquaintances who have been taught the truth; this
hope, this certainty has made its way into the real part
of their hearts, has sunk into their inmost hearts as a
reality.

Accordingly the Passion, the death of Christ does away
with the human side of Christ's nature, and it is just in
connection with this death that the transition is made
into the religious sphere; and here the question comes to
be as to how this death is to be conceived of. On the
one hand, it is a natural death brought about by injustice,
hate, and violence; on the other hand, however, believers
are already firmly convinced in their hearts and feelings
that they are not here specially concerned with morality,
with the thinking and willing of the subject in itself or as
starting from itself, but that the real point of importance
is an infinite relation to God, to God as actually present,

the certainty of the Kingdom of God, a sense of satisfaction not in morality, nor even in anything ethical, nor in the conscience, but a sense of satisfaction beyond which there can be nothing higher, an absolute relation to God Himself.

All other modes of satisfaction imply that in some aspect or other they are of a subordinate sort, and thus the relation of Man to God does not get beyond being a relation to something above, and distant, to something, in fact, which is not actually present at all. The fundamental characteristic of this Kingdom of God is the presence of God, meaning that the members of this Kingdom are not only expected to have love to men, but to have the consciousness that God is Love.

This implies, in fact, that God is present, and that this as personal feeling must be the feeling of the individual Self. This aspect of the truth is represented by the Kingdom of God, or the presence of God, and it is to it that the certainty of the presence of God belongs.   Since it is, on the one hand, a need, a feeling, the subject must, on the other hand, distinguish itself from it, must make a distinction between this presence of God and itself, but in such a way that this presence of God will be something certain, and this certainty can actually exist here only in the form of sensuous manifestation.

The eternal Idea itself means that the characteristic of subjectivity as real, as distinguished from what are simply thoughts, is permitted to appear in an immediate form. On the other hand, it is faith begotten by the sorrow of the world, and resting on the testimony of the Spirit, which explains the life of Christ.   The teaching of Christ and His miracles are conceived of and understood in connection with this witness of the Spirit.   The history of Christ is related, too, by those upon whom the Spirit has been already poured out.   The miracles are conceived of and related under the influence of this Spirit, and the death of Christ is truly understood by this Spirit to mean

that in Christ God is revealed together with the unity of
the Divine and human natures. Christ's death is accordingly the touchstone, so to speak, by means of which
Faith verifies its belief, since it is essentially here that its
way of understanding the appearance of Christ makes
itself manifest. Christ's death primarily means that
Christ was the God-Man, the God who had at the same
time human nature, even unto death. It is the lot of
finite humanity to die ; death is the most complete proof
of humanity, of absolute finitude, and Christ in fact died
the aggravated death of the evil-doer ; He did not only die
a natural death, but a death even of shame and dishonour
on the cross ; in Him humanity was carried to its furthest
point.

In connection with this death we have to notice first of
all what is one of its special characteristics, namely, its
polemical attitude towards outward things. Not only is
the act whereby the natural will yields itself up here
represented in a sensible form, but all that is peculiar to
the individual, all those interests and personal ends with
which the natural will can occupy itself, all that is great
and counted as of value in the world, is at the same time
buried in the grave of the Spirit. This is the revolutionary element by means of which the world is given
a totally new form. And yet in this yielding up of the
natural will, the finite, the Other-Being or otherness, is at
the same time transfigured. Other-Being or otherness
has in fact besides its immediate natural being a more
extended sphere of existence and a further determination.
It belongs essentially to the definite existence of the subject that it should exist for others ; the subject exists not
only on its own account or for itself, but exists also in
the idea formed of it by others, it exists, has value, and
is objective to the extent to which it is able to assert its
claim to exist amongst others and has a valid existence.
Its validity is the idea formed of it by others, and is based
on a comparison with what they hold to be of value

and what is regarded by them as possessing the worth of something potential or essential.

Since, accordingly, the death of Christ, in addition to the fact that it is natural death, is, further, the death of an evil-doer, the most degrading of all deaths, death upon the cross, it involves not only what is natural, but also civil degradation, worldly dishonour; the cross is transfigured, what according to the common idea is lowest, what the State characterises as degrading, is transformed into what is highest. Death is natural, every man must die. But since degradation is made the highest honour, all those ties that bind human society together are attacked in their foundations, are shaken and dissolved. When the cross has been elevated to the place of a banner, and is made a banner in fact, the positive content of which is at the same time the Kingdom of God, inner feeling is in the very heart of its nature detached from civil and state life, and the substantial basis of this latter is taken away, so that the whole structure has no longer any reality, but is an empty appearance, which must soon come crashing down, and make manifest in actual existence that it is no longer anything having inherent existence. Imperial power, on its part, degraded all that was esteemed and valued by men. The life of every individual depended on the caprice of the Emperor, and this caprice was not limited by anything either without or within. But, besides life, all virtue, worth, age, rank, race, everything, in short, was utterly degraded. The slave of the Emperor was next to him the highest power in the State, or had even more power than the Emperor himself; the Senate debased itself in proportion as it was debased by the Emperor. Thus the majesty of world-empire, together with all virtue, justice, veneration for institutions and constituted things, the majesty of everything, in short, held by the world as of value was pitched into the gutter. Thus the temporal ruler of the earth, on his part, changed what was highest into what was most despised, and fundamentally perverted feeling, so that in man's inner life there no longer remained anything to set against the new religion, which in its turn raised what had been most despised to the place of what was highest, and made it a banner. Everything established, everything moral, everything considered by ordinary opinion as of value and possessed of authority, was destroyed, and all that was left to the existing order of things, towards which the new religion took up a position of antagonism, was the purely external, cold power, namely, death, which life, ennobled by feeling that in its inner nature it was infinite now, no longer in any way dreaded.

Now, however, a further determination comes into play—God has died, God is dead,—this is the most frightful of all thoughts, that all that is eternal, all that is true is not, that negation itself is found in God ; the deepest sorrow, the feeling of something completely irretrievable, the renunciation of everything of a higher kind, are connected with this. The course of thought does not, however, stop short here ; on the contrary, thought begins to retrace its steps : God, that is to say, maintains Himself in this process, and the latter is only the death of death. God comes to life again, and thus things are reversed.[1] The Resurrection is something which thus

[1] This is the meaning of the resurrection and the ascension of Christ. Like all that goes before, this elevation of Christ to heaven outwardly appears for the immediate or natural consciousness in the mode of reality. " Thou wilt not leave Thy righteous one in the grave ; Thou wilt not suffer Thine Holy One to see corruption." This is the form, too, in which this death of death, the overcoming of the grave, the triumph over the negative, and this elevation to heaven appear to sense-perception. This triumphing over the negative is not, however, a putting off of human nature, but, on the contrary, is its most complete preservation in death itself and in the highest love. Spirit is Spirit only in so far as it is this negative of the negative which thus contains the negative in itself. When, accordingly, the Son of Man sits on the right hand of the Father, we see that in this exaltation of human nature its glory consists, and its identity with the divine nature appears to the spiritual eye in the highest possible way.— (From the sheets in Hegel's own handwriting belonging to the year 1821.)

essentially belongs to faith. After His resurrection Christ appeared only to His friends; this is not outward history for unbelief, but, on the contrary, this appearing of Christ is for faith only. The resurrection is followed by the glorification of Christ; and the triumph of His exaltation to the right hand of God closes this part of His history, which, as thus understood by believing consciousness, is the unfolding of the Divine nature itself. If in the first division of the subject we conceived of God as He is in pure thought, in this second division we start from immediacy as it exists for sense-perception and for ideas based on sense. The process is accordingly this, that immediate particularity is done away with and absorbed; and just as in the first region of thought, God's state of seclusion came to an end, and His primary immediacy as abstract universality, according to which He is the Essence of Essences, was annulled, so here the abstraction of humanity, the immediacy of existing particularity, is annulled, and this is brought about by death; the death of Christ, however, is the death of death, the negation of the negation. We have had in the Kingdom of the Father the same course and process in the unfolding of God's nature; here, however, the process is explained in so far as it is an object for consciousness. For here there existed the impulse to form a mental picture of the divine nature. In connection with the death of Christ we have finally to emphasise the moment according to which it is God who has killed death, since He comes out of the state of death : this means that finitude, human nature, and humiliation are attributed to Christ as something foreign to His nature, which is that of one who is God pure and simple; it is shown that finitude is something foreign to His nature, and has been adopted by Him from an Other; this Other is represented by men who stand over against the divine process. It is their finitude which Christ has taken upon Himself, this finitude in all its forms, and which at its furthest extreme is represented by Evil; this humanity, which is itself a moment in the divine life, is now characterised as something foreign to God, as something which does not belong to His nature; this finitude, however, in its condition of Being-for-self, or as existing independently in relation to God, is evil, something foreign to God's nature; He has, however, taken our finite nature in order to slay it by His death. His shameful death, as representing the marvellous union of these absolute extremes, is at the same time infinite love.

It is a proof of infinite love that God identified Himself with what was foreign to His nature in order to slay it. This is the signification of the death of Christ. Christ has borne the sins of the world, He has reconciled God to us, as it is said.

This death is thus at once finitude in its most extreme form, and at the same time the abolition and absorption of natural finitude, of immediate existence and estrangement, the cancelling of limits. This abolition and absorption of the natural is to be conceived of in a spiritual sense as essentially meaning that the movement of Spirit consists in comprehending itself in itself, in dying to the natural, that it is therefore abstraction from immediate volition and immediate consciousness, an act of sinking into itself, and then an act whereby it itself draws out of this depth into which it has plunged what is merely its own specific character, its true essence, and its absolute universality. What has for it worth, and all that constitutes its value, it finds only in this abolition of its natural Being and will. The suffering and the sorrow connected with this death which contains this element of the reconciliation of Spirit with itself and with what it potentially is, this negative moment which belongs to Spirit only as Spirit, is inner conversion and change. Here, however, death is not brought before us with this concrete meaning, but is represented as natural death, for in the Divine Idea that negation cannot be exhibited under any other form. When the eternal history of Spirit exhibits itself in an outward way, in the sphere of the natural, Evil which realises itself in the Divine Idea can appear only in the form of the Natural, and thus the reversion which takes place can have only the form of natural death. The Divine Idea cannot proceed beyond this characteristic of the natural. This death, however, although it is natural, is the death of God, and thus sufficient as an atonement for us, since it exhibits the absolute history of the Divine Idea, what has implicitly taken place and takes place eternally.

That the individual man does something, attains to something, and accomplishes it, is owing to the fact that this is how the matter stands regarding the true reality looked at from the point of view of its Notion. The fact, for example, that any particular criminal can be punished by the judge, and that this punishment is the carrying out and expiation of the law, does not imply that it is the judge who does this, or that the criminal does it by undergoing the punishment as a particular outward event; but, on the contrary, what takes place is in accordance with the nature of the thing or true fact, with the necessity of the Notion. We thus have this process before us in a double form : on the one hand, we have it in thought, in the idea embodied in law, and in the Notion ; and, on the other, in one particular instance, and in this particular instance the process is what it is because this belongs to the nature of the thing, and apart from this neither the action of the judge nor the suffering undergone by the criminal would represent the punishment inflicted by the law and the expiation it demands. The fundamental reason, the substantial element, belongs to the nature of the thing.

Accordingly this is how it stands, too, with that satisfaction or atonement for us above referred to, i.e., what lies at the basis of that idea is that this atonement has actually and completely taken place, has taken place

in-and-for-itself; it is not a strange sacrifice, a sacrifice
of what is foreign to man which has been offered, it is
not an Other who has been punished in order that there
might be punishment. Each one must for himself, starting from his own subjectivity and responsibility, do and
be what he ought to be. But what he thus is for himself must not be anything accidental, or be his own
caprice; it must, on the contrary, be something true.
When he thus accomplishes within himself this conversion and the yielding up of the natural will, and lives
in love, this represents the essential fact, the thing in-
and-for-itself. His subjective certainty, his feeling, is
truth, it is the truth and the nature of the Spirit. The
basis of redemption is thus contained in the history
spoken of, for it represents the essential thing or fact,
the thing as it is in-and-for-itself; it is not an accidental
special act and occurrence, but is true and complete.
This proof of its truth is the pictorial view given of it in
the history referred to, and according to that representation the individual lays hold of, appropriates the merit
of Christ. It is not, however, the history of one individual; on the contrary, it is God who accomplishes what
is told in it; *i.e.*, the view which it gives is that this
history is the universal and absolute history, the history
which is for itself.

Other forms, for example, of the sacrificial offering,
with which is connected the false idea that God is a
tyrant who desires sacrifice, reduce themselves to that
conception of sacrifice which has been stated, and are to
be corrected by it. Sacrifice means the abolition and
absorption of naturalness, of Otherness. It is further
said that Christ died for *all*, and this does not represent
an individual act, but the divine eternal history. It is
said in the same way that in Him all have died. This
is itself a moment in the nature of God; it has taken
place in God Himself. God cannot find satisfaction
through anything other than Himself, but only through

Himself. This death is love itself, expressed as a moment of God, and it is this death which brings about reconciliation. In it we have a picture of absolute love. It is the identity of the Divine and the human, it implies that in the finite God is at home with Himself, and this finite as seen in death is itself a determination belonging to God. God has through death reconciled the world, and reconciled it eternally with Himself. This coming-back from the state of estrangement is His return to Himself, and it is because of it that He is Spirit, and the third point accordingly is that Christ has risen. Negation is consequently surmounted, and the negation of the negation is thus a moment of the Divine nature.

Suffering and dying taken in this sense are ideas opposed to the doctrine of moral imputation according to which each individual has to stand for himself only, and each is the doer of his own deeds. The fate of Christ seems to contradict this imputation; this imputation, however, has a place only in the sphere of finitude, where the subject is regarded as a single person, and not in the sphere of free Spirit. The characteristic idea in the region of finitude is that each remains what he is; if he has done evil, he is evil; evil is in him as representing his quality. But already in the sphere of morality, and still more in that of religion, Spirit is known to be free, to be affirmative in itself, so that the element of limit in it which gets the length of evil is a nullity for the infinitude of Spirit; Spirit can make what has happened as if it had not happened; the action certainly remains in the memory, but Spirit puts it away. Imputation, therefore, does not reach to this sphere. For the true consciousness of Spirit the finitude of Man is slain in the death of Christ. This death of the natural gets in this way a universal signification, the finite, evil, in fact, is destroyed. The world is thus reconciled, and through this death the world is implicitly freed from its evil. It is in connection with a true understanding of the death of

Christ that the relation of the subject as such in this way comes into view. Here any mere outward consideration of the history ceases; the subject is itself drawn into the process; it feels the pain of evil and of its own alienation, which Christ has taken upon Himself by putting on humanity, while at the same time destroying it by His death.

Since the content, too, just consists in this, we have here the religious side of the subject, and it is in it that the Spiritual Community, or the Church, first originates. This content is the same thing as what is termed the outpouring of the Holy Spirit. It is Spirit which has revealed this; the relation to men simply as men is changed into a relation which is altered and transformed into a relation which is entirely one of Spirit, and is of such a kind that the nature of God unfolds itself in it, and this truth comes to have immediate certainty in accordance with the form of outward manifestation.

Here, accordingly, he who at first was regarded as a teacher, a friend, a martyr, comes to have a totally different position. Up to this point we have had simply the beginning, which is now carried forward by the Spirit so as to form a result, an end, truth. The death of Christ is in one aspect the death of a man, of a friend who met his death by violence, &c. ; but then it is just this death which, when conceived of in a spiritual way, becomes the means of salvation and the central point of reconciliation.

The perception of the nature of Spirit, that is, the presentation of the satisfaction of the need of Spirit, in a sensuous way, was accordingly what was disclosed to the friends of Christ only after His death. Thus the conviction concerning Him which it was possible for them to get from a study of His life was not yet the real truth ; but, on the contrary, it was the Spirit which first showed them the truth.

Before His death He appeared to them as an individual

under the limitations of sense; the real disclosure of what He was was given to them by the Spirit, of whom Christ said, "He will lead you into all truth." "That will first be the truth into which the Spirit will lead you."

Regarded in this aspect this death consequently assumes the character of a death which is the transition to glory, to a glorified state, which, however, is merely a restoration of the original glorified state. The death, the negative, is the mediating element implying that the original state of majesty is thought of as having been reached. The history of the resurrection and exaltation of Christ to the right hand of God forms part of the history of His death when this comes to have a spiritual signification.

Thus it came about that this little community of believers attained the sure conviction: God has appeared in the form of Man; this humanity in God, and this humanity in its most abstract form, the most complete dependence, weakness in its most extreme form, the final stage of frailty, is just what we have in natural death.

"God Himself is dead," as it is said in a Lutheran hymn; the consciousness of this fact expresses the truth that the human, the finite, frailty, weakness, the negative, is itself a divine moment, is in God Himself; that otherness or Other-Being, the finite, the negative, is not outside of God, and that in its character as otherness it does not hinder unity with God; otherness, the negation, is consciously known to be a moment of the Divine nature. The highest knowledge of the nature of the Idea of Spirit is contained in this thought.

This outward negative changes round in this way into the inner negative. Regarded in one aspect the meaning, the signification attached to death is that in it the human element has been stripped off, and the divine glory comes again into view. But death is itself at the same time also the negative, the furthest point of that experience to which man as a natural being and consequently God Himself are exposed.

In this whole history men have attained to the consciousness of a truth, and this is the truth which they have reached, namely, that the Idea of God has come to be a certainty for them, that the human is God as immediate and present, and this indeed means that we have in this history, as understood by Spirit, the actual representation of the process of what constitutes Man or Spirit. Man as potentially God and dead—that is the mediation whereby the human element is discarded ; or, regarded from another point of view, what has potential or essential Being returns to itself and by this act first comes to be Spirit.

It is with the consciousness of the Spiritual Community, which thus makes the transition from man pure and simple to a God-man, and to a perception, a consciousness, a certainty of the unity and union of the Divine and human natures, that the Church or Spiritual Community begins, and it is this consciousness which constitutes the truth upon which the Spiritual Community is founded.

This then is the explication of the meaning of reconciliation, that God is reconciled with the world, or rather that God has shown Himself to *be* by His very nature reconciled with the world, that what is human is not something alien to His nature, but that this otherness, this self-differentiation, finitude, as it is sometimes expressed, is a moment in God Himself, though, to be sure, it is a vanishing moment ; still He has in this moment revealed and shown Himself to the Church.

This is the form which the history of God's manifestation takes for the Church ; this history is a divine history whereby it reaches a consciousness of the truth. It is this which creates the consciousness, the knowledge, that God is a Trinity.

The reconciliation believed in as being in Christ has no meaning if God is not known as Trinity, if it is not recognised that He *is* but is at the same time the Other, the self-differentiating, the Other in the sense that this

Other is God Himself and has potentially the divine nature in it, and that the abolishing of this difference, of this otherness, this return, this love, is Spirit.

This consciousness involves the truth that faith does not express relation to anything which is an Other, but relation to God Himself. These are the moments with which we are here concerned, and which express the truth that Man has come to a consciousness of that eternal history, that eternal movement which God Himself is.

This is the description of the second Idea as Idea in outward manifestation, and of how the eternal Idea has come to exist for the immediate certainty of Man, *i.e.*, of how it has appeared in history. The fact that it is a certainty for men necessarily implies that it is material or sensuous certainty, but one which at the same time passes over into spiritual consciousness, and for the same reason is converted into immediate sensuousness, but in such a way that we recognise in it the movement, the history of God, the life which God Himself is.

III.

THE IDEA IN THE ELEMENT OF THE CHURCH OR SPIRITUAL COMMUNITY, OR, THE KINGDOM OF SPIRIT.

What was first dealt with was the notion or conception of this standpoint for consciousness; what came second was what was supplied to this standpoint, what actually exists for the Spiritual Community; the third point is the transition into this Community itself.

This third sphere represents the Idea in its specific character as individuality; but, to begin with, it exhibits only the one individuality, the divine, universal individuality as it is in-and-for-itself. One is thus all; once is always, potentially, from the point of view of the Notion, it is simple determinateness. But individuality in its character as independent Being, Being-for-self, is this act of allowing the differentiated moments to reach free immediacy and independence, it shuts them off from each other; individuality just means that it has at the same time to be empirical individuality.

Individuality as exclusive is for others immediacy, and is the return from the Other into self. The individuality of the Divine Idea, the Divine Idea as a person, first attains to completeness in reality, since at first it has the many individuals confronting it, and brings these back into the unity of Spirit, into the Church or Spiritual Community, and exists here as real, universal self-consciousness.

It is just in connection with the act whereby the definite transition of the Idea to the sensuous present is accomplished that we have what is most distinctive in the religion of Spirit, namely, that all the moments are developed till they have reached definiteness and completeness in their most external forms. But even in this condition of extreme opposition Spirit is certain of itself as being absolute truth, and consequently it is afraid of nothing, not even of the sensuous present. It is part of the cowardice of abstract thought that it shuns the sensuous present in a monkish fashion; modern abstraction takes up this attitude of fastidious gentility towards the moment of the sensuous present.

It is next required of the individuals in the Community or Church that they should revere the Divine Idea in the form of individuality, and appropriate it to themselves. For the tender, loving disposition, that of woman, this is easy ; but then, on the other side, we are confronted with the fact that the subject on which this demand is made is in a condition of infinite freedom, and has come to understand the substantiality of its self-consciousness; for the independent Notion, the man, this demand is accordingly infinitely hard. The freedom of the subject rebels against the thought of reverencing a single sensuous individual as God, and against the combination which this implies. The Oriental does not hesitate to comply with this demand, but then he is nothing, he is implicitly thrown aside as of no value, without, however, having thrown himself aside, i.e., without having the consciousness of infinite freedom in himself. Here, however, this love, this recognition of the Divine in an individual is the direct opposite of this, and is just what constitutes the supreme miracle, that miracle which Spirit itself just is.

This region is accordingly the Kingdom of Spirit, implying that the individual is of infinite value in himself, knows himself to be absolute freedom, possesses in himself the most rigid fixedness, and at the same time yields up this fixedness and maintains himself in what is absolutely an Other. Love harmonises all things, even absolute opposition.

The pictorial conception of this religion demands the despising of all that presently exists, of everything which is otherwise regarded as possessed of value, it is that perfect ideality which takes up a polemical attitude towards all the glory of the world; in this single person, in this present immediate individual in whom the Divine Idea appears, everything that belongs to the world has met together, so that it is the individual sensuous present which has value. This individuality or particularity is consequently to be regarded as absolutely universal. Even in ordinary love we find this infinite abstraction from all worldly things, and the loving person centres all his satisfaction in one particular individual; but this satisfaction still belongs essentially to particularity; it is particular contingency and feeling which opposes itself to the Universal, and desires in this way to become objective.

In contrast to this, that individuality in which I will the Divine Idea, is purely universal, it is for this reason directly removed from the sphere of the senses, it passes away of itself, becomes part of a history that is past, this

sensuous mode must disappear and mount into the region
of idea or mental representation. One of the constituent
parts of the formation of the Church is that this sensuous
form passes over into a spiritual element. The mode in
which this purification from immediate Being takes place
implies that the sensuous element in it is preserved ; the
fact that it passes away is negation, as this is posited in
and appears in one particular sensuous individual as such.
It is only in a single individual that this sensuous representation is found, it is not something which can be
inherited, and is not capable of renewal as the manifestation of substance in the Lama is, it cannot appear in such
a way because the sensuous manifestation as a definite
individual manifestation is in its nature momentary ;
it has to be spiritualised, and is therefore essentially a
manifestation that has already been, and so is raised to
the region of idea or mental representation.

It is possible also to occupy a standpoint at which we
do not get beyond the Son and His appearance in time.
This is the case in Catholicism, in which the intercession
of Mary and the Saints is added to the reconciling power
of the Son, and where the Spirit is present, rather in the
Church as a hierarchy merely, and not in the Community
of believers.   Here, however, the second element in the
specification of the Idea is not so much spiritualised, but
rather remains in the region of ordinary thought.   Or to
put it otherwise, Spirit is not so much known as objective,
but merely as the particular subjective form in which it
appears in the sensuous present as the Church and lives
in tradition.   Spirit in this outward form of reality is,
as it were, the Third Person.

For the spirit which stands in need of it, the sensuous
present can be given a permanent existence in pictures,
though these are not indeed works of art, but are rather
miracle-working pictures, regarded, that is to say, as
existing in a definite material form.   It follows from this
that it is not merely the corporeal form and the body of

Christ which is able to satisfy the sensuous need, but rather the sensuous aspect of His bodily presence in general, the cross, the places in which He moved about, and so on. To this, relics, &c., come to be added. There is no lack of such mediate means of satisfying the craving felt. For the Spiritual Community, however, the immediate Present, the Now, is past and gone. The sensuous idea accordingly, above all, integrates the Past, views it from the point of view of the whole, for it the Past is a one-sided moment; the Present contains the Past and the Future in it as moments. Thus the sensuous idea finds the completion of its representation in the Second Advent, but the essentially absolute return is the act of exchanging externality for what is inward : this is the Comforter who can come only when sensuous history as immediate is past.

This, therefore, is the point represented by the formation of the Spiritual Community, or the third point; it is the Spirit. It represents the transition from what is outward, from outward manifestation to what is inward. It occupies itself with the certainty felt by the subject of its own infinite non-sensuous substantiality, and of the fact that it knows itself to be infinite and eternal, knows itself to be immortal.

The retreat into inner self-consciousness which is involved in this conversion is not of the Stoical kind, the value of which consists in the fact that it accomplishes this through the strength of the individual spirit as exercising thought, and seeks for the reality of thought in Nature, in natural things and in comprehending these, and which consequently is devoid of infinite sorrow and stands at the same time in a thoroughly positive relation to the world. On the contrary, it takes the form of the self-consciousness which endlessly yields up its particularity and individuality, and finds its infinite value only in that love which is contained in infinite sorrow and arises out of it. All immediacy in which Man might find some worth is thrown away; it is in mediation alone that he finds such value, but of an infinite kind, and in which subjectivity becomes truly infinite and has an essential existence, is in-and-for-itself. It is only through this mediation that Man is not immediate, and thus at first he is *capable* merely of having such value; but this capacity and possibility is his positive, absolute, essential nature or characteristic.

This characteristic contains the reason why the immortality of the soul becomes a definite doctrine in the Christian religion. The soul, the individual soul, has an infinite, an eternal quality, namely, that of being a citizen in the Kingdom of God. This is a quality and a life which is removed beyond time and the Past; and since it is at the same time opposed to the present limited sphere, this eternal quality or determination eternally, determines itself at the same time as a future. The infinite demand to see God, *i.e.*, to become conscious in spirit of His truth as present truth, is in this temporal Present not yet satisfied so far as consciousness in its character as ordinary consciousness is concerned.

The subjectivity which has come to understand its infinite worth has thereby abandoned all distinctions of authority, power, position, and even of race; before God all men are equal. It is in the negation of infinite sorrow that love is found, and there, too, are first found the possibility and the root of truly universal Right, of the realisation of freedom. The Roman formal life of right or justice starts from the positive standpoint and from the Understanding, and has no principle whereby to maintain absolutely the standpoint of Right, but is thoroughly worldly.

This purity of subjectivity which passes out of infinite sorrow by mediating itself in love, is reached simply by that mediation which has its objective form and pictorial representation in the sufferings, death, and exaltation of

Christ. Regarded from another point of view, this subjectivity likewise possesses this mode of its reality in
itself, inasmuch as it is a multiplicity of subjects and
individuals; but since it is implicitly universal and is
not exclusive, the multiplicity of individuals has to be
absolutely posited as having merely the appearance or
show of reality, and the very fact that it posits itself as
this show of reality is what constitutes the unity of
faith, according to the ordinary idea formed by faith,
and therefore in this third thing. This is the love of
the Spiritual Community, which seems to consist of
many individuals, while this multiplicity is merely a
semblance or illusion.

This love is neither human love, love of persons, the
love of the sexes, nor friendship. Surprise has often
been expressed that such a noble relationship as friendship is does not find a place amongst the duties enjoined
by Christ. Friendship is a relationship which is tinged
with particularity, and men are friends not so much
directly as objectively rather through some substantial
bond of union, in a third thing, in fundamental principles, studies, knowledge; the bond, in short, is constituted by something objective; it is not attachment as
such, like that of the man to the woman as a definite
particular personality. The love of the Spiritual Community, on the other hand, is directly mediated by the
worthlessness of all particularity. The love of the man
for the woman, or friendship, can certainly exist, but
they are essentially characterised as subordinate; they
are characterised not indeed as something evil, but as
something imperfect; not as something indifferent, but
as representing a state in which we are not to remain
permanently, since they are themselves to be sacrificed,
and must not in any way injuriously affect that absolute
tendency and unity which belong to Spirit.

The unity in this infinite love springing out of infinite
sorrow is consequently in no way a sensuous, worldly

connection of things, not a connection of the particularity and naturalness which may still remain over and be held to have value, but unity in the Spirit simply, the love, in fact, which is just the notion or conception of Spirit itself. It is an object for itself in Christ as representing the central point of faith, in which it appears to itself in an infinite, far-off loftiness. But this loftiness is at the same time an infinite nearness to the subject, something peculiar to it and belonging to it, and thus what at first comprised individuals as a Third is also what constitutes their true self-consciousness, their most inner and individual character. Thus this love is Spirit as such, the Holy Spirit. It is in them, and they are and constitute the universal Christian Church, the Communion of saints. Spirit is infinite return into self, infinite subjectivity, not Godhead conceived of in ideas, but the real present Godhead, and thus it is not the substantial potentiality of the Father, not the True in the objective or antithetical form of the Son, but the subjective Present and Real, which, just because it is subjective, is present, as estrangement into that objective, sensuous representation of love and of its infinite sorrow, and as return, in that mediation. This is the Spirit of God, or God as present, real Spirit, God dwelling in His Church. Thus Christ said, "Where two or three are gathered together in My name, there am I in the midst of you." "I am with you always, even to the end of the world."

It is as containing this absolute signification of Spirit, and in this deep sense of being absolute truth, that the Christian religion is the Religion of Spirit, though not in the trivial sense of being a spiritual religion. On the contrary, the true element in the determination of the nature of Spirit, the union of the two sides of the infinite antithesis—God and the world, I, this particular *homuncio*—is what constitutes the content of the Christian religion, and makes it into a religion of Spirit, and this content is also found in it by the ordinary uncultured consciousness.

All men are called to salvation; that is what is highest in the Christian religion and highest in a unique degree. Therefore Christ also says, " All sins can be forgiven to men except the sin against the Spirit." The violation of absolute truth, of the Idea of that union of the two sides of the infinite antithesis, is in these words declared to be the supreme transgression. People have from time to time given themselves a deal of trouble and racked their brains trying to find out what is the sin against the Holy Spirit, and have smoothed down this significant expression in all kinds of ways in order to get entirely rid of it. Everything can be destroyed in the infinite sorrow of love, but this destroying process itself appears only as inner present Spirit. What is devoid of Spirit appears at first to have no sin in it, but to be innocent; but this is just the innocence which is by its very nature judged and condemned.

The sphere of the Spiritual Community is accordingly the region which belongs peculiarly to Spirit. The Holy Spirit was poured out on the disciples, it was their immanent life, from that time onward they joyfully went out into the world as a Spiritual Community, in order to raise it to the condition of a universal Community of believers, and to extend far and wide the Kingdom of God.

We have thus to consider (*a*) the *origin* of the Spiritual Community, or, in other words, its conception or notion; (*b*) its existence in a definite form and its *continued existence*, this is the realisation of its conception; and (*c*) the transition from faith to knowledge, the *alteration*, the *transfiguration* of faith in philosophy.

(*a.*) *The Conception of the Spiritual Community.*

The Spiritual Community consists of the subjects or persons, the individual, empirical subjects who live in the

Spirit of God, though at the same time it is necessary to distinguish between them and the definite content, the history, the truth which confronts them. Faith in this history, in reconciliation, is, on the one hand, immediate knowledge, an act of faith ; on the other hand, the nature of Spirit is in itself this process which has been considered in the universal Idea, and in the Idea in the form of manifestation, and this means that the subject itself is nothing but Spirit, and consequently becomes a citizen of the Kingdom of God owing to the fact that it passes through this process in virtue of what it is. The Other, which exists for the subjects, exists for them objectively in this divine drama in the sense in which the spectator beheld himself objectively in the Chorus.

To begin with, it is undoubtedly the subject, the human subject, Man, in whom is revealed what comes by the aid of Spirit to have for Man the certainty of reconciliation, and comes to be characterised as individual, exclusive, different from others. Thus the representation of the divine history is an objective one so far as the other subjects are concerned ; they have accordingly still to pass through this history and this process in their own selves also.

In order to this, however, they must first presuppose that reconciliation is possible, or, to put it more accurately, that this reconciliation has actually and completely taken place and is a certainty.

This is the universal Idea of God in-and-for-itself ; the other presupposition is that this reconciliation is something certain for Man, and that this truth does not exist for him by means of speculative thought, but is, on the contrary, something certain. This presupposition implies that it is certain that the reconciliation has been accomplished, *i.e.*, it must be represented as something historical, as something which has been accomplished on the earth, in a manifested form. For there is no other mode of representing what is called certainty. This is

the presupposition in which we must believe, to begin
with.

1. The rise of the Spiritual Community appears in the
form of an outpouring of the Holy Spirit. Faith takes
its rise first of all in a man, a human, material manifestation ; and next comes spiritual comprehension, consciousness of the Spiritual. We get spiritual content, a
changing of what is immediate into what has a spiritual
character. The verification here is spiritual, it is not
found in what is sensuous or material ; and it cannot
be brought about in an immediate, material way ; some
objection can always be brought against the material
facts.

As regards the empirical mode of verifying the truth,
the Church is so far right when it refuses to countenance
investigations such as those concerned with the appearances of Christ after His death ; for investigations of
this sort start from a point of view which implies that
the real question is as to the sensuous element in the
appearance of Christ, as to what is historical in it, as if
the verification of Spirit and of *its* truth was contained
in such narratives regarding one who was represented as
an historical person and in an historical fashion. This
truth, however, is sure and certain by itself, although it
has an historical starting-point.

This transition is the outpouring of the Spirit, which
could make its appearance only after Christ had been
taken away out of the flesh, and the sensuous, immediate
present had ceased. It is then the Spirit appears, for
then the entire history is completed, and the entire
picture of Spirit is present to perception. What Spirit
now produces is something different and has a different
form.

The question as to the truth of the Christian religion
directly divides itself into two questions : 1. Is it *really*
true that God does not exist apart from the Son, and that
He has sent Him into the world? And 2. Was *this par-*

ticular individual, Jesus of Nazareth, the carpenter's son, the Son of God, the Christ ?

These two questions are commonly mixed up together, with the result that if this particular person was not God's Son sent by Him, and if this cannot be proved to be true of Him, then there is no meaning at all in His mission. If this were not true of Him, we would either have to look for another, if indeed one is to come, if there is a promise to that effect, *i.e.*, if it is absolutely and essentially necessary, necessary from the point of view of the Notion, of the Idea ; or, since the correctness of the Idea is made to depend on the demonstration of the divine mission referred to, we should have to conclude that there can really be no longer any thought of such a mission, and that we cannot further think about it.

But it is essential that we ask first of all, Is such a manifestation true in-and-for-itself? It is, because God as Spirit is the triune God. He is this act of manifestation, this self-objectifying, and it is His nature to be identical with Himself while thus making Himself objective ; He is eternal love. This objectifying as seen in its completely developed form in which it reaches the two extremes of the universality of God and finitude or death, and this return into self in the act of abolishing the rigidity of the antithesis is—love in the infinite sorrow, which is at the same time assuaged in it.

This absolute truth, this truth in-and-for-itself that God is not an abstraction, but something concrete, is unfolded by philosophy, and it is only modern philosophy which has reached the profound thought thus contained in the Notion. It is not possible at all to discuss this truth in unphilosophical platitudes which suggest an idea of contradiction that is so entirely valueless and is so absolutely wanting in what is spiritual.

But this notion or conception must not be thought of as one which gets a complete form in philosophy only, it is not only potentially true ; on the contrary, it belongs essentially to philosophy to get a grasp of what *is*, of what is actually real in itself. All that is true starts from the form of immediacy as it appears in its mani- festation, *i.e.*, in its Being. The notion or conception must therefore be implicitly present in the self-con- sciousness of men, in the Spirit ; the World-Spirit must have conceived of itself after this fashion. This concep- tion of itself, however, is necessity in the form of the process of Spirit, which was exhibited in the preceding stages of religion, and chiefly in the Jewish, the Greek, and the Roman religions, and had for its result the notion or conception of the absolute unity of the divine and human natures, the reality of God, *i.e.*, God's objectifying of Himself as representing His truth. Thus the history of the world is the setting forth of this truth as a result in the immediate consciousness of Spirit.

We have seen God as a God of free men, though at first as yet in the subjective, limited, national spirit of the various peoples, and in the accidental shape which belongs to imagination ; next we had the sorrow of the world following on the crushing out of the national Spirit. This sorrow was the birthplace of the impulse felt by Spirit to know God as spiritual in a universal form and stripped of finitude. This need was created by the progress of history, by the gradual advance of the World-Spirit. This immediate impulse, this longing which wishes and craves for something definite, the instinct, as it were, of Spirit which is impelled to seek for this, demanded such an appearance in time, the manifestation of God as the infinite Spirit in the form of a real man.

" When the fulness of time was come, God sent His Son," *i.e.*, when Spirit had entered so deeply into itself as to know its infinitude, and to comprehend the Substantial in the subjectivity of immediate self-consciousness, in a subjectivity, however, which is at the same time infinite negativity, and is just, in consequence of this, absolutely universal.

The proof, however, that this particular individual is
the Christ, is of another kind, and has reference only to
the specific statement that this particular individual is
the Christ, and not any other individual, and has not to
do with the question as to whether in this case the Idea
does not exist at all. Christ said, " Run not hither and
thither ; the Kingdom of God is within you." Many
others amongst Jews and heathen were revered as divine
messengers or as gods. John the Baptist went before
Christ ; amongst the Greeks, statues were erected, for
instance, to Demetrius Poliorcetes as if he were a god ;
and the Roman Emperor was revered as God. Apol-
lonius of Tyana and many others passed for being
workers of miracles ; and for the Greeks, Hercules was
the man who by his deeds, which were at the same time
deeds of obedience merely, took his place amongst the
gods, and became God ; without mentioning that great
number of incarnations, and the deification implied in
being raised to Brahma, which we meet with amongst the
Hindus. But it was to Christ only that the Idea, when
it was ripe and the time was fulfilled, could attach itself,
and in Him only could it see itself realised. In the
heroic deeds of Hercules the nature of Spirit is still
imperfectly expressed. But the history of Christ is a
history for the Spiritual Community, since it is absolutely
adequate to the Idea ; while it is only the effort of
Spirit to reach the determination implied in the implicit
unity of the Divine and the Human, which lies at the
basis of those earlier forms, and can be recognised as
present in them. This is what must be regarded as the
essential thing, this is the verification, the absolute proof ;
this is what is to be understood by the witness of the
Spirit ; it is the Spirit, the indwelling Idea which attests
Christ's mission, and for those who believed, and for us
who are in possession of the Notion in its developed
form, this is verification. This is also the kind of verification whose force is of a spiritual kind, and is not

outward force such as that used by the Church against heretics.

This then is (2.) Knowledge or Faith, for faith is also knowledge only in a peculiar form. We have now to consider this point.

Thus what we see is that the divine content appears as self-conscious knowledge of the Divine in the element of consciousness, of inwardness. On the one hand, it is seen that the content is the truth, and that it is the truth of infinite Spirit in general, *i.e.*, is its knowledge, in such a way that it finds its freedom in this knowledge, is itself the Process by which it casts aside its particular individuality, and gets freedom for itself in this content.

To begin with, however, the content exists for the immediate consciousness, and the truth might appear for consciousness in a variety of material forms, for the Idea is one in all things, it is universal necessity; reality can be only the mirror of the Idea, and for consciousness the Idea can accordingly issue forth from everything, for it is always the Idea that is in these infinitely many drops which reflect back the Idea. The Idea is represented figuratively, known and foreshadowed in the seed which is the fruit; the fruit in its final character dies away in the earth, and it is through this negation that the plant first comes into being. A history, a pictorial representation, a description, a phenomenon of this sort can be elevated by Spirit to the rank of something universal, and thus the history of the seed or of the sun becomes a symbol of the Idea, but *only* a symbol, for they are forms which, so far as their peculiar content and specific quality are concerned, are inadequate to express the Idea; what is consciously known through them lies outside of them, the signification they suggest does not exist in them as signification. The object which exists in itself as the Notion is spiritual subjectivity, Man; it is signification in virtue of what it itself is, and this signification does not lie outside of it. It is what thinks everything, knows everything, it is not a symbol, but, on the contrary, its subjectivity, its inner form, its *self* is essentially this very history itself, and the history of the Spiritual is not found in some form of existence, which is inadequate to express the Idea, but rather in its own element. It is therefore necessary for the Spiritual Community that Thought, the Idea, should become objective. At first, however, the Idea appears in a single individual in a material, pictorial form ; this must be discarded, and the real signification, the eternally true essence must be brought into view. This is the faith of the Spiritual Community when it is coming into existence. It starts from faith in the individual, this individual man is changed by the Spiritual Community, He is recognised to be God and is characterised as the Son of God and as comprising all of the finite which attaches to subjectivity as such in its development, but as being subjectivity He is separated from substantiality.

The material or sensuous manifestation is accordingly changed into knowledge of the Spiritual. We thus see the Spiritual Community starting from faith, but regarded in another aspect it appears in the form of Spirit. The different significations of faith and of verification or proof have now to be brought out.

Since faith starts from the sensuous way of viewing things, it has before it a history in time ; what it holds as true is an outward ordinary event, and the verification of the truth of this is conducted according to the historical and juridical mode of verifying a fact, which gives sensuous certainty ; the idea formed of the basis upon which truth rests takes as a foundation the material certainty of other persons regarding certain material facts, and brings other facts into connection with these.

The history of the life of Christ is thus the outward form of verification ; but faith alters its meaning, that is to say, we have not merely got to do with faith as faith in a certain external history, but with the fact that this particular man was the Son of God.

The sensuous content thus becomes something wholly different, it becomes altered into another kind of content, and what is demanded is that this should be proved to be true. The object has undergone a complete alteration, and from being a material, empirically existing element, it has become a divine moment, an essentially supreme moment in God Himself. This content is no longer anything material, and therefore when the demand is made that it should be verified in the material fashion just referred to, this method is at once seen to be insufficient, because the object is of a wholly different nature.

If miracles are supposed to contain the immediate verification of the truth, still in-and-for-themselves they supply a merely *relative* verification or a proof of a subordinate sort. Christ says, by way of reproof, " Unless ye see miracles, ye will not believe." " Many will come and say to Me : Have we not done many signs in Thy name ? And I will say to them : I have not known you ; depart from Me." What is the kind of interest that can here any longer attach to this working of miracles ? The relative element could have an interest or importance only for those who stood outside, for the instruction of Jews and heathen. But the Spiritual Community, which has taken a definite form, no longer stands in need of this relative kind of proof, it has the Spirit in itself, which leads into all truth, and which, by means of its truth as Spirit, exercises upon Spirit the true kind of force, a power in which Spirit has left to it its absolute freedom. The miracle represents a force which influences the natural connections of things, and is consequently a force which is exercised only upon Spirit when it is confined within the consciousness of this limited connection between things. How is it possible that the eternal Idea itself could reach consciousness through the conception of a force of this kind ?

When the content is defined to mean that the miracles of Christ are themselves material phenomena

which can be attested historically, and when His resurrection and ascension are in the same way considered
as occurrences perceived by the senses, so far as the Sensuous is concerned we are not dealing with the sensuous
attestation of these phenomena, and it is not suggested
that the miracles of Christ, His resurrection and ascension,
in their character as themselves outward phenomena and
sensuous occurrences, have not sufficient evidence of their
truth ; but, on the contrary, what we are concerned with
is the relation of the sensuous verification and the
sensuous occurrences taken together, to Spirit, to the
spiritual content. The verification of the Sensuous,
whatever be its content, and whether it is based on evidence or direct perception, is always open to an infinite
number of objections, because it is based on what is
sensuous and external, and this is an Other so far as
Spirit or consciousness is concerned ; here consciousness
and its object are separated, and what holds sway is
this underlying separation, which carries with it the
possibility of error, deception, and a want of the culture
necessary to form a correct conception of a fact, so that
one may have doubts, and look on the Holy Scriptures,
as regards what in them has reference to what is merely
external and historical, as profane writings, without mis-
trusting the goodwill of those who give the personal
evidence. The sensuous or material content is not
certain in itself, because it does not originate with Spirit
as such, because it belongs to another sphere and does not
come into existence by means of the Notion. It may be
thought that we ought to come to our conclusions by a
comparison of all the evidence and the circumstances,
or that there must be reasons why we should decide
for the one or for the other, only, this entire method of
proof and the sensuous content as such ought to be
given a subordinate place in comparison with the need
of Spirit. What is to be true for Spirit, what it is
necessary for it to believe must have no connection with

sensuous faith ; what is true for Spirit is something for
which sensuous manifestation has only a secondary value.
Since Spirit starts from what is sensuous, and attains
to this lofty estimate of itself, its relation to the Sensuous
is a directly negative relation.   This is a fundamental
principle.

Still, spite of this, there always remains a certain
curiosity in this matter, and a desire to know how in
this case we are to understand miracles, how we are to
explain them and conceive of them—to conceive of them,
that is to say, in the sense that they are not miracles at
all, but, on the contrary, are natural effects.   A curiosity
of this kind, however, presupposes doubt and unbelief,
and would like to find some plausible grounds whereby the persons concerned might still be held to be
morally virtuous and preserve their character for truth-
fulness ; so next it is maintained that there was no
intention to deceive, *i.e.*, that no deception actually was
practised, and that in any case it was so moderate and
well meant that Christ and His friends ought still to be
considered as honourable persons.   The shortest way of
settling the matter would be entirely to *reject* miracles ;
if we do not believe in any miracles at all, and find
that they are opposed to reason, the fact of their being
proved will do no good ; the evidence for them must
rest on sense-perception, but there is in the human mind
an insurmountable objection to regard as truth what is
attested solely after this fashion—for here the proofs
are nothing but possibilities and probabilities, *i.e.*, they
are merely subjective and finite reasons.

Or we must give the advice : simply don't have doubts
and then they are solved !   But I *must* have them, I
cannot rid myself of them, and the necessity there is for
answering them rests on the necessity of *having* them.
Reflection advances these claims as absolute, it fixes on
these finite reasons ; but by piety, by true faith, these
finite reasons, these methods of the finite understanding

have long since been set aside. Curiosity of this sort really has its origin in unbelief; faith, however, rests on the witness of the Spirit—not on miracles, but on the absolute truth, on the eternal Idea. Thus so far as the true content is concerned, and regarding them from this standpoint, miracles are of small importance, they may with equal propriety either be used as subjective reasons with the minor purpose of edification, or else be let alone. There is the further fact that miracles, if they are to attest the truth of anything, must first be attested themselves. But what has to be attested by them is the Idea which has no need of them, and because of this has no need to attest *them*.

It has further to be observed that miracles are, speaking generally, effects produced by the power exercised by Spirit upon the natural connection of things, are an interference with the course and the eternal laws of Nature. But the truth is that it is Spirit which is this miracle, this absolute interference. Life is already an interference with these so-called eternal laws of Nature ; it destroys, for instance, the eternal laws of mechanism and chemistry. The power of Spirit, and also its weakness, have still more effect on life. Terror can produce death, anxiety, illness, and so in all ages infinite faith and trust have enabled the lame to walk and the deaf to hear, &c. Modern unbelief in occurrences of this sort is based on a superstitious belief in the so-called force of Nature and its independence relatively to Spirit.

This, however, is merely the first and accidental method of attesting truth employed by faith. The real kind of faith rests on the Spirit of truth. The former kind of verification still involves a relation to the sensuous immediate present ; faith proper is spiritual, and in Spirit truth has the Idea for its basis, and, since the Idea is at the same time represented in a temporal and finite way existing in a single definite individual, it can appear as realised in this individual only after his death and after he has been removed from the temporal sphere when the process through which the manifestation passes has itself reached the form of spiritual totality, *i.e.*, the very fact of believing in Jesus implies that this faith has no longer before it the sensuous manifestation as such, the sensuous perception of which would in that case have constituted the proof of the truth.

What happens here is what happens in connection with all knowledge in so far as it has reference to a Universal. Kepler, as is well known, discovered the laws of the Heavens. They are valid for us in a double way, they are the Universal. A start was made from single instances; certain movements were referred back to laws. But these are only single instances, and we would be free to think that there may be millions more of instances, that there may be bodies which don't move like those we know of, and thus this is not a universal law even in the case of the heavenly bodies themselves. We have certainly become acquainted with these laws by means of induction; but for Spirit, the interest lies in the fact that such a law is true in-and-for-itself, *i.e.*, in its own nature, that reason finds in it its counterpart, and then recognises it to be true in-and-for-itself. In comparison with this absolute knowledge, the sensuous knowledge referred to accordingly takes a secondary place, it is indeed a starting-point, a point of departure which has to be gratefully recognised, but a law such as that just mentioned holds good for itself—and thus accordingly the proof of its truth is of a different kind from that supplied by the senses, it is the Notion, and sensuous existence is now lowered to the condition of a dream-like vision of the earthly-life, above which exists a higher region with a fixed content of its own.

The same kind of thing is seen in connection with the proofs of the existence of God which start from the finite. The defect in them is that the finite is conceived of in an affirmative way only; but the transition from the finite

to the Infinite is at the same time of such a character
that the region of the finite is left behind, and the finite
is reduced to the condition of something subordinate, to
being a far-away picture, which has its real existence
only in the past and in memory, and not in Spirit, which
is above all things present, and which has left that
starting-point behind, and belongs to a region the value
of which is of a totally different sort. The pious man
can thus take advantage of everything in order to edify
himself, and in that case this is the starting-point. It
has been proved that several of the quotations made by
Christ from the Old Testament are incorrect, and that
the meaning extracted from them is not based on the
immediate sense of the words. The Word, according to
this view, is to be regarded as something fixed ; but Spirit
makes out of it something that is true. Thus the material
history is the starting-point for Spirit, for faith, and these
two characteristics must be distinguished from each other,
and what we are first of all concerned with is the return
of Spirit into itself, spiritual consciousness.

It thus becomes clear that it is the Church or Spiritual
Community which of itself produces this faith, and that
it is not, so to speak, created by the *words* of the Bible,
but, on the contrary, by the Spiritual Community. So,
too, it is not the material Present but the Spirit which
teaches the Spiritual Community that Christ is the Son
of God, that He sits eternally at the right hand of the
Father in heaven. That is the interpretation, the witness,
the decree of Spirit. If grateful peoples have only placed
their benefactors amongst the stars, Spirit has recognised
subjectivity as an absolute moment of the divine nature.
The person of Christ has been decreed by the Church to
be the Son of God. We have nothing to do in this connection with the empirical method of stating this, with
the ecclesiastical method of determining the truth, with
councils and such like. The real question is as to what
the content essentially is, is in-and-for-itself. The true

Christian content of faith is to be justified by philosophy, not by history. What Spirit does is no history; it takes to do only with what exists on its own account, is in-and-for-itself, not with something past, but, on the contrary, simply with what is present.

3. But this has appeared in time, too, it has a relation to the subject, it exists for it, and it has a no less essential relation to the fact that the subject is intended to be a citizen of the Kingdom of God.

This fact that the subject itself is to become a child of God involves the truth that reconciliation has actually been completely accomplished in the Divine Idea, and that it has accordingly appeared in time, that the truth has become a matter of certainty to men. It is just this fact of certainty which is the manifestation, the Idea, in the manifested form in which it comes to consciousness.

The relation of the subject to this truth is that the subject reaches this very consciousness of unity, thinks itself worthy of it, produces it in itself, is filled with the Divine Spirit.

This takes place by means of mediation in itself, and this mediation means that the subject has this faith; for faith is the truth, the presupposition that reconciliation is essentially and absolutely accomplished and is certain. It is only by means of this belief that reconciliation has been essentially and absolutely accomplished and is certain, that the subject is capable of placing itself in this unity, and is in a position to do this. This mediation is absolutely necessary.

In the blissful feeling thus reached by means of this act of apprehending the truth, the difficulty is removed which is directly involved in the circumstance that the relation of the Spiritual Community to this Idea is a relation of individual particular subjects to the Idea; this difficulty is, however, done away with in this very truth itself.

Speaking more strictly, the difficulty is that the subject is *different* from the Divine Spirit, and appears as something which is its finitude. This finite element is taken away, and the reason of this is that God looks on the heart of Man, on the substantial will, on the most inward all-embracing subjectivity of Man, on the inner, true, earnest act of will.

Besides this inner will, and as distinguished from this inner substantial reality, there further exists in Man an element of externality, of defectiveness, which shows itself in the fact that he commits mistakes, that he can exist in a way which is not in conformity with this inner, substantial, essential nature, this substantial, essential inwardness.

But externality, otherness—in short, finitude, or imperfection as it may further be defined, is degraded to the condition of something unessential, and is known as such. For in the Idea the otherness, or Other-Being of the Son, is a passing, disappearing moment, and not at all a true, essential, permanent, and absolute moment.

This is the notion or conception of the Spiritual Community in general ; the Idea, which so far is the process of the subject within and in itself—this subject being taken up into the Spirit—is spiritual, in the sense that the Spirit of God dwells in it. This pure self-consciousness which thus belongs to it is at the same time a consciousness of the truth, and this pure self-consciousness which knows and wills the truth is just the Divine Spirit in it. Or, this self-consciousness taken as faith which rests on the Spirit, *i.e.*, on a mediation which does away with all finite mediation, is the faith wrought in Man by God.

(*b.*) *The Realisation of the Spiritual Community.*

The real Spiritual Community is what we in general call the Church. This no longer represents the rise of the Spiritual Community, but the Spiritual Community as actually existing and as maintaining itself.

The actual, permanent existence of the Spiritual Community is its continuous, eternal becoming, which is based on the fact that it is the very nature of Spirit to know itself as eternal, to liberate itself so as to form those finite flashes of light which make the individual consciousness, and then to collect itself again out of this finitude and comprehend itself, and in this way the knowledge of its essence and consequently the divine self-consciousness appear in finite consciousness. Out of the ferment of finitude, and while it changes itself into foam, Spirit rises like a vapour.

In the Spiritual Community as actually existing, the Church is emphatically the institution in virtue of which the persons composing it reach the truth and appropriate it for themselves, and through it the Holy Spirit comes to be in them as real, actual, and present, and has its abode in them; it means that the truth is in them, and that they are in a condition to enjoy and give active expression to the truth or Spirit, that they as individuals are those who give active expression to the Spirit.

The Church viewed in its universal aspect means that the truth is here presupposed as already existing—not as if it were just originating, and the Holy Spirit were being poured out for the first time, and was being brought into existence for the first time, but rather that the truth exists as actually present truth. For the subject this means an alteration of the relation in which it stood to the truth at the beginning.

1. This truth which is thus presupposed is actually present; it is the doctrine of the Church, the Faith, and we know what the content of this doctrine is; it is, in one word, the doctrine of reconciliation. We have no longer to do with the fact that this one man has been elevated by the outpouring, the decree of the Spirit, so as to have an absolute signification, but with the fact that this signification is consciously known and recognised.

This represents the absolute capacity possessed by the subject for taking a share in the truth, both as it exists in itself and as it exists in an objective form, the capacity for reaching the truth, for being in the truth, for attaining to a consciousness of the truth. This consciousness of doctrine is here presupposed and actually exists.

It is clear from this, both that some kind of doctrine is necessary, and that the doctrine is already formed when the Spiritual Community definitely exists. It is this doctrine which is represented in a pictorial way, and constitutes a content in which we see and have shown in an absolutely completed form what ought to be accomplished in the individual as such.

This doctrine is thus regarded as something presupposed so far as its main elements are concerned, as something already formed, while it is in the Spiritual Community itself that it first gets a matured form. The Spirit which is poured out is the beginning, what makes the beginning, that in which the doctrine takes its rise. The Spiritual Community is the consciousness of this Spirit, the expression of what the Spirit has discovered, and by which it has been laid hold of, namely, that Christ is for the Spirit. The distinction involved in the question as to whether the Spiritual Community gives expression to its consciousness on the basis of a written document, or attaches its own self-determinations to tradition, is not at all an essential one ; the main point is, that by means of the Spirit, which is present in it, this Community is the infinite power and authority whereby its doctrine is further developed and gets a more specific form. This authority makes its presence felt in both of those different cases. The exposition of a document which lies at the basis of any doctrine is always in its turn a form of knowledge, and develops into new specific truths; and even if, as in the case of tradition, it attaches itself to something given or taken for granted, the tradition itself, in its historical development, is essentially a positing or making explicit of some implicit truth. Thus doctrine is essentially worked out and matured in the Church. It exists, to begin with, as intuition, feeling, as the felt, flash-like witness of the Spirit. But the determination implied in the act of producing or bringing into existence is itself merely a one-sided determination, for truth is at the same time implicitly present or presupposed. The subject is already taken up into the content.

The confession of faith or dogma accordingly is something which has been essentially formed in the Church first of all, and it is consequently Thought, developed consciousness which asserts its rights in connection with it, and it applies all that it has gained from trained thinking and philosophy, to these thoughts and on behalf of this truth thus consciously perceived ; doctrine is constructed out of foreign concrete elements which have still an impure element mixed with them.

This actually existing doctrine must accordingly be preserved in the Church, and all that is considered as doctrine must be taught. In order to remove it out of the region of caprice and of accidental opinions and views, and to preserve it as absolute truth and as something fixed, it is deposited or stated in creeds. It *is*, it exists, it has value, it is recognised immediately yet not in a material fashion that the apprehension of this doctrine takes place through the senses, just as the world, too, is something presupposed as existing, and to which we are related as to something material.

Spiritual truth exists only as something consciously known ; the mode in which it outwardly appears consists in the fact that it is taught. The Church is essentially the institution which implies the existence of a teaching body to which is committed the duty of expounding this doctrine.

The subject is born within the circle of this doctrine ;

he begins in this condition of established existing truth
and in the consciousness of it. That is his relation to
this truth, which actually exists, and is presupposed as
having an absolute and essential existence.

2. Since the individual is thus born in the Church, he
is forthwith destined, although, to be sure, unconsciously,
to share in this truth and to become a partaker of it; he
is destined for this truth. The Church expresses this in
the Sacrament of Baptism, Man is in the fellowship of
the Church, in which Evil is essentially, in-and-for-itself,
overcome, and God is essentially, or in-and-for-Himself,
reconciled.

Baptism shows that the child has been born in the
fellowship of the Church, not in sin and misery; that he
has not come into a hostile world, but that the Church
is his world, and that he has only to train himself in the
Spiritual Community which already actually exists as
representing his worldly condition.

Man must be born twice, once naturally, and then
again spiritually, like the Brahman. Spirit is not immediate, it exists only in so far as it brings itself out of
itself; it exists only as the regenerate Spirit.

This regeneration is no longer that infinite sadness
which is in general the birth sorrow of the Spiritual
Community; the subject is not indeed spared the infinitely real sorrow, but this is softened; for there still
exists the opposing factor of particularity, of special
interests, passions, selfishness. The natural heart which
encompasses Man is the enemy that has to be fought;
this is, however, no longer the real battle out of which
the Spiritual Community sprang.

The doctrine of the Church is related to this individual
as something external. The child is, to begin with, Spirit
implicitly only, it is not yet realised Spirit, does not
actually exist as Spirit, but has only the capability, the
faculty of being Spirit, of becoming Spirit actually; thus
the truth comes to it at first as something taken for

granted, recognised, valid, *i.e.*, truth necessarily presents itself at first to men in the form of authority.

All truth, even material truth—this, however, is not truth properly so-called—comes to men in this form, to begin with.   In our sense-perception the world presents itself to us as authority, it is, we find it as it is, we take it as something which has existence, and we are related to it as something which exists.   It exists in a certain way, and its existence in this form is valid for us.

Doctrine, the spiritual element does not actually exist in the form of material authority of this sort, but must be taught as established truth.   Custom is something established or valid, a definitely formed conviction ; but because it is something spiritual we do not say : it is ; but rather, it is valid.   Since it comes to us as something which exists, it is, and since it thus comes to us as something having valid worth, we call the mode in which it thus appears authority.

Just as man has to learn about material things on authority and because they are there and exist, has to be content with them—the sun is there, and because it is there I must be content with it—so, too, is it with doctrine or truth ; it does not, however, come to us by means of sense-perception, by the active exercise of the senses, but through teaching, as something which actually exists, through authority.   What is in the human spirit, *i.e.*, in its true spirit, is in this way brought into its consciousness as something objective, or what is in it is developed so that it knows it to be the truth in which it exists.   In such education, practice, training, and appropriation, the whole interest centres merely in getting accustomed to the Good and the True.   So far we are not concerned with overcoming Evil, for Evil has implicitly and actually been overcome.

We are concerned merely with contingent subjectivity. With the one characteristic of faith, namely, that the subject is not what it is meant to be, there is joined the absolute possibility that it may fulfil its destiny and be received into favour by God. This belongs to faith. The individual must lay hold of the truth of the implicit unity of divine and human nature, and he lays hold of this truth by faith in Christ; God is thus no longer for the individual something beyond this world, and the apprehension of this truth is in direct contrast to the first fundamental characteristic, according to which the subject is not what it ought or is intended to be. The child, inasmuch as it has been born in the Church, has been born in freedom and to freedom; there no longer exists for it any absolute Other-Being, this Other-Being is considered as something overcome and conquered.

This education in the truth is concerned only with preventing evil from appearing, for there is in Man, looked at from a general point of view, a possibility that it will appear; but in so far as evil appears when a man does what is evil, it is at the same time something which is implicitly a nullity over which Spirit has power, and this power is of such a character that Spirit is able to make evil to cease to exist, to undo it.

Repentance, Penitence signifies, that the transgression has come to be recognised owing to a man's elevation to the truth, as something which has been virtually overcome and has no longer power in itself. That what has happened can be made as though it had not happened, cannot take place in a sensuous or material way, but in a spiritual and inward way. He is pardoned, he passes for one who has been adopted by the Father amongst men.

This is the business of the Church, this training whereby the education of the spirit becomes ever more inward, and this truth becomes identical with his Self, with the will of Man, becomes his act of will, his Spirit. The battle is past, and Man is conscious that it is not a case of battle, as it is in the Persian religion or the Kantian Philosophy, in which Evil is indeed to be overcome, but

in which it confronts the Good in virtue of its own
essential nature, and in which infinite progress is what
is highest of all.

If we get no further than the idea of what ought to
be, then effort becomes endless, and the solution of the
problem is removed infinitely far away.

Here, on the contrary, the contradiction is already
implicitly solved; evil is known as something which in
the Spirit is virtually and absolutely overcome, and in
virtue of the fact of its being thus overcome the subject
has only to make its will good, and evil, the evil action,
disappears.

Here there is the consciousness that there is no sin
which cannot be forgiven if the natural will is surren-
dered, unless the sin against the Holy Spirit, the denial
of Spirit; for it alone is the power which can cancel
everything.

Very many difficulties arise in connection with this
point, and they all spring from the conception of Spirit
and of freedom. On the one hand, Spirit is regarded as
universal Spirit, and, on the other hand, as Man's independent existence, as the independent existence of the
single individual. It is necessary to say that it is the
divine Spirit which effects regeneration; this is divine
free grace, for all that is divine is free; it is not fate, it
is not destiny. On the other hand, however, there is
the self of the soul existing in a positive way, and it is
sought accordingly to ascertain how much Man's share
in the matter is; a *Velleitas*, a *Nisus* is left to him, but
persistence in firmly remaining in such a relation is itself
unspiritual. The first condition of Being, the Being of
the Self, is potentially the Notion, potentially Spirit, and
what has to be abolished is the form of its immediacy, of
its isolated, particular, independent Being or Being-for-
self. This cancelling of self and coming to self on the
part of the Notion is not, however, limited, universal
Spirit. The act implied in belief in implicit reconcilia-

tion, is, viewed in one aspect, the act of the subject, and, viewed in another aspect, it is the act of the Divine Spirit : faith is itself the Divine Spirit which works in the individual ; but this latter is not in this case a passive receptacle, but, on the contrary, the Holy Spirit is equally the Spirit of the subject, since it has faith ; in the exercise of this faith it acts against its natural life, discards it, puts it away. The difference between the three ways of representing this truth which have been employed may also serve to throw light on the antinomy which is involved in the course thus pursued by the soul.

(*a*.) There is first the moral view which finds its antithesis in the absolutely external relation of self-consciousness, in a relation which, taken by itself, might appear either as first or as fourth, namely, in the oriental despotic relation which involves the annihilation of individual thought and will ; this moral view places the absolute end, the essence of Spirit, in an end connected with volition, and with volition, in fact, simply as *its* volition, so that this subjective aspect is the main point. Law, the Universal, the Rational is *my* rationality in me, and so, too, the willing of the end and its realisation which make it my own, my subjective end, are also *mine ;* and inasmuch as the idea of something higher or highest, of God and the Divine, enters into this view, this is itself merely a postulate of my reason, something posited by me. It *ought*, it is true, to be something which has not been posited, something which is a purely independent power ; still, although it is thus something not posited, I do not forget that this very fact of its not being posited is something which has been posited by me. It comes to the same thing whether this be stated in the form of a postulate, or whether we say, my feeling of dependence or of the need of salvation is what comes first, for in both cases the peculiar objectivity of truth has been abolished.

(*b*.) In reference to the good resolve, and still more in

reference to the Universal or Law, the pious man further adds that this is the divine will, and that the power of making the good resolution is itself really something divine, and he does not go beyond the universal relation here implied.

Finally, (c.) The mystical and ecclesiastical view gives greater definiteness to this connection between God and the subjective act of will and Being, and brings it into the relation which is based on the nature of the Idea. The various ways in which this truth has been conceived of in the Church are simply attempts to solve the antinomy. The Lutheran conception of it is, without doubt, the most brilliant, even if it has not perfectly reached the form of the Idea.

3. What comes last in this sphere of thought is the enjoyment of what is thus appropriated, the enjoyment of the presence of God. What we have here is the consciously felt presence of God, unity with God, the *unio mystica*, the feeling of God in the heart.

This is the Sacrament of the Supper, in which Man has given him in a sensible immediate way the consciousness of his reconciliation with God, the abiding and indwelling of the Spirit in him.

Since this is a feeling in the individual heart, it is also a movement, it presupposes the abolition of differences whereby this negative unity comes into existence as the result. If the permanent preservation of the Spiritual Community, which is at the same time its unbroken creation, is itself the eternal repetition of the life, passion, and resurrection of Christ, then this repetition gets a complete expression in the Sacrament of the Supper. The eternal sacrifice here just is, that the absolute substantial element, the unity of the subject and of the absolute object is offered to the individual to enjoy in an immediate way, and since the individual is reconciled, it follows that this complete reconciliation is the resurrection of Christ. Consequently the Supper is

the central point of Christian doctrine, and it is from
it that all the differences in Christian doctrine get their
colour and peculiar character. The conceptions formed
of it are of three kinds :—

(1.) According to one conception the host, this outward, material, unspiritual thing is, owing to the act of
consecration, the actually present God—God as a thing,
and in the form of an empirical thing, and thus, too,
as empirically enjoyed by Man. Since God is thus
known as something outward in the Supper which is the
central point of doctrine, this externality is the basis of
the whole Catholic religion. There arises from this a
slavishness of knowledge and action ; this externality
runs through all further definitions of the truth owing
to the fact that the True is represented as something
fixed and external. Being thus something which has a
definite existence outside of the subject, it can come to
be in the power of others ; the Church is in possession
of it as it is of all the means of grace ; the subject is in
this respect something passive and receptive which does
not know what is true, right, and good, but has to accept
it merely from others.

(2.) According to the Lutheran conception the movement starts from something external which is an ordinary
common thing, but the act of communion takes place and
the inner feeling of the presence of God arises to the
extent to which, and in so far as, the externality is eaten
not simply in a corporal fashion, but in spirit and faith.
It is only in spirit and in faith that we have the present
God. The sensible presence is in itself nothing, nor does
consecration make the host into an object worthy of
adoration ; but, on the contrary, the object exists in faith
only, and thus it is in the consuming and destroying of
the sensuous that we have union with God and the consciousness of this union of the subject with God. Here
the grand thought has arisen that, apart from the act
of communion and faith, the host is a common, material

thing; the process truly takes place only in the spirit of the subject.

In this case there is no transubstantiation—transubstantiation there certainly is, but it is of the kind by which what is external is absorbed and abolished; while the presence of God is of a purely spiritual sort, and is directly connected with the faith of the subject.

(3.) According to this third conception God is present only in the conception we form of Him, only in memory, and thus His presence is so far merely immediate and subjective. This is the conception of the Reformed Church, an unspiritual and merely lively remembrance of the Past, not a divine Presence, not a really spiritual existence. Here the Divine, the Truth has got lowered to the prose of the Enlightenment and of the mere Understanding, and expresses a merely moral relation.

(c.) *The Realisation of the Spiritual culminating in Universal Reality.*

This directly involves the transformation and remodelling of the Spiritual Community.

Religion is here the spiritual religion, and the Spiritual Community exists primarily in what is inward, in Spirit as such. This inner element, this subjectivity which is present to itself as inward, not developed in itself, is feeling or sensation; the Spiritual Community has also as an essential part of its character, consciousness, ordinary thought or mental representation, needs, impulses, a worldly existence in fact, but this brings with it disunion, differentiation; the divine objective Idea presents itself to consciousness as an Other outside of it which is given partly through authority and is partly appropriated in acts of devotion—to put it otherwise, the moment of communion is merely a single moment, or the divine Idea, the divine content is not actually seen, but is only represented in the mind. The Now or actuality of communion as thus represented is transferred partly to a region beyond, to a heaven beyond the present, partly to the past and partly to the future. Spirit, however, is above all things present, and demands a real and complete presence; it demands more than love merely, than sad ideas or mental pictures, it demands that the content should itself be present, or that the feeling, the sensation experienced should be developed and expanded.

Thus the Spiritual Community, in its character as the Kingdom of God, has standing over against it, objectivity in general. Objectivity in the shape of an external immediate world is represented by the heart with its interests; another form of objectivity is the objectivity of Reflection, of abstract Thought, of the Understanding; and the third and true form of objectivity is that of the Notion; and we have now to consider how Spirit realises itself in these three elements.

1. In religion the heart is implicitly reconciled; this reconciliation has thus its place in the heart, it is spiritual —is the pure heart which attains this enjoyment of the presence of God in it, and consequently reconciliation, the enjoyment of being reconciled. This reconciliation is, however, abstract; the self, the subject, that is to say, represents at the same time that aspect of this spiritual presence according to which a worldly element in a developed form is actually found in the self, and thus the Kingdom of God, the Spiritual Community, has a relation to the worldly element.

In order that the reconciliation be real, it is necessary that in this development, in this totality, the reconciliation should also be consciously known, be present, and be brought forward into actuality. The principles which apply to this worldly element actually exist in this spiritual element.

The truth of the worldly element is the Spiritual, or, to put it more definitely, it means that the subject as an object of divine grace, as a being who is reconciled with

God, has an infinite value by the very character which is essentially his, and which is further developed in the Spiritual Community. In accordance with this its essential character, the subject is accordingly recognised as being the infinite certainty of Spirit itself, as the eternity of Spirit.

So far as this subject which is thus inherently infinite is concerned, the fact of its being determined or destined to infinitude is its freedom, and just means that it is a free person, and thus is also related to this world, to reality as subjectivity which is at home with itself, reconciled within itself, and is absolutely fixed and infinite subjectivity. This is the substantial element; this specific character which thus belongs to it must form the basis in so far as it brings itself into relation with this world.

The rationality, the freedom of the subject means that the subject is this something which has been freed and has attained to this condition of freedom through religion, that it is essentially free in virtue of its religious character. What we are concerned with is to see how this reconciliation takes place within the worldly sphere itself.

(1.) The first form of reconciliation is the immediate one, and just because of its being immediate it is not yet the true mode of reconciliation. This reconciliation shows itself as follows. At first the Spiritual Community, as representing the fact of reconciliation, the Spiritual, the fact of reconciliation with God in itself, stands aloof from the worldly sphere in an abstract way; the Spiritual renounces the worldly sphere by its own act, takes up a negative relation to the world, and consequently to itself; for the world in the subject shows itself as the impulse to Nature, to social life, to art and science.

The concrete element in the self, namely, the passions, is not able to justify itself in reference to the religious element by the fact of its being natural; while ascetic withdrawal from the world implies that the heart does not get a concrete expansion and is to remain undeveloped, or, in other words, that the spiritual element, the state of reconciliation, and the life in which this reconciliation is to show itself, is to be, and is to continue to be, concentrated in itself and undeveloped. It is, however, the very nature of Spirit to develop itself, to differentiate itself until it reaches the worldly sphere.

(2.) The second form of this reconciliation implies that the interests of the world and religious interests continue to be external to one another, and that still they ought to come into relation to each other. Thus the relation in which both stand is merely an external one, and it means that the one prevails over the other, and thus there is no reconciliation : the religious element, it is felt, should be the ruling element ; what has been reconciled, the Church namely, should rule the secular element, which is unreconciled.

There is a union with the worldly element which is unreconciled, the worldly element in its purely crude state, and which in its purely crude state is merely brought under the sway of the other ; but the element which thus holds sway absorbs this worldly element into itself, all tendencies, all passions, everything, in short, which represents worldly interests devoid of any spiritual element, make their appearance in the Church owing to the position of sovereignty thus attained, because the secular element is not reconciled in itself.

Thus a sovereignty is reached by means of what is unspiritual, in which what is external is the ruling principle, and in which Man is in his general relationships directly outside of himself ; it is, in fact, the relation or condition of want of freedom. The element of disunion enters into everything that can be called human, into all kinds of impulses, and into all those relationships which have reference to the family, to active life, and life in the State ; and the ruling principle is that Man is not at home with himself, is in a region foreign to his nature.

Man, in fact, in all these forms is in a condition of servitude, and all those forms which his life takes are held to be worthless, unholy, and he himself, by the very fact of his connection with them, is essentially something finite, disunited, and thus has no valid worth, since what possesses validity is an Other.

This reconciliation is connected with worldly interests and with Man's own heart in such a way that it becomes the direct opposite of reconciliation. The further development of this condition of rupture in reconciliation itself, is accordingly what takes the form of the corruption of the Church—the absolute contradiction of the Spiritual within itself.

(3.) The third characteristic is that this contradiction cancels itself in Morality, that the principle of freedom has forced its way into secular life ; and since secular life so constructed is itself in conformity with the Notion, reason, truth, eternal truth, it is a freedom which has become concrete, the rational will.

It is in the organisation of the State that the Divine has passed into the sphere of reality ; the latter is penetrated by the former, and the existence of the secular element is justified in-and-for-itself, for its basis is the Divine Will, the law of right and freedom. The true reconciliation whereby the Divine realises itself in the region of reality is found in moral and legal life in the State ; this is the true disciplining of the secular life.

The institutions of morality are divine, are holy, not in the sense in which what is holy is opposed to what is moral, as when it is held that celibacy represents what is holy as opposed to family life, or voluntary poverty as opposed to active acquisition by one's own efforts, to what is lawful. In the same way blind obedience passes for being something holy ; while, on the contrary, what makes morality is obedience in freedom, free, rational will, the obedience of the subject in respect of what is moral. In morality the reconciliation of religion with reality, with the secular life, is an actual and accomplished fact.

2. The second point is that the ideal side now emerges here on its own account. In this state in which Spirit is reconciled with itself, what is inward knows itself as being within the sphere of its own nature, knows that it is together with itself, and this knowledge that it is together with itself, not outside of itself, is just Thought, which is the state of reconciliation, the being together with self, the being at peace with self, but in a wholly abstract undeveloped condition of peace with itself. There thus arises the infinite demand that the content of religion should verify its truth for Thought as well, and this is a necessary requirement which cannot be set aside.

Thought is the Universal, the active expression of the Universal, and stands in contrast to the concrete in general, which represents the external.

It is the Freedom of Reason which has been won in religion, and which knows itself in Spirit as existing for itself. This freedom accordingly opposes itself to the purely unspiritual externality, to servitude ; for servitude is directly opposed to the conception of reconciliation and liberation, and thus thought enters in and destroys and bids defiance to externality in whatever form it may appear.

This represents the negative and formal act which in its concrete form has been called the " Enlightenment," and which implies that thought sets itself to oppose externality, and that the freedom of Spirit, which is involved in reconciliation, is asserted. This thought, when it first appears, appears in the form of this abstract Universal, and sets itself against the concrete in general, and consequently against the Idea of God, against the theory that God is the Triune God and not a dead abstraction, but a Being related to Himself, who is at home with Himself and returns to Himself. Abstract thought attacks this doctrinal content, as held by the Church, with its principle of identity ; for this concrete content is in contradiction with this law of identity. In the concrete there are determinations, differences ; since abstract thought turns against externality in general, it is also opposed to difference as such, the relation of God to Man, the unity of the two, divine grace and human freedom ; for all this is the union of opposed determinations. The rule, however, for the Understanding, for this abstract thought, is abstract identity ; this kind of thought thus aims at dissolving all that is concrete, all determinations, all content in God, and accordingly reflection has as its final resultant merely the objectivity of identity itself, this, namely, that God is nothing but the Supreme Essence, without definite character or determination, empty ; for every determination makes what is determined concrete. He is for cognition something beyond the present, for cognition or reasoned knowledge is knowledge of a concrete content. Reflection in this its complete form is the antithesis of the Christian Church ; and as everything concrete in God is destroyed, this fact is expressed somewhat in this fashion—Man cannot know God ; for to know God is to know Him in accordance with His attributes or determinations, but according to this view He remains a pure abstraction. This formula certainly contains the principle of freedom, of inwardness, of religion even ; but it is, to begin with, conceived of in a merely abstract way.

The Other, by means of which determination enters into this universality which exists alongside of this abstraction, is nothing but what is contained in the natural inclinations, the impulses of the subject. Regarding the matter from this standpoint, it is accordingly said that Man is by nature good. Inasmuch as this pure subjectivity, this ideality, is pure freedom, it is certainly brought into connection with the essential character of the Good, but the Good itself must in this case equally remain an abstraction.

The determination of the Good here is the arbitrariness, the accidental nature of the subject in general, and this latter is thus the extreme or culminating point of this subjectivity, the freedom which renounces its claim to truth and to the development of truth, which thus moves within itself and knows that what it considers as having validity is simply its own determinations, and that it has the mastery over all that is called good and evil.

This is an inner self-enclosed life which may indeed coexist with calm, lofty, and pious aspirations, but may as readily appear as hypocrisy or as vanity in its most extreme form. It is what is called the pious life of feeling, to which Pietism also restricts itself. Pietism recognises no objective truth, sets itself in opposition to dogmas, to the content of religion, and though it does indeed preserve the element of mediation, and still maintains a certain relation to Christ, yet this relation is supposed to remain in the sphere of feeling, in the sphere of inner sentiment. Each person has thus *his own* God, Christ, &c. The element of particularity in which each has his own individual religion, his own theory of the Universe, &c., does undoubtedly exist in Man; but in religion it is absorbed by life in the Spiritual Community, and for the truly pious man it has no longer any real worth and is laid aside.

On this side of the empty essence of God there thus stands a finitude which is free on its own account and has become independent, which has an absolute value in itself, *e.g.*, in the shape of the righteousness of individuals. The further consequence is, that not only is the objectivity of God thus put in a sphere beyond the present and negated, but all other objective characteristics which have validity in-and-for-themselves, and which have appeared in the world as Right, as what is moral, &c., absolutely disappear. Since the subject thus retreats to the extreme point of its infinity, the Good, all that is right, &c., are contained only in it, it takes all this as constituting its own subjective character, it is only *its* thought. What gives body to this Good is accordingly taken from natural caprice, from what is accidental, from passion, &c. This subject is further the consciousness that objectivity is shut up within it itself, and that this objectivity has no permanent existence; it is only the principle of identity which has for it validity; this subject is something abstract, it can be filled up with any kind of content, since it has the power to subsume every content which is thus planted in the heart of Man. Subjectivity is thus caprice itself, and is, in short, the knowledge of that power belonging to it whereby it produces objectivity or the Good and gives it a content.

The other development of this point of view, accordingly, is that the subject has no independent existence, is not for itself in reference to the unity which it has reached by emptying itself, it does not preserve its particularity as against it, but has for its specific aim self-absorption in the unity of God. The subject has thus no particular end, nor any objective end beyond simply the glory of the one God. What we have here is religion; there is in it an affirmative relation to its Essence which is constituted by this One, in it the subject yields itself up. This religion has the same objective content as the Jewish religion, but the relation in which men stand to one another is broadened; there is no particularity left in it, the Jewish idea of national value which establishes the relation in which Man stands to the One, is wanting here. Here there is no limitation, Man is related to this One as a purely abstract self-consciousness. This is the characteristic of the Mohammedan religion. It forms the antithesis of Christianity, because it occupies a like sphere with the Christian religion. It is, as it were, the Jewish spiritual religion, but this God exists for self-consciousness in Spirit which has merely abstract knowledge, and occupies a stage which is one with that occupied by the Christian religion, inasmuch as in it no kind of particularity is retained. The man who fears God is acceptable to Him, and Man has value only in so far as he finds his truth in the knowledge that this God is the One, the Essence. There is no recognition of the existence of any wall of partition between believers themselves or between them and God. Before God all specific distinction of the subject according to his standing or rank is done away with ; rank may exist, there may be slaves, but this is to be regarded as merely accidental.

The contrast between the Christian and Mohammedan religions consists in the fact that in Christ the spiritual element is developed in a concrete way, and is known as Trinity, *i.e.*, as Spirit, and that the history of Man, the relation in which he stands to the One, is a concrete history. It takes its start from the natural will, which is not as it ought to be, and the yielding up of this will is the act whereby it reaches this its essence by means of this negation of itself. The Mohammedan hates and proscribes everything concrete, God is the absolute One, and as against Him Man retains for himself no end, no particularity, no interests of his own. Man as actually existing does undoubtedly particularise himself in his natural inclinations and interests, and these are here all the more savage and unrestrained that reflection is want-ing in connection with them ; but this again involves something which is the complete opposite, namely, the tendency to let everything take its course, an indifference in respect of every kind of end, absolute fatalism, in-difference in respect of life, while no practical end is regarded as having any essential worth. Since, how-ever, Man is as a matter of fact practical and active, the end to be pursued can only be to bring about the wor-ship of the One amongst all men, and accordingly the Mohammedan religion is essentially fanatical.

Reflection, as we have seen, occupies the same stand-point as Mohammedanism in so far as it maintains that

God has no content, is not concrete. Thus the manifestation of God in the flesh, the exaltation of Christ to the position of Son of the God, the transfiguration of the finitude of the world and of self-consciousness until they appear as the infinite self-determination of God, have no place here. Christianity is held to be a system of teaching or set of doctrines, and Christ an ambassador from God, a divine teacher, and so a teacher like Socrates, only a still more distinguished teacher, since he was without sin. This, however, is to go only half way, it is a compromise. Christ was either merely a man, or he was the "Son of Man." There would thus be nothing left of the divine history, and Christ would be spoken of as he is in the Koran. The difference between this standpoint and Mohammedanism consists merely in the fact that the latter, the conceptions of which are bathed in the ether of illimitableness, and which represents this infinite independence, directly gives up all particular interests, enjoyment, position, individual knowledge, all "vanity" in short. On the other hand, rationalistic Enlightenment gives Man an abstract standing on his own account, since for it God is beyond this world and has no affirmative relation to the subject, so that Man recognises the affirmative Universal only in so far as it is in him, and yet has it in him in a merely abstract way, and accordingly what gives it body or substance is taken only from what is accidental and arbitrary.

Still we must recognise the presence of reconciliation in this last form too, and thus this final manifestation is also a realisation of Faith. Since, in fact, all content, all truth perishes in this particular subjectivity which knows itself infinitely in itself, the principle of subjective freedom has as a consequence come to be consciously known. What is called in the Spiritual Community the inner life, is now developed in itself; it is not only something inward, conscience, but it is subjectivity which differentiates itself makes distinctions within itself, is concrete ;

it appears as its own objectivity, it knows the Universal as being in itself, as something which it produces out of itself, it is the subjectivity which is independent, for itself, self-conscious, determines itself within itself, and is thus the complete development of the subjective extreme until it has reached the Idea in itself. The defect here is that this is merely formal, that it misses having true objectivity, it represents the extreme point of formal spiritual development without inner necessity. If the Idea is to get a truly complete form, it is necessary that the objectivity should be set free, should be the totality of objectivity in itself.

The result of this objectivity, therefore, is, that everything in the subject is refined away, without objectivity, without fixed character, without development in God. This final and culminating point thus reached by the formal culture of our day is at the same time the most extreme crudeness, because it possesses merely the form of culture.

We have so far recognised the presence of these two mutually opposing extremes in the development of the Spiritual Community. The one was that unfreedom, that servitude of the Spirit in the absolute region of freedom ; the other was abstract subjectivity, subjective freedom without content.

3. What we have finally still to consider is, that subjectivity develops the content out of itself, but does this in accordance with necessity—knows and recognises the content to be necessary and that it is objective, that it has an essential existence of its own, is in-and-for-itself. This is the standpoint of philosophy, according to which the content takes refuge in the Notion and by means of thought gets its restoration and justification.

This thought is not merely the process of abstraction and determination which is governed by the law of identity ; this thought is itself essentially concrete, and thus it is comprehension, grasping in the Notion, it means that

the Notion so determines itself as to take on the form
of totality, of the Idea.

It is free reason which has an essential existence,
is in-and-for-itself, which develops the content of truth
and justifies it in knowledge, recognises and cognises one
truth. The purely subjective standpoint, the volatilisation
of all content, the Enlightenment of the Understanding,
together with Pietism, do not recognise any content, and
consequently no truth.

The Notion, however, *produces* the truth—this is subjective freedom—but at the same time recognises this content to be something not produced, to be something which
is inherent and essentially true, true in-and-for-itself.
This objective standpoint is alone capable of expressing
and attesting the witness of the Spirit in a way which
betokens intellectual training and thought, and it is involved in the position taken up by the better kind of
dogmatic theology of our day.

This standpoint consequently supplies us with the
justification of religion, and in particular of the Christian
or true religion ; it knows the content in accordance
with its necessity, in accordance with its reason, and so,
too, it knows the forms also in the development of this
content.

What these forms are we have already seen, namely,
the manifestation of God, that representation for the sensuous, spiritual consciousness which has arrived at universality, at thought, that complete development which
exists for Spirit.

In the act of justifying the content and the forms,
in getting a rational knowledge of the specific character
of the manifestation, thought at the same time also
knows the limits of the forms. Enlightenment knows
only of negation, of limit, of determinateness as such,
and because of this is unjust to the content.

Form or determinateness is not merely finitude, or
limit, but rather the form, as totality of the form is

itself the Notion, and these forms are necessary and essential.

Owing to the fact that reflection has invaded the domain of religion, thought or reflection takes up a hostile attitude to the ordinary or popular idea in religion and to its concrete content. Thought, when it has thus begun, never pauses again, but goes on its way, empties feeling, heaven, and the knowing mind, and the religious content accordingly takes refuge in the Notion. Here it must get its justification, here thought must conceive of itself as concrete and free, preserving the differences not as if they were only posited or dependent on something, but allowing them to appear as free, and consequently recognising the content as objective.

It is the business of philosophy to establish the relation in which thought stands to the two preceding stages. Religion, the need felt by the pious mind, can take refuge in " experience," in feeling, as well as in the Notion, and limit itself to this, and thus give up the search after truth, renounce the possibility of knowing any content, so that the Holy Church has no longer any communion in it, but splits up into atoms. For what communion there is is in doctrine ; but here each individual has a feeling of his own, has his own sensations or experiences, and his particular theory of the universe. This form does not answer to Spirit which also wishes to know what its relation is to doctrine. Philosophy thus stands opposed to two points of view. On the one hand, it appears to be opposed to the Church, and has this in common with culture and reflection, that in comprehending the popular religious idea it does not keep to the forms of the popular idea, but has to comprehend it in thought, though in doing this it recognises that the form of the popular idea is also necessary. But the Notion is that higher element which also embraces within it different forms and allows their right to exist. The second way in which it takes up an attitude of opposition is when it appears in antagonism to Enlightenment, to the theory which holds that the content is of no consequence, to opinion, to the despair which renounces the truth. The aim of philosophy is to know the truth, to know God, for He is the absolute truth, inasmuch as nothing else is worth troubling about save God and the unfolding of God's nature. Philosophy knows God as essentially concrete, as spiritual, real universality which is not jealous but imparts itself. Light by its very nature imparts itself. Whoever says that God cannot be known, says He is jealous, and so makes no earnest effort to believe in Him, however much he may speak of God. Enlightenment, that conceit, that vanity of the Understanding is the most violent opponent of philosophy, and is displeased when the latter points to the element of reason in the Christian religion, when it shows that the witness of the Spirit, of truth, is lodged in religion. Philosophy, which is theology, is solely concerned with showing the rationality of religion.

In philosophy, religion gets its justification from thinking consciousness. Piety of the naïve kind stands in no need of this, it receives the truth as authority, and experiences satisfaction, reconciliation by means of this truth.

In faith the true content is certainly already found, but there is still wanting to it the form of thought. All forms such as we have already dealt with, feeling, popular ideas, and such like, may certainly have the form of truth, but they themselves are not the true form which makes the true content necessary. Thought is the absolute judge before which the content must verify and attest its claims.

Philosophy has been reproached with setting itself above religion ; this, however, is false as an actual matter of fact, for it possesses this particular content only and no other, though it presents it in the form of thought ; it sets itself merely above the form of faith, the content is the same in both cases.

The form of the subject as an individual who feels, &c., concerns the subject as a single individual; but feeling as such is not rejected by philosophy. The question merely is as to whether *the content* of feeling is the truth, whether it can prove itself to be true in thought. Philosophy *thinks* what the subject as such *feels*, and leaves it to the latter to settle with its feeling. Feeling is thus not rejected by philosophy; on the contrary, it simply gets through philosophy its true content.

But, in so far as thought begins to place itself in opposition to the concrete, the process of thought then consists in carrying through this opposition until it reaches reconciliation. This reconciliation is philosophy; so far philosophy is theology, it sets forth the reconciliation of God with Himself and with Nature, and shows that Nature, Other-Being is divine, that it partly belongs to the very nature of finite Spirit to rise into the state of reconciliation, and that it partly reaches this state of reconciliation in the history of the world.

This religious knowledge thus reached through the Notion is not universal in its nature, and it is further only knowledge *in* the Spiritual Community, and thus we get in reference to the Kingdom of God three stages or positions: the first position is that of immediate naïve religion and faith; the second, the position of the Understanding, of the so-called cultured, of reflection and Enlightenment; and finally, the third position, the stage of philosophy.

But if now, after having considered the origin and permanent existence of the Spiritual Community, we see that in attaining realisation in its spiritual reality it falls into this condition of inner disruption, then this realisation appears to be at the same time its disappearance. But ought we to speak here of destruction when the Kingdom of God is founded eternally, when the Holy Spirit as such lives eternally in its Spiritual Community, and when the gates of Hell are not to prevail against the

Church ?   To speak of the Spiritual Community passing away is to end with a discordant note.

Only, how can it be helped ?   This discordant note is actually present in reality.   Just as in the time of the Roman Empire, because universal unity in religion had disappeared, and the Divine was profaned, and because, further, political life was universally devoid of principle, of action, and of confidence, reason took refuge only in the form of private right, or, to put it otherwise, because what was by its very nature essential, what existed in-and-for-itself was given up, individual well-being was elevated to the rank of an end, so, too, is it now.   Moral views, individual opinion and conviction without objective truth, have attained authority, and the pursuit of private rights and enjoyment is the order of the day.   When the time is fulfilled in which speculative justification, justification by means of the Notion, is what is needed, then the unity of the outer and inner no longer exists in immediate consciousness, in the world of reality, and in the sphere of *Faith* nothing is justified.   The rigidity of an objective command, an external direction, the power of the State can effect nothing here ; the process of decay has gone too deep for that.   When the Gospel is no longer preached to the poor, when the salt has lost its savour, and all the foundations have been tacitly removed, then the people, for whose ever solid reason truth can exist only in a pictorial conception, no longer know how to assist the impulses and emotions they feel within them.   They are nearest to the condition of infinite sorrow ; but since love has been perverted to a love and enjoyment from which all sorrow is absent, they seem to themselves to be deserted by their teachers.   These latter have, it is true, brought help to themselves by means of reflection, and have found their satisfaction in finitude, in subjectivity and its virtuosity, and consequently in what is empty and vain, but the substantial kernel of the people cannot find its satisfaction there.

For us philosophical knowledge has harmonised this discord, and the aim of these lectures has just been to reconcile reason and religion, to show how we know this latter to be in all its manifold forms necessary, and to rediscover in revealed religion the truth and the Idea.

But this reconciliation is itself merely a partial one without outward universality. Philosophy forms in this connection a sanctuary apart, and those who serve in it constitute an isolated order of priests, who must not mix with the world, and whose work is to protect the possessions of Truth. How the actual present-day world is to find its way out of this state of disruption, and what form it is to take, are questions which must be left to itself to settle, and to deal with them is not the immediate practical business and concern of philosophy.

LECTURES ON THE PROOFS OF THE

EXISTENCE OF GOD

F

FIRST LECTURE

THESE Lectures are devoted to the consideration of the proofs of the existence of God. The occasion for them is this. I had at first to make up my mind to give only one set of lectures in this summer session on philosophical knowledge as a whole, and then afterwards I felt I would like to add a second set on at least one separate subject of knowledge. I have therefore chosen a subject which is connected with the other set of lectures which I gave on logic, and constitutes, not in substance, but in form, a kind of supplement to that set, inasmuch as it is concerned with only a particular aspect of the fundamental conceptions of logic. These lectures are therefore chiefly meant for those of my hearers who were present at the others, and to them they will be most easily intelligible.

But inasmuch as the task we have set ourselves is to consider the proofs of the existence of God, it would appear as if only one aspect of the matter belongs to the subject of logic, namely, the *nature* of proof. The other, again, the content, which is God Himself, belongs to a different sphere, that of religion, and to the consideration of it by thought, to the philosophy of religion. In point of fact, it is a portion of this branch of knowledge which has to be set apart and treated by itself in these lectures. In what follows it will more clearly be seen what relation this part bears to the entirety of the doctrine of religion ; and further, that this doctrine in so far as it is scientific, and what belongs to the sphere of logic, do not fall outside one another to the extent that would appear from the first statement of our aim, and that what is logical does not constitute the merely formal side, but, in fact, occupies the very centre point of the content.

The first thing we encounter when we seek to make a beginning with the execution of our design is the general, and, so far as this design is concerned, repugnant, point of view of the prepossessions of present-day culture. If the object, God, is in itself capable of producing exaltation of mind by its very name, and of stirring our soul to its innermost depths, our lofty expectation may just as quickly die away when we reflect that it is the proofs of the existence of God with which we are about to concern ourselves. For the *proofs* of the existence of God are to such an extent fallen into discredit that they pass for something antiquated, belonging to the metaphysics of days gone by; a barren desert, out of which we have escaped and brought ourselves back to a living faith; the region of arid Understanding, out of which we have once more raised ourselves to the warm feeling of religion. The attempt to renovate, by means of new applications and artifices of an acute Understanding, those rotten props of our belief that there is a God, which have passed for proofs, or to improve the places which have become weak through attacks and counter-proofs, could of itself gain no favour merely by its good intention. For it is not this or that proof, or this or that form and way of putting it, that has lost its weight, but the very proving of religious truth has so much lost credit with the mode of thought peculiar to our time that the impossibility of such proof is already a generally accepted opinion. Nay more, it has come to be regarded as irreligious to place confidence in such reasoned knowledge, and to seek by such a path to reach a sure conviction regarding God and His nature, or even regarding His mere existence. This business of proof, therefore, is so much out of date, that the proofs themselves are barely even historically known here and there; and even to theologians, that is to say, people who desire to have a scientific acquaintance with religious truths, they are sometimes unknown.

The proofs of the existence of God have originated in the necessity of satisfying thought and reason. But this necessity has assumed, in modern culture, quite a different position from that which it had formerly, and those points of view must first of all be considered which have presented themselves in this reference. Yet since they are known in their general aspects, and this is not the place to follow them back to their foundations, we need only recall them, and, in fact, limit ourselves to the form which they assume within the sphere of Christianity. It is in this region that the conflict between faith and reason in Man himself first finds a basis, and that *doubt* enters his soul, and can reach the fearful height of depriving him of all peace. Thought must indeed touch the earlier religions of imagination, as we may shortly call them ; it must turn itself with its opposite principles directly against their sensuous pictures and all else in them. The contradictions, the strife and enmity which have thus arisen belong to the external history of philosophy. But the collisions between philosophy and religion here get the length of hostility merely, and have not come to be that inner division of mind and feeling, such as we see in Christianity, where the two sides which come into contradiction get possession of the depth of the Spirit as their single and consequently common source, and in this position, bound together in their contradiction, are able to disturb this spot itself, the Spirit in its inmost nature. The expression " faith " is reserved for Christianity ; we do not speak of Greek or Egyptian faith, or of a faith in Zeus or Apis. Faith expresses the inwardness of certainty, and certainty of the deepest and most concentrated kind, as distinguished from all other opinion, conception, persuasion, or volition. This inwardness, at once as being what is deepest and at the same time most abstract, comprises thought itself ; a contradiction of this faith by thought is therefore the most painful of all divisions in the depths of the Spirit.

Yet such misery is happily, if we may so express ourselves, not the only form in which the relation of faith
and knowledge is to be found. On the contrary, this relation presents itself in a peaceful form, in the conviction
that revelation, faith, positive religion, and, on the other
hand, reason and thought in general, must not be in contradiction, and not only that they may be in harmony,
but also that God does not so contradict Himself in His
works, cannot so contradict Himself, as that the human
Spirit in its essence, in its thinking reason, in that which
it must have come from the very first to regard as divine
in itself, could get into conflict with what has come to it
through greater enlightenment about the nature of God
and Man's relation to that nature. During the whole of
the Middle Ages, theology was understood to mean nothing else than a scientific knowledge of Christian truths,
that is to say, a knowledge essentially connected with
philosophy. The Middle Ages were far enough away from
taking the historical knowledge of faith for scientific
knowledge ; in the Fathers and in what may be reckoned
generally as historical material, they sought only authori-
ties, edification, and information on the doctrines of the
Church. The opposite tendency is simply to search out
the human origin of the articles of faith by the historical
treatment of the older evidences and works of every kind,
and in this way to reduce them to the minimum of their
most primitive form. This form must be regarded as
wholly unfruitful in deeper knowledge and development,
because it is in contradiction with that Spirit, which, after
the removal of that primitive form as something immediately present, had been poured out on the adherents of
these doctrines, in order to lead them now, for the first
time, into all truth. The tendency here described was
unknown in these times. In the belief in the unity
of this Spirit with itself, the whole of these doctrines,
even those which are most abstruse for reason, are regarded from the point of view of thinking, and the

attempt is made, in the case of all of these which are recognised as in themselves the content of belief, to *prove* them on rational grounds. The great theologian Anselm of Canterbury, whom we shall have to consider elsewhere, declares in this sense that, if we are firm in the faith, it is idleness, *negligentiæ mihi esse videtur*, not to know what we believe. In the Protestant Church it has in the same way come about that the rational knowledge of religious truths is cherished and held in honour in combination with theology or along with it. The point of interest was to see how far the natural light of reason, human reason by itself, could progress in the knowledge of the truth, with the important reservation that through religion Man can learn higher truths than reason is in a position to discover of itself.

Here we come upon two distinct spheres, and, to begin with, a peaceful relation between them is justified by means of the distinction that the teachings of positive religion are *above* but not *against* reason. This activity of thinking knowledge found itself stimulated and supported from without through the example which lay before its eyes in the pre-Christian, or, speaking generally, non-Christian religions. This showed that the human spirit, even when left to itself, has attained to deep insight into the nature of God, and with all its errors has arrived at great truths, even at fundamental truths, such as the existence of God and the purer idea, free from sensuous ingredients, of that existence, the immortality of the soul, providence, and such like. Thus positive doctrine and the rational knowledge of religious truths have been peacefully pursued alongside of one another. This position of reason in relation to dogma was, however, different from that confidence of reason which was first considered, which dared to approach the highest mysteries of doctrine, such as the Trinity, and the incarnation of Christ; whereas, on the contrary, the point of view referred to after the one just mentioned

timidly confined itself to the business of merely venturing
through the medium of thought to deal with what the
Christian religion possesses in common with heathen and
non-Christian religions in general, and what must therefore remain a part merely of what is abstract in religion.

But when once we have become conscious of the difference of these two spheres, we must pronounce the relation
of equality in which faith and reason are to be regarded
as standing each alongside of the other, to be unintelli-
gible, or else to be a misleading pretence. The tendency
of thought to seek unity leads of necessity to the comparison of these spheres first of all, and then when they
once pass for different, to the agreement of faith with
itself alone, and of thought with itself alone, so that each
sphere refuses to recognise the other and rejects it. It
is one of the commonest self-deceptions of the Understanding to regard the element of difference, which is
found in the one central point of Spirit, as though it
must not necessarily advance to opposition and so to
contradiction. The point at which the conflict on the
part of Spirit begins has been reached as soon as what
is concrete in Spirit has, by means of analysis, attained
to the consciousness of difference. All that partakes of
Spirit is concrete ; in this we have before us the Spiritual
in its most profound aspect, that of Spirit as the concrete
element of faith and thought. The two are not only
mixed up in the most manifold way, in immediate passing
over from one side to the other, but are so inwardly bound
up together that there is no faith which does not contain
within itself reflection, argumentation, or, in fact, thought,
and, on the other hand, no thinking which does not,
even if it be only for the moment, contain faith,—for
faith in general is the form of any presupposition, of any
assumption, come whence it may, which lies firmly at the
foundation—momentary faith. This means that even in
free thinking that which now exists as a presupposition, is
a comprehended result, thought out either before or after,

but in this transformation of the presupposition into a result, again has a side which is a presupposition, an assumption or unconscious immediacy of the activity of the Spirit.

Yet the explanation of the nature of free self-conscious thought we must here leave on one side, and rather remark that for the attainment of this essentially and actually existent union of faith and thought a long time has been necessary—more than fifteen hundred years—and that it has cost the most severe toil to reach the point at which thought has escaped from its absorption in faith, and attained to the abstract consciousness of its freedom, and thereby of its independence and its complete self-sufficiency, in the light of which nothing can have validity for thought which has not come before its judgment-seat, and been then justified as admissible. Thought thus taking its stand upon the extreme point of its freedom—and it is only completely free in this extreme point—and rejecting authority and faith in general, has driven faith in like manner to take its stand in an abstract fashion upon itself, and to attempt entirely to free itself from thought. At all events, it has arrived at the point of declaring itself to be freed from and not to require thought. Wrapped up in unconsciousness of the at all events small amount of thought which must remain to it, it goes on to declare thought to be incapable of reaching truth and destructive of it, so that thought is capable of comprehending one thing only, its incapacity to grasp the truth and see into it, and of proving to itself its own nothingness, with the result that suicide is its highest vocation. So completely has the relation in the view of the time been reversed, that faith has now become exalted as immediate knowledge in opposition to thought, as the only means of attaining to the truth, just as formerly, on the other hand, only that could give peace to Man of which he could become conscious as truth through proof by thought.

This standpoint of opposition cannot better show how important and far-reaching it is than when it is considered in relation to the subject which we have set ourselves to discuss, the knowledge of God. In the working out into opposition of the difference between faith and thought, it is immediately apparent that they have reached formal extremes in which abstraction is made from all content, so that in the first instance they are no longer opposed as concretely defined religious faith and thought about religious subjects, but abstractly, as faith in general, and as thought in general, or knowledge, in so far as this last does not yield merely forms of thought, but gives us a content in and with its truth. From this point of view the knowledge of God is made dependent on the question as to the nature of knowledge in general, and before we can pass to the investigation of the concrete it seems necessary to ascertain whether the consciousness of what is true can and must be thinking knowledge, or, faith.   Our proposed consideration of the knowledge of the existence of God thus changed into this general consideration of knowledge, just as the new philosophical epoch has made it the beginning and foundation of all philosophical speculation that the nature of knowledge itself is to be examined before the actual, *i.e.*, concrete knowledge of an object.   We thus incurred the danger—a danger, however, necessary in the interests of thoroughness—of having to trace the subject further back than the time at our disposal for carrying out the aim of these lectures would permit of our doing.   If, however, we look more closely at the demand which appears to have met us, it becomes perfectly plain that it is only the subject that has changed with it, not the thing.   In both cases, either if we admitted the demand for that inquiry, or stuck directly to our theme, we should have to *know*, and in that case we should have a subject, too, in the shape of knowledge itself.   And as in doing so we should not have emerged from the activity of knowledge, from real knowledge, there is nothing to hinder our leaving the other subject which it is not our aim to consider, alone, and thus stick to our own subject. It will further appear, as we follow out our purpose, that the knowledge of our subject will also in itself justify itself as knowledge. That in true and real knowledge the justification of knowledge will and must lie, might admittedly be said in advance, for to say so is simply a tautology, just as we may know in advance that the desired way round, the desiring to know knowledge before actual knowledge, is superfluous just because it is inherently absurd. If under the process of knowledge we figure to ourselves an external operation in which it is brought into a merely mechanical relation with an object, that is to say, remains outside it, and is only externally applied to it, knowledge is presented in such a relation as a particular thing for itself, so that it may well be that its forms have nothing in common with the qualities of the object; and thus when it concerns itself with an object, it remains only in its own forms, and does not reach the essential qualities of the object, that is to say, does not become real knowledge of it. In such a relation knowledge is determined as finite, and as of the finite; in its object there remains something essentially inner, whose notion is thus unattainable by and foreign to knowledge, which finds here its limit and its end, and is on that account limited and finite. But to take such a relation as the only one, or as final or absolute, is a purely made-up and unjustifiable assumption of the Understanding. Real knowledge, inasmuch as it does not remain outside the object, but in point of fact occupies itself with it, must be immanent in the object, the proper movement of its nature, only expressed in the form of thought and taken up into consciousness.

We have now provisionally indicated those standpoints of culture which in the case of such material as we have before us ought in the present day to be taken into account. It is pre-eminently, or, properly speaking, only here that it is self-evident that the proposition already laid down, according to which the consideration of knowledge is not different from the consideration of its object, must hold good without limitation. I will therefore at once indicate the general sense in which the proposed theme, the proofs of the existence of God, is taken, and which will be shown to be the true one. It is that they ought to comprise the elevation of the human spirit to God, and express it for thought, just as the elevation itself is an elevation of thought and into the kingdom of thought.

And to begin with, as regards knowledge, Man is essentially consciousness, and thus what is felt, the content, the determinateness which a feeling or sensation has, is also in consciousness as something presented in the form of an idea. That in virtue of which feeling is religious feeling, is the divine content; it is therefore essentially something of which we have knowledge. But this content is in its essence no sensuous perception or sensuous idea; it does not exist for imagination, but only for thought; God is Spirit, only for Spirit, and only for pure Spirit, that is, for thought. This is the root of such a content, even though imagination and even sense-perception may afterwards accompany it, and this content itself may enter into feeling. It is the elevation of the thinking Spirit to that which is the highest thought, to God, that we thus wish to consider.

This elevation is besides essentially rooted in the nature of our mind. It is necessary to it, and it is this necessity that we have before us in this elevation, and the setting forth of this necessity itself is nothing else than what we call proof. Therefore we have not to prove this elevation from the outside ; it proves itself in itself, and this means nothing else than that it is by its very nature necessary. We have only to look to its own process, and we have there, since it is necessary in itself, the necessity, insight into the nature of which has to be vouched for by proof.

SECOND LECTURE

IF the undertaking which is commonly called proof of the existence of God has been understood in the form in which it was set forth in the first lecture, the chief objection to it will have been got rid of. For the nature of proof was held to consist in this, that it is only the consciousness of the proper movement of the object in itself. If this thought might be attended with difficulties in its application to other objects, these difficulties would necessarily disappear in the case of the object with which we are concerned, for it is not a passive and external object, but really a subjective movement, the elevation of the Spirit to God, an activity, the following of a certain course, a process, and thus has in it that necessary procedure which constitutes proof, and which has only to be taken up and studied in order that it may be seen to involve proof. But the expression proof carries with it too definitely the idea of a merely subjective line of thought to be followed on our behoof, to allow of the conception of it just stated being considered sufficient in itself apart from any attempt to expressly examine and get rid of this contrasted idea. In this lecture, then, we must first come to an understanding about the nature of proof in general, and with especial definiteness as regards that aspect of it which we here put aside and exclude. It is not our business to assert that there is no proof of the kind indicated, but to assign its limits, and to see that it is not, as is falsely thought, the only form of proof. This is bound up with the contrast drawn between immediate and mediated knowledge, in which in our time the chief interest centres in connection with religious knowledge, and even the religious frame of mind itself, which must accordingly be likewise considered.

The distinction, which has already been touched upon in connection with knowledge, implies that two kinds of proof must be taken into account, of which the one is clearly that which we use simply as an aid to knowledge, as something subjective, whose activity and movement have their place within ourselves, and are not the peculiar movement of the thing considered. That this kind of proof finds a place in the scientific knowledge of finite things and their finite content, becomes apparent when we examine the nature of the procedure more closely. Let us take for this purpose an example from a science in which this method of proof is admittedly applied in its most complete form. If we prove a geometrical proposition every part of the proof must in part carry its justification within itself, so also when we solve an equation in algebra. In part, however, the whole course of procedure is defined and justified through the aim which we have in connection with this, and because that end is attained by such procedure. But we are very well aware that that of which the quantitive value has been developed out of the equation, has not as an actual thing run through these operations in order to reach the quantity which it possesses, and that the magnitude of the geometrical lines, angles, and so on, has not gone through and been brought about by the series of propositions by which we have arrived at it as representing a result. The necessity which we see in such proof corresponds indeed to the individual properties of the object itself, these relations of quantity actually belong to it; but the progress in connecting the one with the other is something which goes on entirely within us; it is a process for realising the aim we have in view, namely, to see into the meaning of the thing, not a course in which the object arrives at its inherent relations and their connection. It does not thus create itself, and is not created, as we create it and its relations in the process of attaining insight into it.

Besides proof proper, of which the essential characteristic—for this is all that is necessary for the purpose of our investigation—has been brought out, we find further, that in the region of finite knowledge the term proof is also applied to what, when more closely examined, is only the indicating of something, the pointing out of an idea, a proposition, a law, and so on in experience. Historical proof we do not require from the point of view from which we here consider knowledge, to elaborate in detail ; it depends for its material on experience, or rather perception. Looked at in one light, it makes no difference that it has reference to foreign perceptions and their evidences ; argumentation, that is to say, the exercise of understanding proper regarding the objective connection of circumstances and actions, makes these data into presuppositions and fundamental assumptions, just as its criticism of evidences has done in drawing its conclusions. But in so far as argument and criticism constitute the other essential side of historical proof, such proof treats its data as being the ideas of other people ; the subjective element directly enters into the material, and the reasoning about and combination of that material is likewise subjective activity ; so that the course and activity of knowledge has quite different ingredients from the course followed by the circumstances themselves. As regards the pointing things out in everyday experience, this is certainly concerned, in the first instance, with individual perceptions, observations, and so on, that is to say, with the kind of material which is only pointed out, but its interest is by so doing to prove further that there are in Nature and in Spirit such species and kinds, such laws, forces, faculties, and activities as are mentioned in the sciences. We pass by the metaphysical or common psychological reflections about that subjective element of

sense, external and internal, which accompanies perception.   But the material, however, in so far as it enters into
the sciences, is not so left to itself as it is in the senses
and in perception.   On the contrary, the content of the
sciences—the species, kinds, laws, forces, and so on—is
built up out of that material, which is, perhaps, already
called by the name of phenomena, by putting together
through analysis what is common, the leaving aside of
what is not essential, the retention of what is called essential, without any certain test having been applied to distinguish between what is to be regarded as non-essential
and what as essential.   It is admitted that what is perceived does not itself make these abstractions, does not
compare its individuals (or individual positions, circumstances, and so on), or put what is common in them
together ; that therefore a great part of the activity of
knowledge is a subjective affair, just as in the content
which has been obtained a part of its definitions, as being
logical forms, are the product of this subjective activity.
The expression " predicate," or mark (*Merkmal*), if people
will still use this stupid expression, directly indicates a
subjective purpose of isolating properties for our use in
marking distinctions, while others, which likewise exist
in the object, are put aside.   This expression is to be
called stupid, because the definitions of species and kinds
directly pass for something essential and objective, and
not as existing merely for us who mark distinctions.
We may certainly also express ourselves by saying that
the species leaves aside, in one kind, properties which it
places in another, or that energy in one form of its
manifestation leaves aside circumstances which are present in another, that these circumstances are thus shown
by it to be unessential, and it of itself gives up the form
of its manifestation, and withdraws itself into inactivity
or self-containedness ; that thus, for example, the law of
the motion of the heavenly bodies penetrates to every
single place and every moment in which the heavenly

body occupies that place, and just by this continual abstraction shows itself to be a law. If we thus look on abstraction as objective activity, which it so far is, it is yet very different from subjective activity and its products. The former leaves the heavenly body to fall back again after abstraction from this particular place and this particular moment into the particular changing place and moment of time, just as the species may appear in the kind in other contingent or unessential forms and in the external particularity of individuals. On the other hand, subjective abstraction raises the law like the species into its universality as such, and makes it exist and preserves it in this form, in the mind.

In these forms of the knowledge which progresses from mere indication to proof, from immediate objectivity to special products, the necessity may be felt of considering explicitly the method, the nature, and fashion of the subjective activity, in order to test its claims and procedure; for this method has its own characteristics and kind of progress which are quite different from the characteristics and process of the object in itself. And without entering more particularly into the nature of this method of knowledge, it becomes immediately apparent, from a single characteristic which we observe in it, that inasmuch as it is represented as being concerned with the object in accordance with subjective forms, it is only capable of apprehending relations of the object. It is therefore idle to start the question whether these relations are objective and real or only subjective and ideal, not to mention the fact that such expressions as subjectivity and objectivity, reality and ideality, are simply vague abstractions. The content, be it objective or merely subjective, real or ideal, remains always the same, an aggregate of relations, not something that is in-and-for-itself, the notion of the thing, or the infinite, with which knowledge must have to do. If that content of knowledge is taken by perverted sense as containing relations only, and these are understood to be phenomena or relations to a faculty of subjective knowledge, it must, so far as results are concerned, always be recognised as representing the great intellectual advance which modern philosophy has achieved, that the mode of thinking, proving, and knowing the infinite, which has been described, is proved incapable of reaching what is eternal and divine.

What has been brought out in the preceding exposition regarding knowledge in general, and especially what relates to thinking knowledge (which is what alone concerns us), and to proof, the principal moment in that knowledge, we have looked at from the point of view from which it is seen to be a movement of the activity of thought which is outside the object and different from the development of the object itself. This definition may in part be taken to be sufficient for our purpose, but partly, too, it is to be taken as what is essential in opposition to the one-sidedness which lies in the reflections about the subjectivity of knowledge.

In the opposition of the process of knowledge to the object to be known lies the finiteness of knowledge. But this opposition is not on that account to be regarded as itself infinite and absolute, and its products are not to be taken to be appearances only because of the mere abstraction of subjectivity; but in so far as they themselves are determined by that opposition, the content as such is affected by the externality referred to. This point of view has an effect upon the nature of the content, and yields a definite insight into it; while, on the contrary, the other way of looking at the question gives us nothing but the abstract category of the subjective, which is, moreover, taken to be absolute. What we thus get as the result of the way in which we look at the proof, for the otherwise quite general quality of the content, is, speaking generally, just this, that the content, inasmuch as it bears an external relation to knowledge, is itself determined as something external, or, to put it

more definitely, consists of abstractions from finite properties. Mathematical content as such is essentially
magnitude. Geometrical figures pertain to space, and
have thus in themselves externality as their principle,
since they are distinguished from real objects, and represent only the one-sided spatiality of these objects,
as distinguished from their concrete filling up, through
which they first became real. So number has the unit
for its principle, and is the putting together of a multiplicity of units which are independent, and is thus a
completely external combination. The knowledge which
we have here before us can only attain its greatest
perfection in this field, because that field contains only
simple and definite qualities, and the dependence of these
upon each other, the insight into the nature of which is
proof, is thus stable, and ensures for proof the logical
progress of necessity. This kind of knowledge is capable
of exhausting the nature of its objects. The logical
nature of the process of proof is not, however, confined
to mathematical content, but enters into all departments
of natural and spiritual material; but we may sum up
what is logical in knowledge in connection with proof
by saying that it depends on the rules of inference;
the proofs of the existence of God are therefore essentially inferences. The express investigation of these
forms belongs, however, partly to logic, and for the rest
the nature of the fundamental defect must be ascertained
in the course of the examination of these proofs which is
about to be taken in hand. For the present it is enough
to remark further, in connection with what has been said,
that the rules of inference have a kind of foundation
which is of the nature of mathematical calculation.
The connection of propositions which are requisite to
constitute a syllogistic conclusion depends on the relations of the sphere which each of them occupies as
regards the other, and which is quite properly regarded
as greater or smaller. The definite extent of such

a sphere is what determines the correctness of the subsumption. The older logicians, such as Lambert and Ploucquet, have been at the pains of inventing a notation by means of which the relation in inference may be reduced to that of identity, that is, to the abstract mathematical relation of equality, so that inference is shown to be the mechanism of a kind of calculation. As regards, however, the further nature of knowledge in such an external connection of objects, which in their very nature are external in themselves, we shall have to speak of it presently under the name of mediate knowledge, and to consider the opposition in its more definite form.

As regards these forms which are called species, laws, forces, and so on, knowledge does not stand to them in an external relation ; they are rather its products. But the knowledge which produces them, as has been shown, produces them only by abstraction from what is objective ; they have their root in this, but are essentially separated from what is actual ; they are more concrete than mathematical figures, but their content differs essentially from that from which the start was made, and which must constitute their only foundation of proof.

The defective element in this mode of knowledge has thus attention drawn to it in a different form from that shown in the way of looking at it, which declares the products of knowledge to be mere phenomena, because knowledge itself is only a subjective activity. But the general result, however, is the same, and we have now to see what has been set over against this result. What is determined as insufficient for the aim of the Spirit, which is the absorption into its very nature of what is infinite, eternal, divine, is the activity of the Spirit which in thinking proceeds by means of abstraction, inference, and proof. This view, itself the product of the mode of thought characteristic of the period, has jumped straight over to the other extreme in giving out a proofless, immediate knowledge, an unreasoning faith, a feeling devoid of thought, as the only way of grasping and having within oneself divine truth. It is asserted that that kind of knowledge which is insufficient for the higher kind of truth is the exclusive and sole kind of knowledge. The two assumptions are most closely connected. On the one side, we have, in the investigation of what we have undertaken to consider, to free that knowledge from its one-sidedness, and in doing so at the same time to show by facts that there exists another kind of knowledge than that which is given out as the only kind. On the other side, the pretension which faith as such sets up against knowledge is a prejudice which occupies too firm and sure a position not to make a stricter investigation necessary. In view of this pretension it must be borne in mind that the true, unsophisticated faith, the more it in case of dire necessity might reasonably make pretensions, the less it does make them, and that the case of necessity exists only for the merely rationalising, dry, and polemical assertion of faith.

But I have elsewhere already explained how the matter stands as regards that faith or immediate knowledge. It is not possible that in the forefront of any attempt to deal at the present time with the proofs of the existence of God, the position taken up by faith can be set aside as done with; the chief points from which it is to be criticised, and the place to be assigned to it, must at least be called to mind.

THIRD LECTURE

It has already been remarked that the assertion of faith, of which we have to speak, is found outside of genuine simple faith. This latter, in so far as it has advanced to conscious knowledge, and has consequently acquired a consciousness of knowledge, accedes to knowledge with full confidence in it, because it is pre-eminently full of confidence in itself, is sure of itself, and firmly established in itself. We are rather concerned with faith in so far as it takes up a polemical attitude towards rational knowledge, and expresses itself in a polemical fashion even against knowledge in general. It is thus not a faith which opposes itself to another kind of faith. Faith (or belief) is what is common to both; it is therefore the content which fights against the content. But this fact of having to do with content at once brings knowledge with it. If it were otherwise, the overthrow and defence of the truth of religion would not be carried out with external weapons, which are just as foreign to faith and religion as to knowledge. The faith which rejects knowledge as such, is just because of this devoid of content, and is, to begin with, to be taken abstractly as faith in general, as it opposes itself to concrete knowledge, to rational knowledge, without reference to content. As thus abstract, ·it is removed back into the simplicity of self-consciousness. This is in its simplicity, in so far as it has any fulness at all, feeling, and what is content in knowledge is definiteness of feeling. The assertion of abstract faith thus leads immediately to the form of feeling, in which the subjectivity of knowledge intrenches itself as in an inaccessible place. The standpoints of both must therefore be briefly indicated, from which their one-sidedness,

and consequently the untruth of the fashion in which they
are asserted to be ultimate and fundamental determinations, becomes apparent. Faith, to begin with it, starts
from this, that the nullity of knowledge, so far as absolute truth is concerned, has been demonstrated. We
wish so to proceed as to leave faith in possession of this
assumption, and to see accordingly what it is in itself.

To begin with, if the opposition is conceived of as being
of such an absolutely general kind as that between faith
and knowledge, as we often hear it put, this abstraction
must be directly found fault with. For faith belongs to
consciousness; we know about what we believe; nay, we
know about it with certainty. It is thus at once apparent
that it is absurd to wish to separate faith and knowledge
in such a general fashion.

But faith is now called *immediate* knowledge, and is
accordingly to be distinguished radically from mediate
and mediating knowledge. Since at this stage we leave
on one side the speculative examination of these conceptions, in order to keep within the proper sphere of this
kind of assertion, we will oppose to this separation, which
is asserted to be absolute, the fact that there is no act
of knowledge, any more than there is any act of sensation, conception, or volition, no activity, property, or condition pertaining to Spirit, which is not mediated and
mediating; just as there is no other object in Nature or
Spirit, be it what it may, in heaven or the earth, or under
the earth, which does not include within itself the quality
of mediation as well as that of immediacy. It is thus
as a universal fact that logical philosophy presents it—
we might add, along with the exhibition of its necessity,
to which we need not here appeal—in the completed
circle of the forms of thought. As regards the matter of
sense, whether it belongs to outer or inner perception, it
is admitted that it is finite, that is, that it exists only as
mediated through what is other than sense. But of
this matter itself, and still more of the higher content of

Spirit, it will be admitted that it derives its essential character from categories, and that the nature of this character is shown in logic to be the possession of the moment of mediation above indicated inseparably in itself. But we pause here to call attention to the absolutely universal fact, in whatever sense and with whatever meaning the facts may be understood. Without digressing into examples, we abide by the one object which here lies nearest to us.

God is activity, free activity relating itself to itself, and remaining with itself. The essential element in the notion or conception of God, or, for that matter, in every idea of God, is that He is Himself, the mediation of Himself with Himself. If God is defined merely as the Creator, His activity is taken only as going out of itself, as expanding itself out of itself, as sensible or material producing, without any return into itself. The product is something different from Him, it is the world; the introduction of the category of mediation would at once bring with it the idea that God must be through the medium of the world; one might, at all events, say with truth that He is Creator only by means of the world, or what He creates. Only this would be mere empty tautology; for the category, "that which is created," is itself directly involved in the first category, that of the Creator. On the other hand, what is created remains, so far as the ordinary idea of it is concerned, as a world outside God, as an Other over against Him, so that He exists away beyond that world, apart from it, in-and-for-Himself. But in Christianity least of all is it true that we have to know God only as creation, activity, not as Spirit. The fact rather is that to this religion, the explicit consciousness that God is Spirit is peculiar, the consciousness that He, even as He is in-and-for-Himself, relates Himself, as it were, to the Other of Himself (called the Son), to Himself, that He is related to Himself in Himself as love, essentially as this love is mediation with itself. God is indeed the

Creator of the world, and is so sufficiently defined. But God is more than this; He is the true God in that He is the mediation of Himself with Himself, and is this love.

Faith, then, inasmuch as it has God as the object of its consciousness, has this mediation for its object; just as faith, as existing in the individual, only exists through teaching and training, the teaching and training of men, but still more through the teaching and training of the Spirit of God, and exists only through this process of mediation. But faith, like consciousness in general, this relation of the subject to an object, is quite abstract, whether God is its object, or whatever thing or content may be the object, and so faith or knowledge only exists through the medium of an object. Otherwise we have empty identity, a faith in or knowledge of nothing.

But conversely there is to be found here the other fact that, in like manner, there can be nothing which is only and exclusively the product of mediation. If we examine into what we understand by immediacy, it will be seen that it must exist in itself without any difference, such as that through which mediation is at once posited. It is simple reference to self, and is thus in its immediate form merely Being. Now all knowledge, mediate and immediate, and indeed everything else, at all events *is;* and that *it is,* is itself the least and most abstract thing that one can say of anything. If it is even only subjective, as faith or knowledge is, at all events it is, the predicate of Being belongs to it, just as such Being appertains to the object which exists only in faith or knowledge. The insight involved in this view is of a very simple kind. Yet we may be impatient with philosophy just because of this simplicity, in so far as we pass from the fulness and warmth which belong to faith, over to such abstractions as Being and immediacy. But, in point of fact, this is not the fault of philosophy; on the contrary, it is that assertion of faith and immediate knowledge which takes its stand on these abstractions. In this fact, that faith is not mediate knowledge, there lies the entire value of the matter, and the verdict passed upon it. But we come also to the content, or rather, we may likewise come only to the relation of a content, to knowledge.

It is further to be remarked that immediacy in knowledge, which is faith, has this further quality, that faith knows that in which it believes, not merely generally, not merely in the sense of having an idea or knowledge from without of it, but knows it with certainty. It is in certainty that the nerve of faith lies. And here we encounter a further distinction, we further distinguish truth from certainty. We know very well that much has been known, and is known for certain, which is nevertheless not true. Men have long enough known it to be certain, and millions still know it to be certain, to take a trivial example, that the sun goes round the earth. And what is more, the Egyptians believed, and knew it for certain, that Apis was a great or the greatest god; while the Greeks thought the same regarding Jupiter; just as the Hindus still know for certain that the cow, and other inhabitants of India, the Mongols and many races, that a man, the Dalai-Lama, is God. That this certainty is expressed and asserted is admitted. A man may quite well say, I know something for certain, I believe it, it is true. But, at the same time, every one else must be allowed the right to say the same thing, for every one is " I," every one knows, every one knows for certain. But this unavoidable admission expresses the truth that this knowledge, knowledge for certain, this abstraction, may have a content of the most diverse and opposite kind, and the proof of the content must lie just in this assurance of being certain, of faith. But what man will come forward and say, Only that which I know and know as certain is true; what I know as certain is true just because I know it as certain. Truth stands eternally over against mere certainty, and neither certainty, nor immediate knowledge, nor faith decides what is truth. Christ directed the minds of the Apostles and His friends

away from the genuinely immediate visible certainty
which they derived from His immediate presence, from
His own sayings and spoken words heard with their ears
and apprehended through their senses and feelings, away
from such a faith and such a source of faith to the
truth, into which they were to be led only in the further
future and through the Spirit. For the attainment of
anything more in addition to this highest certainty, derived
from the source above indicated, there exists nothing except just what is in the content itself.

Faith, in so far as it is defined to be immediate knowledge, as distinguished from what is mediate, reduces
itself to the abstract formalism above mentioned. This
abstraction makes it possible not only to rank as faith
the sensuous certainty which I have that I possess a body,
and that there are things outside me, but to deduce or
prove from it what the nature of faith is. But we should
do gross injustice to what in the sphere of religion is
termed faith if we were to see in it only this abstraction.
Faith must rather be full of substance; it must be a
content, and this is to be a true content; it must be far
removed from such a content as the sensuous certainty
that I have a body, that things perceived by the senses
surround me. It must contain the truth, and quite a
different truth from that last mentioned, the truth of
finite things of sense, and derived from quite a different
source. The tendency above indicated to formal subjectivity must find faith as such even too objective, for this
latter has always to do with ideas of things, with a knowledge of them, with a state of conviction regarding some
content. This extreme form of the subjective, in which
the definite form of the content and the conception and
knowledge of it have vanished, is that of feeling. We
cannot, therefore, avoid speaking of it too; it is this
form, moreover, which is asked for in our times, not
feeling of the simple or naïve kind, but as a result of
culture, derived from grounds or reasons which are the
same as those already referred to.

FOURTH LECTURE

As has been shown in the preceding lecture, the form of feeling is closely related to mere faith as such. It is the yet more intensive forcing back of self-consciousness into itself, the development of the content to mere definiteness of feeling.

Religion must be felt, must exist in feeling, otherwise it is not religion; faith cannot exist without feeling, otherwise it is not religion. This must be admitted to be true, for feeling is nothing but my subjectivity in its simplicity and immediacy—myself as this particular existent personality. If I have religion only as idea, faith takes the form of certainty about these ideas; its content is before me, it is still an object over against me; it is not yet identical with me as simple self; I am not so penetrated through and through with it that it constitutes my qualitative, determinate character. The very inmost unity of the content of faith with me is requisite in order that I may have quality or substance, its substance. It thus becomes my feeling. As against religion Man must hold nothing in reserve for himself, for it is the innermost region of truth. Religion must therefore possess not only this as yet abstract "I," which even as faith is yet knowledge, but the concrete "I" in its simple personality, comprehending the whole of it in itself. Feeling is this inwardness which is not separated in itself.

Feeling is, however, understood to have the property of being something purely individual, lasting for a single moment, just as one individual thing in the process of alternation with another exists either after that other or alongside of it. But the heart signifies the all-embracing unity of the feelings, both in their quantity and also as regards their duration in time. The heart is the ground or basis which contains in itself and preserves the essential nature of feelings, independent of the fleeting nature of their succession in consciousness. In this their unbroken unity—for the heart expresses the simple pulse of the living spirit—religion is able to penetrate the different kinds of feeling, and to become for them the substance which holds, masters, and rules them.

But this brings us at once to the reflection that feeling and heart as such are only the one side, definite forms of feeling and heart being the other. And, accordingly, we must at once go further and say, that just as little is religion true, because it exists in our feelings or hearts, as because it is believed and known immediately and for certain. All religions, even the most false and unworthy, exist in our feelings and hearts just as much as those that are true. There are feelings which are immoral, unjust, and godless, just as much as there are feelings which are moral, just, and pious. Out of the heart proceed evil thoughts, murder, adultery, backbiting, and so forth; that is to say, the fact that thoughts are not bad, but good, does not depend on their being in the heart and proceeding out of it. We have to do with the definite form which is assumed by the feeling which is in the heart. This is a truism so trivial that one hesitates to give it expression, but it is part of philosophical culture to carry the analysis of ideas even to the length of questioning and denying what is most simple and most commonly received. To that shallow type of thought or Enlightenment which is vain of its boldness, it appears unmeaning and unseemly to recall trivial truths, such, for instance, as that which may be here once more brought to mind, the truth that Man is distinguished from the brute by the faculty of thought, but shares that of feeling with it. If feeling is religious feeling, religion is its definite quality. If it is wicked, bad feeling, what is bad and wicked is its definite quality. It is this determinate quality which forms the content for consciousness, what in the words already used is called thought. Feeling is bad on account of its bad content; the heart, because of its sinful thoughts. Feeling is the common form for the most different kinds of content. It can on that account just as little serve as a justification for any of its determinate qualities, for its content, as can immediate certainty.

Feeling makes itself known as a subjective form, as being something in me, while I am the subject of something. This form is that which is simple, which remains equal to itself, and therefore potentially indeterminate in every difference of content—the abstraction of my existence as a single individual. The determinateness or special character of the feeling is, on the contrary, to begin with, difference in general, the being unlike some other, being manifold. It must therefore be explicitly distinguished from the general form whose particular and definite quality it is, and be regarded on its own account. It has the form of the content which must be regarded " on its own merits," and judged on its own account; on this value depends the value of the feeling. This content must be true, to begin with, and independently of the feeling, just as religion is true on its own account— it is what is in itself necessary and universal—the Thing or true fact which develops itself to a kingdom of truths and of laws, as well as to a kingdom of their knowledge and their final ground, God.

I shall indicate only in outline the consequences which ensue if immediate knowledge and feeling as such are elevated into a principle. It is their very concentration which carries with it for the content, simplification, abstraction, and indefiniteness. Thus they both reduce the divine content, be it religious as such, or legal and moral, to a minimum, to what is most abstract. With this the determination of the content becomes arbitrary, for in that minimum there exists nothing determinate. This is a weighty consequence, from a theoretical as well as a practical point of view. Chiefly from a practical, for since, for the justification of disposition and action, reasons are necessary, the faculty of argument must still be very untrained, and very little skilled in its work, if it does not know how to assign good reasons for what is arbitrary.

Another feature in the situation, which the withdrawal into immediate knowledge and into feeling brings into view, concerns the relation of men to other men, and their spiritual fellowship. The objective, the true fact or Thing, is what is in-and-for-itself universal, and is so, therefore, for all. As what is most universal, it is implicitly thought in general ; and thought is the common basis. The man who betakes himself to feeling, to immediate knowledge, to his own ideas or his own thoughts, shuts himself up, as I have already said, in his own particularity, and breaks off any fellowship or community with others—the only way is to leave him alone. But this kind of feeling and heart lets us see more closely into the nature of feeling and heart. Restricting itself in accordance with its first principle to its own feeling, the consciousness of a content degrades it to the determinate form belonging to itself ; it maintains itself rigidly as self-consciousness, in which this determinateness inheres ; the self is for consciousness the object which it sets before itself, the substance which has the content only as an attribute, as a predicate in it, so that it is not the independent element in which the subject is sublated, or loses itself. The subject is itself in this way a fixed condition, which has been called the life of feeling. In the so-called Irony, which is connected with it, the "myself" is abstract only in relation to itself; in the distinction of itself from its content it stands as pure consciousness of itself, and as separated from it.

In the life of feeling this subject exists rather in the above-mentioned identity with the content, it is definite consciousness in it, and remains as this individual "I," object and end to itself. As the religious individual "I," it is end to itself; this individual " I " is object and end in general; in the expression, for instance, that I am blessed, and in so far as this blessedness is brought about through belief in the truth, the "I" is filled with truth and penetrated by it. Filled in this way with yearning, it is unsatisfied in itself; but this yearning is the yearning of religion; it is, accordingly, satisfied in having this yearning in itself; in it it has the subjective consciousness of itself, and of itself as the religious self. Carried beyond itself only in this yearning, it is just in it that it preserves itself and the consciousness of being satisfied, and in close connection with this the consciousness of its contentment with itself. But this inwardness involves at the same time the opposite condition which consists in that most unhappy sense of division experienced by the pure hearted. While I regard myself strictly as this particular and abstract " I," and compare my particular impulses, inclinations, and thoughts, with what ought to fill my nature, I am able to feel that this contrast is a painful contradiction within myself, which becomes permanent, owing to the fact that "I," as this particular subjective " me," have it as my aim and object to concern myself about myself as my individual self. It is just this fixed reflection which prevents me from being filled by the substantial content, by the Thing or true fact, for in the true fact I forget myself; in the very act of becoming absorbed in it that reflection upon myself disappears of itself. I am characterised as subjective only in that opposition to the Thing which remains with me through reflection on myself. In thus keeping myself outside of the Thing or true fact, and since this Thing constitutes my end, the real interest is transferred from the attentive observation of the Thing back to myself. I thus go on unceasingly

emptying myself, and continue in this condition of emptiness. The hollowness which thus attaches to the highest
end pursued by the individual, namely, pious effort and
anxiety about the welfare of his own soul, has led to the
most inhuman manifestations of a feeble and spiritless
reality, ranging from the quiet anxiety of a loving disposition to the suffering caused to the soul by despair
and madness. This was still more the case in former
times than in these later days when the sense of satisfaction in the yearning has gained the upper hand of the
sense of division, and has produced in the soul a feeling of
contentment and even a sense of irony itself. Unreality in
the heart, such as that referred to, is not only emptiness,
but is also narrow-heartedness. It is its own formal,
subjective life with which it is filled.; it always has this
particular " I " as its object and end. It is only the
truly Universal, the Universal in-and-for-itself, which is
broad, and the heart inwardly extends only by entering
into this, and expanding within this substantial element,
which is at once the religious, the moral, and the legal
element. Speaking generally, love is the abandonment
on the part of the heart of limitation to a particular point
of its own, and its reception of the love of God is the
reception of that development or unfolding of His Spirit
which comprehends in itself all true content, and swal-
lows up in this objectivity whatever is merely peculiar to
the heart. In this substantial element the subjectivity,
which is for the heart itself a one-sided form, is given up,
and this at the same time supplies the impulse to throw
off the subjectivity. This is the impulse to action in
general, or, more strictly speaking, it is the impulse to
take part in the action of the content which is divine
in-and-for-itself, and is therefore the content which has
absolute power and authority. It is this, accordingly,
which constitutes the reality or real existence of the heart,
and it is indivisibly both that inner reality and also outer
reality.   G

When we have thus distinguished between what, because it is buried in and absorbed into the Thing or true object, is the unsophisticated heart, and the heart which in reflection is consciously occupied with itself, we find that the distinction constitutes the relation in which the heart stands to the substantial element. So long as the heart remains within itself, and consequently remains outside of this element, it is by its own act in an external and contingent relation to this element. This connection, which leads the heart to declare what is just, and to lay down the law in accordance with its own feeling, has been already mentioned. To the objectivity of action, that is, to action which originates in the truly substantial element, subjectivity opposes feeling, and to this substantial element and to the thinking knowledge of it it opposes immediate knowledge. Here, however, we do not stay to consider the nature of action, but simply remark that it is just this substantial element, represented by the laws of justice and morality and the commandments of God, which is by its very nature the true Universal, and has consequently its root and basis in the region of thought. If sometimes the laws of justice and morality are regarded merely as arbitrary commands of God—which would mean, in fact, that they were irrational—still it would take us too far to make that our starting-point. But the putting on a permanent basis and the investigation of the conviction, on the part of the conscious subject, of the truth of the principles which ought to constitute for him the basis of his action, is thinking knowledge. While the unsophisticated heart yields itself up to these principles, its insight is as yet so undeveloped, and any pretension on its part to independence is so foreign to it, that it reaches them rather by the road of authority, and thus this part of the heart in which they are implanted is alone the place of conscious thought, for they are themselves the thoughts of action, and are inherently universal principles. This heart cannot, therefore, offer any opposition to the development of what is its own objective basis, any more than it can to that of those truths which belong to it, and which at first appear in themselves rather as theoretical truths pertaining to its religious faith. As, however, this possession, and the intensity which characterises it, are already in the heart only through the mediation of education, which has asserted its influence upon its thought and knowledge just as it has upon its volition, so, in a still greater degree, the further developed content, and the alteration in the circle of its ideas which are implicitly native to the place where they are found, also represent mediating knowledge mediated into the conscious form of thought.

FIFTH LECTURE

WE may sum up what has gone before as follows. The heart ought not to have any dread of knowledge; the determinateness of feeling, the content of the heart, ought to have a substantial form. Feeling or the heart must be filled by the Thing or true object by what actually exists, and consequently be broad and true in character. But this Thing, this substantial element, is simply the truth of the Divine Spirit, the Universal in-and-for-itself, though just because of this it is not the abstract Universal, but the Universal in the development which belongs essentially to ˜itself. The substantial element is thus essentially implicit thought, and exists in thought. But thought, what constitutes the really inner nature of faith itself, if it is to be known as essential and true—in so far as faith is no longer something implicit and merely natural, but is regarded as having entered into the sphere of knowledge with all its requirements and claims—must at the same time be known as something necessary, and must have gained a consciousness of itself and of the connected nature of its development. It thus extends and proves itself at the same time; for, speaking generally, to prove simply means to become conscious of the connection, and consequently of the necessity of things, and in relation to our present design it means the recognition of the particular content in the Universal in-and-for-itself, and of how this absolute truth itself is the result, and is consequently the final truth of all particular content. This connection, which is thus present to consciousness, must not be a subjective movement of thought outside of reality, but must follow this latter, and must simply unfold its meaning and necessity. Knowledge is just this unfolding of the objective movement of the content, of the inner necessity which essentially belongs to it, and it is true knowledge since it is in unity with the object. For us this object must be the elevation of our spirit to God, and is thus what we have referred to as the necessity of absolute truth in the form of that final result into which everything returns in the Spirit.

But because it contains the name of God, the mention of this end may easily have the effect of rendering worthless all that was urged against the false ideas of knowledge, cognition, and feeling, and all that was gained in the way of a conception of true knowledge.

It has already been remarked that the question as to whether our reason can know God, was made a formal one; that is to say, it was referred to the criticism of knowledge, of rational knowledge in general, and connected with the nature of faith and feeling in such a way that what is included under these special heads is to be understood apart altogether from any content. This is the position taken up by immediate knowledge, which itself speaks with the fruit of the tree of knowledge in its mouth, and transfers the problem to the formal sphere since it bases the justification of such knowledge, and of this exclusively, on the reflections which it makes regarding proof and philosophical knowledge, and as a consequence it has to put the true and infinite content outside of the range of its reflections, because it does not get beyond the idea of finite knowledge and cognition. With this presupposition of a knowledge and cognition which are merely finite, we contrasted the knowledge which does not remain outside of the Thing or true reality, but which, without introducing any of its own qualities, simply follows the course of true reality, and we have directed· attention to the substantial element in feeling and the heart, and have shown that, speaking generally, it exists essentially for consciousness and for conscious thought, in so far as its truth has to be worked out in what constitutes its most inner nature. But owing to the mention of the name of God, this object defined as knowledge in general, as well as the study of it, have been forced into an inferior position, and connected with that subjective way of looking at things for which God is something *above*. Since, in what has gone before, this aspect of the matter has received sufficient elucidation, and can be here indicated merely, rather than examined in detail, the only other thing to do would be to explain the relation of God in and to knowledge as deduced from the nature of God. In connection with this it may be remarked, first of all, that our subject, namely, the elevation of the subjective spirit to God, directly implies that in this very act of elevation the one-sidedness of knowledge, that is, its subjectivity, is abolished, and that it is itself essentially this process of abolition and absorption. Consequently, the knowledge of the other side of the subject, namely, the nature of God, and, together with this, His relation in and to knowledge, comes in here of itself. But there is one drawback connected with what is of an introductory and incidental character, and is yet necessary here, and it is this, that any thorough treatment of the subject renders it superfluous. Still we may so far anticipate as to say that there can be no thought here of carrying our treatment of the subject to the point reached by the explanation so intimately connected with it, of the self-consciousness of God, and of the relation of His knowledge of Himself to the knowledge of Himself in and through the human spirit. Without referring you here to the more abstract and systematic discussions on this subject to be found in my other works, I may call attention to a very remarkable book which has recently appeared, entitled, "Aphorisms on Agnosticism and Absolute Knowledge in Relation to the Science of Christian Faith," by C. Fr. G——l (Berlin: C. Franklin). It

makes reference to my statement of philosophical principles, and contains quite as much thoroughly grounded
Christian belief as it does speculative and philosophical
depth. It throws light on all the points of view from
which the Understanding directs its attack on the Christianity of knowledge, and answers the objections and
counter - arguments which the theory of agnosticism
(Nichtwissen) has brought against philosophy. It shows
in particular the misunderstanding and the want of
understanding of which the pious consciousness is guilty
when it ranges itself on the side of the explaining
Understanding in connection with the principle of
agnosticism, and thus makes common cause with it in
its opposition to speculative philosophy. What is there
advanced regarding the self-consciousness of God, His
knowledge of Himself in men, and Man's knowledge of
himself in God, has direct reference to the point of view
just indicated, and it is marked by speculative thoroughness while casting light on the false opinions which have
been attributed alike to philosophy and to Christianity in
connection with these subjects.

But even in connection with the purely general ideas
to which we here confine ourselves, in order that, taking
God as the starting-point, we may discuss the relation in
which He stands to the human spirit, we are met more
than anywhere else by an assumption which is in contradiction with any such design—namely, that we do not
know God; that even in the act of believing in Him we
do not know what He is, and therefore cannot start from
Him. To take God as the starting-point would be to
presuppose that we were able to state, and had stated,
what God is in Himself as being the primary object.
That assumption, however, permits us to speak merely of
our relation to Him, to speak of religion and not of God
Himself. It does not permit of the establishment of a
theology, of a doctrine of God, though it certainly does
allow of a doctrine of religion.

If there is not exactly any such doctrine, we at least hear much talk—an infinite amount of it, or rather, little talk with infinite repetitions—about religion, and therefore all the less about God Himself. This everlasting explanation of religion, of its necessity, its usefulness, and so on, together with the insignificant attempts to explain God, or the prohibition even of any attempt at explaining His nature, is a peculiar phenomenon of the culture of our time. We get off most easily when we rest contented with this standpoint, so that we have nothing before us but the barren characterisation of a relation in which our consciousness stands to God. As thus understood, religion means at least that our spirit comes into contact with this content, and our consciousness with this object, and is not merely, so to speak, a drawing out of the lines of longing into empty space, an act of perception which perceives nothing and finds nothing actually confronting it. Such a relation implies, at all events, this much, that we not only stand in a certain connection with God, but that God stands also in a certain connection with us. This zeal for religion expresses, hypothetically at least, something regarding our relation to God, if it does not express exclusively what would be the really logical outcome of the principle of the impossibility of knowing God. A one-sided relation, however, is not a relation at all. If, in fact, we are to understand by religion nothing more than a relation between ourselves and God, then God is left without any independent existence. God would, on this theory, exist in religion only, He would be something posited, something produced by us. The expression that God exists in religion only, an expression which is both frequently employed and found fault with, has, however, the true and important meaning that it belongs to the nature of God in His condition of complete and perfect independence that He should exist for the spirit of Man, and should communicate Himself to Man. The meaning here expressed is totally different from that

previously referred to, according to which God is merely
a postulate, a belief. *God is,* and gives Himself to men
by coming into a relation with them. If this word *is* is
limited to the expression of the truth that we do indeed
know or recognise the *fact* that God is, but do not know
what He is, and is thus used with a constantly recurring
reflection on knowledge, then this would imply that no
substantial qualities can be attributed to Him. Thus we
should not have to say we know that *God* is, but could
merely speak of *is ;* for the word God introduces an idea,
and consequently a substantial element, a content with
definite characteristics, and apart from these God is an
empty word. If in the language of this agnosticism
(Nichtwissen) those characteristics to which we must
still find it possible to refer are limited to express something negative—and for this the expression the Infinite
is peculiarly appropriate, whether by it is meant the
Infinite in general or those so-called attributes extended
into infinity—then all that this gives us is merely indeterminate Being, abstraction, a kind of supreme or
infinite Essence which is expressly our product, the product of abstraction, of thought, and does not get beyond
being mere Understanding.

If, however, God is not thought of as existing in subjective knowledge merely, or in faith, but if it is seriously
meant that He exists, that He exists for us, and has on
His part a relation to us, and if we do not get beyond
this merely formal characteristic, it is all the same implied
that He communicates Himself to men, and this is to
admit that God is not jealous. The Greeks of purely
ancient times attributed jealousy to God when they
represented Him as putting down all that was generally
regarded as great and lofty, and as wishing to have and
actually placing everything on a level. Plato and Aristotle were opposed to the idea of divine jealousy, and
the Christian religion is still more opposed to it since it
teaches that God humbled Himself even to taking on the

form of a servant amongst men, that He revealed Himself to them; that, consequently, far from grudging men what is high, nay even what is highest, He, on the contrary, along with that very revelation, laid on them the command that they should know God, and at the same time indicated that this was Man's highest duty. Without appealing to this part of the teaching of Christianity, we may take our stand on the fact that God is not jealous, and ask, Why should He not communicate Himself to Man? It is recorded that in Athens there was a law according to which any man who had a lighted candle and refused to allow another to light his at it, was to be punished with death. This kind of communication is illustrated even in connection with physical light, since it spreads and imparts itself to some other thing without itself diminishing or losing anything; and still more is it the nature of Spirit itself to remain in entire possession of what belongs to it, while giving another a share in what it possesses. We believe in God's infinite goodness in Nature, since He gives up those natural things which He has called into existence in infinite profusion, to one another, and to Man in particular. And is He to bestow on Man what is thus merely material and which is also His, and withhold from him what is spiritual, and refuse to Man what alone can give him true value? It is as absurd to give such ideas a place in our thoughts as it is absurd to say of the Christian religion that by it God has been revealed to Man, and to maintain at the same time that what has been revealed is that He is not now revealed and has not been revealed.

On God's part there can be no obstacle to a knowledge of Him through men. The idea that they are not able to know God must be abandoned when it is admitted that God has a relation to us, and since our spirit has a relation to Him, God exists for us, or, as it has been expressed, He communicates Himself and has revealed Himself.

God reveals Himself, it is said, in Nature; but God cannot reveal Himself to Nature, to the stone, to the plant, to the animal, because God is Spirit; He can reveal Himself to Man only, who thinks and is Spirit. If there is no hindrance on God's side to the knowledge of Him, then it is owing to human caprice, to an affectation of humility, or whatever you like to call it, that the finitude of knowledge, the human reason is put in contrast to the divine knowledge and the divine reason, and that the limits of human reason are asserted to be immovable and absolutely fixed. For what is here suggested is just that God is not jealous, but, on the contrary, has revealed and is revealing Himself; and we have here the more definite thought that it is not the so-called human reason with its limits which knows God, but the Spirit of God in Man, it is, to use the speculative expression previously employed, the self-consciousness of God which knows itself in the knowledge of Man.

This may suffice by way of calling attention to the main ideas which are floating about in the atmosphere of the culture of our time as representing the results of the " Enlightenment," and of an understanding which calls itself reason. These are the ideas which directly meet us, to begin with, when we undertake to deal with the general subject of the knowledge of God. It was possible only to point out the fundamental moments of the worthlessness of those categories which are opposed to this knowledge, and not to justify this knowledge itself. This, as being the real knowledge of its object, must receive its justification along with the content.

Note.—The rendering of *Nichtwissen* in this Lecture by "Agnosticism" involves something of an anachronism, and is not technically strictly accurate ; but we have no other English word which seems so well to suggest the meaning.—E. B. S.

SIXTH LECTURE

ALL questions and investigations regarding the formal element in knowledge we for the present consider as settled or as put on one side. We at the same time escape the necessity of putting in a merely negative form the exposition of what is known as the metaphysical proofs of the existence of God. Criticism which leads to a negative result is not merely a sorry business, but, in confining itself to the task of showing that a certain content is vain, it is itself a vain exercise, an exertion of vanity. In defining those proofs as the grasping in thought of what we have called the elevation of the soul to God, we declared that in criticism we must directly reach an affirmative content.

And so, too, our treatment of the subject is not to be historical. Since time will not permit of me doing otherwise, I must partly refer you to histories of philosophy for the literary portion of the subject, and, indeed, the range of the historical element in these proofs may be held to be of the greatest possible extent, to be universal in fact, since every philosophy has a close connection with the primary question or with subjects which are most intimately related to it. There have, however, been times when this question was treated of in the express form of these proofs, and the interest which was felt in refuting atheism directed attention to them in a supreme degree and secured for them thorough treatment—times when the insight of thought was considered indispensable even in theology in connection with those of its parts which were capable of being known in a rational way. Besides, the historical element in anything which is a substantial

content for itself, can and should have an interest for us
when we are clear about the thing itself, and that thing
which we have got to consider here deserves above
anything else to be taken up for itself, apart from any
interest which might otherwise attach to it by its being
connected with material lying outside of it. To occupy
ourselves too exclusively with the historical element in
subjects which are in themselves eternal truths for Spirit,
is a proceeding rather to be disapproved of, for it is only
too frequently an illusion which deceives us as to what
is of real interest. Historical study of this kind has the
appearance of dealing with the Thing or actual reality;
while, on the contrary, we are as a matter of fact dealing
with the ideas and opinions of others, with external circumstances, with what, so far as the actual reality is
concerned, is past, transitory, and vain. We may certainly
meet with historically learned persons who are what is
called thoroughly conversant with all the details of what
has been advanced by celebrated men, Fathers of the
Church, philosophers, and such like, regarding the fundamental principles of religion, but who, on the other hand,
are strangers to the true object or Thing itself. If such
people were to be asked what they considered to be the
reality and the grounds of their conviction regarding the
truth they possessed, they would very likely be astonished
at such a question as something which did not concern
them here, their real concern being, on the contrary, with
others, with theories and opinions, and with the knowledge
not of something actual but of theories and opinions.

It is the metaphysical proofs which we are considering
here. I make this further remark inasmuch as it has
been the custom to deduce a proof of the existence of
God, *ex consensu gentium*, a popular category over which
Cicero long ago waxed eloquent. The knowledge that
all men have imagined, believed, known this, carries with
it a tremendous authority. How could any man resist
it and say, I alone contradict all that all men picture to

themselves as true, what many of them have perceived to
be the truth by means of thought, and what all feel and
believe to be the truth. If, to start with, we leave out of
account the force of such a proof, and look at the dry
substance of it which is supposed to rest on an empirical
and historical basis, it will be seen to be both uncertain
and vague. All that about *all* nations, *all* men who are
supposed to believe in God, is on a level with similar
appeals to all generally; they are usually made in a very
thoughtless fashion. A statement, which is necessarily
an empirical statement, is made regarding *all* men, and
which covers all individuals, and consequently *all* times
and places; future ones, too, if strictly taken, for we are
supposed to be dealing with *all* men. But it is not
possible to get historical evidence regarding all nations.
Such statements regarding *all* men are in themselves
absurd, and are to be explained only by the habit people
have of not treating seriously such meaningless and
trite ways of speaking. But apart from this, nations,
or if you choose to call them tribes, have been discovered, whose dull minds, being limited to the few
objects connected with their outward needs, had not
risen to a consciousness of anything higher which might
be called God. What is supposed to be the historical
element in the religion of many peoples rests principally
on uncertain explanations of sensuous expressions, outward actions, and the like. Of a great many nations,
even such as are otherwise highly civilised, and with
whose religion we have a more definite and thorough
acquaintance, it may be said that what they call God is
of such a character that we may well hesitate to recognise
it as God. A dispute of the most bitter kind has been
carried on between two Roman Catholic monastic orders
as to whether the names Thiän and Chang-ti, which
occur in the Chinese State-religion, the former meaning
heaven, and the latter lord, might be used to designate
the Christian God, that is to say, as to whether these

names did not express ideas which are utterly opposed
to our ideas of God, so opposed that they contain nothing
in common with ours, not even the common abstract
idea of God. The Bible makes use of the expression,
" the heathen who know not God," although these heathen
were idolaters, *i.e.*, as it is well put, although they had a
religion. Here, all the same, we draw a distinction between God and an idol, and spite of the broad meaning attached in modern times to the name religion, we
would perhaps shrink from giving the name God to an
idol. Are we to call the Apis of the Egyptians, the
monkey, the cow, &c., of the Hindus and other nations,
God? Even if we were to speak of the religion of these
peoples, and consequently allow that they had something
more than a superstition, still we might hesitate to
speak of their having belief in God. Otherwise God
would be represented by the purely indeterminate idea
of something higher of an entirely general character, and
not even of something invisible and above sense. One
may take up the position that even a bad or false religion
should still be called a religion, and that it is better that
the various nations should have a false religion rather
than none at all, which reminds us of the story of the
woman who, to the complaint that it was bad weather,
replied that such weather was at least better than no
weather at all. Closely connected with this position is
the thought that the value of religion is to be found only
in the subjective element, in the fact of having a religion,
it being a matter of indifference what idea of God is
contained in it. Thus belief in idols, just because such
a belief can be included under the abstract idea of God
in general, is regarded as sufficient, just as the abstract
idea of God in general is considered satisfactory. This
is certainly the reason, too, why such names as idols and
heathen are regarded as something 'antiquated, and are
considered as objectionable because of their invidious
meaning. As a matter of fact, however, this abstract

antithesis of truth and falsehood demands a very different solution from that given in the abstract idea of God in general, or, what comes to the same thing, in the purely subjective view of religion.

In any case the *consensus gentium* with regard to belief in God turns out to be a perfectly vague idea, both as regards the element of fact as such expressed in it, and also as regards the substantial element composing it. But neither is the force of this proof binding in itself, even if the historical basis had been of a firmer and more definite kind. A proof of this kind does not amount to being an individual inner conviction, since it is a matter of accident whether or not others agree with it. Conviction, whether in the form of faith or knowledge based on thought, certainly takes its start from something outside, from instruction, from what is learnt, from authority in fact; still it is essentially an inner act of self-remembrance on the part of Spirit. The fact that the individual himself is satisfied is what constitutes Man's formal freedom, and is the one moment in presence of which authority of every kind entirely falls away; and the fact that he finds satisfaction in the Thing, in the actual reality, is what makes real freedom, and is the other factor in presence of which, in the very same manner, all authority sinks out of sight. They are truly inseparable. Even in the case of faith the one absolutely valid method of proof referred to in the Scriptures does not consist of miracles, credible accounts and the like, but of the witness of the Spirit. With regard to other subjects we may yield to authority, either from confidence or from fear; but the exercise of the right referred to is at the same time the higher duty laid upon us. In connection with the kind of conviction implied in religious belief in which the innermost nature of Spirit is directly involved, both as regards the certainty of itself (conscience) and because of its content, the individual, in consequence of this, has the absolute right to demand that his own witness and not that of outside minds should be what decides and gives confirmation.

The metaphysical method of proof which we are here considering, constitutes the witness of thinking Spirit in so far as this latter is thinking Spirit not merely potentially, but actually. The object with which it takes to do, exists essentially in thought, and even if, as was previously remarked, it is taken in the sense of something represented in feeling, still the substantial element in it belongs to thought, which is its pure self, just as feeling is the empirical self, the self which has become specialised or separate. In reference to this object an advance was made at an early period to the stage of thinking, witnessing, that is, proving, so soon, in fact, as thought emerged from its condition of absorption in sensuous and material conceptions and ideas of the sky, the sun, the stars, the sea, and so on, and disengaged itself, so to speak, from its wrapping of pictures of the imagination which were still permeated by the sensuous element—so that Man came to be conscious of God as essentially objectivity which was to be *thought* of, and which had been reached by thought. So, too, the subjective action of Spirit by a process of recollection brought itself back from feeling, picture-thought, and imagination, to its essence, namely, thought, and sought to have before it what belongs peculiarly to this sphere, and to have it in its pure form as it exists in this sphere. The elevation of the soul to God in feeling, intuition, imagination, and thought— and as being subjective it is so concrete that it has in it something of all these elements—is an inner experience. In regard to it we have likewise an inner experience of the fact that accidental and arbitrary elements enter into it. Consequently there arises on external grounds the necessity for analysing that elevation, and for bringing into clear consciousness the acts and characteristic qualities contained in it, in order that it may be purified from other contingent elements, and from the contingency which attaches to thought itself ; and in accordance with the old belief that what is substantial and true can be reached only by reflection, we effect the purification of this act of elevation whereby it attains to substantiality and necessity, by explaining it in terms of thought, and give thought the satisfaction of realising that the absolute right possessed by it has a right to satisfaction totally different from that belonging to feeling and sense-perception or ordinary conception.

SEVENTH LECTURE

THE necessity we feel of understanding the elevation of the spirit to God from the point of view of thought, is suggested by a formal characteristic which meets us at the very first glance when we consider what direction is taken by the proof of the existence of God, and which has to be taken notice of first of all. The study of a subject from the point of view of thought is an exposition, a differentiation of what in our very first experience we arrive at by a single stroke. In connection with the belief that God is, this analysis comes into direct contact with a point which has already been incidentally touched upon, and is to be dealt with more thoroughly here, namely, the question as to the distinction to be drawn between *what* God is and the fact *that* He is. God *is ;* what then does this mean ? what is it supposed to be ? God is, to begin with, a figurative idea, a name. So far as the two determinations contained in the proposition, namely, God and Being, are concerned, the most important thing is to determine or define the subject for itself, all the more that here the predicate of the proposition which would otherwise be indicated by the peculiar determination of the subject, namely, *what* this subject is, contains merely dry Being. But then God is for us more than mere Being. And, conversely, just because He is an infinitely richer content than mere Being, and is infinitely different from it, the important thing is to add to it this determination as representing a determination which is different from that of Being. This content which is thus distinguished from Being is an idea, a thought, a conception which is to be explained for itself, and have its meaning determined afterwards. Thus in the Metaphysic of God, or what is known as natural theology, we start by unfolding the meaning of the notion or conception of God. This is in accordance with the ordinary mode of dealing with the subject, since we consider what our previously formed idea of God contains, and in so doing further presuppose that we *all* have this idea which we express by the term God. The notion, accordingly, for itself, and apart altogether from the question of its reality, brings with it the demand that it should be true in itself as well, and consequently, as being the notion, that it should be logically true. Since logical truth, in so far as thought takes the form of Understanding merely, is reduced to identity, to what does not contradict itself, nothing more is demanded than that the notion should not contradict itself, or, as it is otherwise expressed, that it be *possible*, since possibility is itself nothing more than the identity of an idea with itself. The second thing, accordingly, is to show that this notion exists, and this is the proof of the existence of God. But because that possible notion is, in this very matter of identity, of bare possibility, reduced to this the most abstract of categories, and becomes no richer by means of existence, the product thus reached does not answer to the fulness of the idea of God, and we have accordingly a third division of the subject, in which we treat still further of the attributes of God and of His relations to the world.

These are the distinctions which meet us when we begin to examine the proofs of the existence of God. It is the work of the Understanding to analyse what is concrete, to distinguish and to define the elements belonging to it, then to hold firmly to them and abide by them. If at a later stage it once more frees them from their isolation, and recognises that it is their union which constitutes the truth, still they are from this standpoint to be regarded as being true before their union as well, and consequently when outside of this condition of unity. It is accordingly the interest of the Understanding to show that Being essentially belongs to the notion or conception of God, and that this notion must necessarily be thought of as being or existing. If this is the case, then the notion must not be thought of as separate from Being ; it has no real truth apart from Being. The result thus reached is opposed to the idea that the notion should be regarded as true in itself, and as something the existence of which must be assumed, to begin with, and then established. If the Understanding here declares that this first separation made by it and what arises from the separation have no truth, then the comparison, the other separation which further arises in connection with this, is proved to be without any foundation. The notion, that is to say, is to be first considered, and then afterwards the attributes of God are to be dealt with. It is the notion or conception of God which constitutes the content of Being ; it can be, and ought also to be, nothing else than the " substance of its realities." But how then should the attributes of God be anything but realities and *His* realities. If the attributes of God are supposed to express rather His relations to the world, the mode of His action in and towards an Other different from Himself, then the idea of God involves this much at least, that God's absolute independence does not permit Him to come out of Himself, and shows us what happens to be the condition of the world, which is supposed to be outside of Him and to be contrasted with Him, and which we have no right to suppose is already separate from Him. Thus His attributes, His action and mode of existence, remain shut up within His notion, find their determination in it alone, and are essentially nothing more than its relation to itself ; the attributes are merely the determinations of the notion itself. But, again, if we start from the world looked at in itself as something which is external so far as God is concerned, so that the attributes of God describe His relations to it, then the world, as a product of His creative power, gets a definite character only through His notion, in which again, consequently, we find, after having followed this unnecessary and roundabout road through the world to God, that the attributes get their definite character, while the notion, if it is not to be something empty, but, on the contrary, is to be something full of content, is made explicit only through them.

It results from this that the differences which we have met with are so formal that they cannot be taken as the basis of any substantial element, or of any particular spheres of existence which, if regarded apart from each other, could be considered as representing something true. The elevation of the spirit to God is found in one thing, in the determination of His notion, of His attributes, and of His Being ; or God as notion or idea is the absolutely Indeterminate, and it is only when there is a transition, namely, to Being—and this is the transition in its very first and most abstract form—that the notion and the idea enter on the stage of determinateness.   This determinateness, to be sure, is poor enough, but the reason of this just is that the Metaphysic referred to begins with possibility, a possibility which, although it is meant to be that of the notion of God, comes to be the mere possibility of the Understanding, which is devoid of all content, simple identity.   Thus we find that in reality we are dealing merely with the final abstractions of thought in general and Being, and with their opposition as well as with their inseparableness, such as we have seen these to be.   Since we have pointed out the nullity of the differences with which the metaphysical principle in question starts, we have to remember that only one result follows so far as the process involved in them is concerned, this, namely, that along with the differences we give up the process.   One of the proofs which we have to consider will have for its content the very contrast of thought and Being, which we already see making its appearance here, and which will therefore be examined in its proper place in accordance with the value which it itself possesses.   Here, however, we might give prominence to the affirmative element which it contains for the knowledge of the at first absolutely general and formal nature of the notion. We must pay attention to this so far as it has reference to the speculative basis and connection of our treatment of the subject in general. This is an aspect of the question which we merely indicate, whereas in itself it can indeed be nothing else but the truly leading one; but it is not our intention to follow it out in our treatment of the subject, or to confine ourselves to it alone.

It may therefore be remarked by way of preliminary, that what was previously called the notion or conception of God for itself and its possibility, is now to be called thought simply, and indeed abstract thought. A distinction was drawn between the notion of God and the possible existence of God. It was only such a notion which was in harmony with possibility, with abstract identity; and so, too, of what was intended to be taken not as the Notion in general but as a particular notion, in fact as the notion of God, nothing remained but simply this very abstract characterless identity.

It is already implied in what has been said that we cannot take any such abstract determination of the Understanding as applicable to the Notion, but rather that we must simply regard it as concrete in itself, as a unity which is not indeterminate but essentially determinate, and thus only as a unity of determinations; and this unity itself, which is thus joined on to its determinations, is therefore nothing but the unity of itself and its determinations, so that apart from the determinations the unity is nothing and disappears, or, more strictly speaking, it is even degraded to the condition of what is merely an untrue determinateness, and requires to get into relation in order to be true and real. To what has just been said, we may further add that such a unity of determinations —and it is they which constitute the content—is therefore not to be taken as a subject to which they are attached as representing several predicates which would

have their bond of union only in it as in a third thing,
but would be in themselves outside of this unity and
mutually opposed.   On the contrary, their unity is to be
regarded as belonging essentially to them, that is to say,
as a unity which is constituted solely by the determinations themselves, and, conversely, the separate determinations as such are to be considered as in themselves
inseparable from each other, and able to pass over into
each other, and as having no meaning taken by themselves apart from one another, so that as they constitute
the unity this latter is their soul and substance.

It is this which constitutes the concrete element of
the Notion in general.   We cannot engage in philosophical speculation regarding any object whatever without
employing universal and abstract categories of thought,
least of all when God, the profoundest subject of thought,
the absolute Notion, is the object, so that it was not
possible to avoid pointing out what the speculative
notion or conception of the Notion itself is.   Here it
will be possible to develop this notion only in the way
of an historical sketch ; that its content is true in-and-for-
itself is shown in the logical part of philosophy.   Some
examples might make it plainer for ordinary thought, and
not to go too far—and Spirit, certainly, is always what
is nearest—it is sufficient to think of the life-force
which is the unity, the simple unit of the soul, and
which is at the same time so concrete in itself that it
appears only in the form of the process of its viscera, of
its members and organs, which are essentially different
from it and from each other, and which, yet, when separated from it, perish, and cease to be what they are,
namely, life, that is, they no longer have the meaning
and signification which belong to them.

We have still to trace in detail the result of the notion
or conception of the speculative Notion in the same
fashion in which we have dealt with the conception
itself.   That is to say, since the characteristics of the

Notion exist only in its unity, and are therefore inseparable—and in conformity with the character of our object
we shall call it the Notion of God—each of these characteristics themselves, in so far as it is taken in itself,
and as distinct from any other, must be regarded not as
an abstract characteristic, but as a concrete notion or
conception of God. But God is at the same time one
only, and accordingly no other relation exists between
these notions except the relation which was previously
declared to exist among them as characteristics ; that is
to say, they are to be regarded as moments of one and
the same notion, as being necessarily related to each
other, as mutually mediating each other, as inseparable,
so that they exist only in virtue of their relationship to
each other, and this relation is the living unity which
comes into existence through them, and is regarded as
their hypothetical basis. It is with a view to their thus
appearing in different forms that they are implicitly
the same notion, only posited differently, and that, in
fact, this different way in which they are posited, or
different mode of appearance, is in necessary connection
with the other, so that the one comes out of the other,
and is posited by means of it.

The difference between the Notion in this form and
the Notion as such consists, accordingly, merely in this,
that the latter has in it abstract determinations representing the aspects it presents, while the Notion in its more
determinate form, the Idea namely, has itself concrete
aspects within itself for which those universal determinations merely supply a basis. These concrete aspects or
sides are, or rather seem to be, a complete whole existing
for itself. When it is conceived of as differentiated in
them, within the sphere which constitutes their specific
determinateness, and likewise in itself, then we get the
further determination of the Notion, a multiplicity not
only of determinations, but a wealth of definite forms
which are accordingly purely ideal, and are posited and

contained in the one Notion, in the one subject. And the unity of the subject with itself becomes the more intensive the greater the number of differences developed in it. The further continuous determination or specification which takes place is at the same time a going into itself on the part of the subject, a going down into or absorption of itself in itself.

When we say that it is one and the same Notion which is merely further determined, we are employing a formal expression. Any further and continued determination of what is one and the same adds several determinations to what is thus further defined. This richness in increased determination or specification must not, however, be thought of simply as a multiplicity of determinations, but rather as concrete. These concrete aspects regarded in themselves even take on the form of a complete self-existing whole. But when posited in one notion, in one subject, they are not independent and separate from one another in it, but rather exist ideally, and the unity of the subject accordingly becomes all the more intensive. The greatest intensity of the subject in the ideality of all concrete determinations, of the most complete antitheses, is Spirit. By way of giving a clearer conception of this, we shall refer to the relation of Nature and Spirit. Nature is contained in Spirit, is created by it, and spite of its apparently immediate Being, of its apparently independent reality, it is in itself something merely posited or dependent, something created, something having an ideal existence in Spirit. When in the course of knowledge we advance from Nature to Spirit, and Nature is defined as simply a moment of Spirit, we do not reach a true multiplicity, a substantial two, the one of which would be Nature, and the other Spirit; but, on the contrary, the Idea which is the substance of Nature, having taken on the deeper form of Spirit, retains in itself that content in this infinite intensity of ideality, and is all the richer because of the determination of this ideality itself, which is in-and-for-itself, self-conscious, or Spirit. In connection with this mention of Nature regarded in reference to the several characteristics which we have to treat of in the course of our investigation, we may mention, by way of preface, that it does indeed appear in this shape as the totality of external existence, but at the same time as one of those characteristics above which we are to raise ourselves. Here we do not go on either to consider that speculative ideality, nor to a study of the concrete shape in which the thought-determination in which it has its root, appears as Nature. The peculiar feature of the stage it occupies certainly forms one of the characteristics of God, a subordinate moment in the same notion. Since in what follows we mean to confine ourselves to its development, and to how the differences continue to be thoughts as such, moments of the Notion, the stage referred to will be regarded not as Nature but as necessity, and life as a moment in the notion or conception of God, which, however, may further be conceived of as Spirit, and possessed of the deeper quality of freedom, in order that it may be a notion or conception of God which would be worthy of Him and also of us.

What has just been said regarding the concrete form of a moment of the notion reminds us of a peculiar aspect of the matter, according to which the characteristics or determinations increase in the course of their development. The relation of the characteristics of God to one another is a difficult subject in itself, and is all the more difficult for those who are not acquainted with the nature of the Notion. But without some acquaintance at least with the notion of the Notion, or, at all events, without having some idea of it, it is not possible to understand anything about the Essence of God as representing Spirit in general. What has been said, however, will get its direct application in that part of our treatment of the subject which immediately follows.

EIGHTH LECTURE

In the preceding lecture the speculative fundamental characteristics connected with the nature of the Notion, and its development into the manifoldness of specific qualities and definite forms, have been indicated. If we look once more at the special problem we are dealing with, we find that there, too, we are at once met by a multiplicity. We find that there are several proofs of the existence of God. There is an external empirical multiplicity or difference, which presents itself, first of all, as something which has had an historical origin, and which has nothing to do with the differences which follow from the development of the Notion, and which we take, accordingly, in the form in which we directly come upon it. We may, however, have a feeling of distrust in reference to that multiplicity if we happen to reflect that here we have not to do with a finite object, and remember that our study of an infinite object must be philosophical, and that we are not to deal with it and expend labour upon it in a haphazard and external fashion. An historical fact, nay even a mathematical figure, contains a number of references within it, and relations to what is outside of it, in accordance with which a conception is formed of it, and from which we reason syllogistically to the principal relation upon which they themselves depend, or to another specific quality which is of importance here and which is closely connected with them. It is said that some twenty proofs of the Pythagorean problem have been discovered. The more important an historical fact is, the more points of connection it presents with the circumstances of the time and with other historical events, so that in showing the necessity for accepting the fact as true we may start from any one of these points. The direct testimonies may also be very many in number, and each testimony in so far as it is not otherwise self-contradictory has in this sphere the force of a proof. If in the case of a mathematical proposition one single example is held to be sufficient, it is principally in connection with historical subjects and juridical cases that a multiplicity of proofs must be held to strengthen the force of the proof itself. In the region of experience or phenomena, the object, as being an empirical and individual thing, has the quality of contingency, and thus the particularity of the knowledge we have of it gives the object the same mere appearance of Being. It is its connection with other facts which gives the object its necessary character, and each of these again belongs in itself to this contingent sphere. Here it is the extension and repetition of such connection which gives to objectivity the kind of universality which is possible in this region. The verification of a fact or a perception by means of the mere number of the observations taken, relieves the subjectivity of perception from the reproach of being an illusion, a deception, or any one of those forms of error which it may by way of objection be declared to be.

In dealing with God since we presuppose the existence of an absolutely general idea of Him, it is found, on the one hand, that He infinitely transcends that region in which all objects whatsoever stand in a connected relation with one another ; and that, on the other hand, since God exists only for the inner element of Man's nature in general, we directly meet in this sphere with the contingency of thought, conception, and imagination, in the most varied forms and with what is expressly allowed to be contingency, namely, that of sensations, emotions, and such like. We thus get an infinite number of starting-points from which it is possible to advance to God, and from which we must necessarily advance, and hence the infinite number of such essential transitions which must have the force of proofs. So, too, the verification and confirmation of conviction by means of the repetition of the experiences gained of the way to truth, must appear to be necessary in order to counteract the infinite possibility of deception and error which, on the other hand, lurks in the way to truth. The individual's trust and the intensity of his belief in God are strengthened by the repetition of the essential elevation of his spirit to God, and by the experience and knowledge he gains of God's wisdom and providence as shown in countless objects, events, and occurrences. In proportion to the inexhaustible number of the relations in which things stand to the one object is the inexhaustible need felt by Man as he enters more and more deeply into the infinitely manifold finitude of his outward surroundings and his inner states, to continuously repeat his experience of God, that is, to bring before his eyes by new proofs the fact of God's working in the world.

When we are in presence of this species of proof we at once feel that it belongs to a different sphere from that of the scientific proof. The empirical life of the individual, composed as it is of the most varied changes of mood and of conditions of feeling consequent on its entrance into different external states, takes occasion both from these states and when it is in them to multiply the result it has arrived at that there is a God, and seeks more and more anew to make this belief its own, and to make it a living belief for itself as being an individual existence subject to change. The scientific field, however, is the sphere of thought. Here the "many times" of the repetition, and the "at all times" which really represents the result, are united together in what is "once." We have to deal with the one thought-determination, which, being one, comprises in itself all those special forms of the empirical life split up as it is into the infinite particularities of existence.

But these different spheres are different only as regards form ; the matter of them is the same. Thought only brings the manifold content into a simple shape. It epitomises it without depriving it of its value or of anything that is essential to it. Its peculiar work rather is to bring this essential element into prominence. But here, too, we get various different determinations. First of all, the thought-determination is seen to be related to the starting-point from which Spirit rises from the finite up to God. Even if it reduces the innumerable characteristics to a few categories, these categories are still several in number. The finite, which has been called in a general way the starting-point, has various characteristics, and these consequently are the source of the different metaphysical proofs of the existence of G,od, that is to say, the proofs belonging to the sphere of thought only. In accordance with the historical form of the proofs, as we have to deal with them, the categories of the finite in which the starting-points get their definite character are, first, the contingency of earthly things, and next, the teleological relation which they have in themselves and to one another. But besides this finite beginning, finite so far as the content is concerned, there is yet another starting-point, namely, the Notion of God, which so far as its content is concerned is infinite and something that ought to be, and the only finite element in which is that it can be something subjective, an element of which it has to be divested. We may without prejudice admit a variety of starting-points. This does not in itself in any way conflict with the demand which we considered ourselves justified in making that the true proof should be one only ; in so far as this proof is known by thought to represent the inner element of thought, thought can also show that it represents one and the same path, although starting from different points. Similarly the result is one and the same, namely, the Being of God. This, however, is a kind of indeter-

minate Universal. A difference, however, emerges here
to which we must give somewhat closer attention. It
is intimately connected with what we have called the
beginnings or starting-points. These differ according to
their starting-points, each of which has a definite content;
they are definite categories ; the act whereby the spirit
rises from them to God is in itself the necessary course
of thought, which, in accordance with an expression
commonly used, is called a syllogistic argument. This
has necessarily a result, and this result is defined in
accordance with the definite character which attaches to
the starting-point, for it follows only from this. Thus
it comes about that the different proofs of the existence
of God result in giving different characteristics or aspects
of God. This is opposed to what is considered most
probable, and to the opinion that in the proofs of the
existence of God the interest centres in the fact of
existence only, and that this one abstract characteristic
or determination ought to represent the common result
of all the different proofs. The attempt to get out of
them determinations of the content is rendered unnecessary by the fact that the whole content is found ready
to hand in the ordinary idea of God, and this idea thus
presupposed, whether in a more definite or in a vaguer
form, or in accordance with the ordinary procedure of
Metaphysics above referred to, is definitely laid down
beforehand, and made to represent the so-called Notion
of God. The reflection that the characteristics of the
content result from the transitions which take place in
the course of reasoning, is not expressly made here, and
least of all in connection with the proof which descends
to the particular after having started from what had
been previously determined, namely, the notion or conception of God, and which is expressly intended merely
to satisfy the demand that the abstract characteristic of
Being should be attached to that conception.

But it is self-evident that the different premises, and

the variety of syllogisms which are constructed by means of these, will also yield several results differing in content. If, accordingly, the starting-points seem to permit us to take the fact of their being distinct from one another as implying a relation of equality or indifference between them, this indifference is of a limited character in view of the results which a multiplicity of characteristics of the conception of God yields; and indeed the primary question regarding their mutual relations crops up of itself in this connection, since God is one. The relation most readily thought of here is that according to which God is defined as being in His several characteristics one subject consisting of several predicates, as, for instance, when we are in the habit of speaking not only of finite objects which are described by a variety of predicates, but also when we attribute to God a variety of attributes, and speak of Him as being all-powerful, all-wise, as righteousness, goodness, and so forth. The Orientals speak of God as the many-named, or rather as the infinite-all-named, and imagine that the demand to declare what He is can be exhausted only by the inexhaustible statement of His names, that is, of His characteristics or specific qualities. We have already said of the infinite number of starting-points that they are comprised by means of thought in simple categories, and so here the necessity is still greater for reducing the multiplicity of attributes to a smaller number, or rather to one notion, all the more that God is one notion which has in it several inseparable notions; and while we allow with regard to finite objects that each in itself is certainly only one subject, an individual, that is, something indivisible, a notion or conception, we still regard this unity as being in itself manifold, made up of many things external to one another and separable, a unity which is in conflict with itself by the very fact of its existence. The finitude of living beings consists in this, that in them body and soul are separable, and, still more, that the members, nerves, muscles, and so on, the colouring matter, oil, sweat, &c., &c., are also separable ; in fact, that what we regard as predicates existing in an actual subject or individual, such as colour, smell, taste, and so on, can separate from each other as independent materials, and that it belongs to the very nature of the unity that it should thus break up into parts. Spirit reveals its finitude in its variety, and in general in the want of correspondence between its Being and its notion. It becomes manifest that the intelligence does not adequately correspond to the truth, the will to the Good, the Moral, and the Right, the imagination to the understanding, and both these to the reason, and so on, and, besides, that the sense-consciousness with which the whole of existence is always kept supplied, or at any rate nearly so, consists of a quantity of momentary, transitory, and so far untrue elements. This very thorough separability and separateness of the activities, tendencies, aims, and actions of Spirit, which we meet with in empirical reality, may in some degree serve as an excuse for conceiving of the Idea of Spirit as something which breaks up into faculties, capacities, activities, and the like ; for it is as an individual form of existence, a definite single being, that it is this particular finite existence which is thus found in a separate form of existence external to itself. But it is God only who is this particular One, and only as He is this One is He God ; thus subjective reality is inseparable from the Idea, and consequently cannot be separated in itself. It is here that we see the variety, the separation, the multiplicity of the predicates which are knit into a unity by the subject only, but which in themselves would be in a condition of difference which would result in their coming into opposition and consequently into antagonism with each other, and which would show in the most decided way that they were something untrue, and that multiplicity of characteristics was an unsuitable category.

The next shape taken by the reduction of the several

characteristics of God resulting from the several proofs, to the one notion or conception which is to be conceived of as being one in itself, is the ordinary one, according to which they are to be carried back to a *higher* unity, as it is called, *i.e.*, a more abstract unity, and, since the unity of God is the highest of all, to what is consequently the most abstract form of unity. The most abstract unity, however, is unity itself, and from this it would result that the Idea of God means simply that God is unity— and to express this in terms implying a subject, or at least something which has Being—that He is the One in fact, a description, however, which implies that He is One only as against many, so that the One in Himself might still also be a predicate of the many, and therefore be unity in Himself, the One Substance rather, or, if you like, Being. But such an abstract form of determination would simply bring us back to this, that what would result from the proof of the existence of God would be simply the Being of God in an abstract sense, or, what comes to the same thing, that God Himself would simply be the abstract One (neuter) or Being, the empty Essence of the Understanding, over against which would be placed the concrete idea of God, which cannot find satisfaction in any such abstract characterisation. But not only is the ordinary idea not satisfied with this abstraction, the Notion looked at in its general aspect is by its very nature concrete itself, and what appears outwardly as difference and multiplicity of characteristics is simply the development of its moments, which all the while remains within itself. It is therefore the inner necessity of reason which shows itself active in thinking Spirit, and produces in it this multiplicity of characteristics; only, since this thought has not yet got a grasp of the nature of the Notion itself, nor consequently of the nature of its relation and the necessity of the connection, what are virtually stages in development appear to be simply an accidental multiplicity, the various elements of which follow on one another and are outside of one another, just as this thought also, moving within the circle occupied by each one of these character-istics, so conceives of the nature of the transition which is called Proof, that the characteristics, while connected with each other, still remain outside of each other, and mediate with each other merely as independent. It does not recognise that mediation with self is the true and final relation in any such process. And it will become evident that this is the formal defect in these proofs.

NINTH LECTURE

IF we look at the difference which exists between the proofs of the existence of God with which we are dealing, as it actually presents itself, we come upon a distinction which is of an essential kind. One set of the proofs goes from the Being to the thought of God, that is, to put it more definitely, from determinate Being to true Being as representing the Being of God; the other set proceeds from the thought of God, from truth in itself, to the Being of this truth. This distinction, although it is brought forward as one which merely happens to exist in this form, and is of a contingent character, is based on a necessary principle which requires to be taken notice of. We have before us two characteristics—the thought of God and the Being of God. We *may* start from the one or from the other indifferently in following out the course of reasoning which is supposed to result in their union. Where it is thus a question merely of possible choice, it appears to be a matter of indifference from which we start; and further, too, if the one leads to their being brought into connection, the other appears to be superfluous.

But what thus at first appears to be an indifferent duality and an external possibility has a connection in the Notion, so that neither are the two ways of arriving at the truth indifferent to one another, nor is the difference between them merely of an external character, nor is one of them superfluous. This necessity is not of the nature of an accessory circumstance. It is closely connected with the deepest part of our subject, and chiefly with the logical nature of the Notion. So far as the Notion is concerned, the two paths are not merely different in a general way,

but are one-sided, both in reference to the subjective elevation of the spirit to God, and also in reference to the nature
of God Himself.   We wish to exhibit this one-sidedness in
its more concrete form in reference to our subject.   We
have before us, to begin with, merely the abstract categories
of Being and Notion, the contrast between them and their
mode of relationship.   It will be shown at the same time
how these abstractions and their relations to one another
constitute and determine the basis of what is most concrete.

That I may be able to put this thought in a more
definite form, I may, by way of anticipation, refer to a
further distinction, according to which there are three
fundamental modes in which the connection of the two
sides or characteristics appears.   The first represents the
passing over of the one characteristic into its Other; the
second, their relativity, or the appearance of the one implicitly or actually in the Being of the Other ; the third
mode, again, is that of the Notion or the Idea, according
to which the characteristic preserves itself in its Other in
such a way that this unity, which is itself implicitly the
original essence of the two, is considered as their subjective unity.   Thus neither of them is one-sided, and they
both together constitute the appearance of their unity,
which is, to begin with, merely their substance, and
thus eternally results from them as being the immanent appearance of totality, and is distinguished from
them for itself as their unity, as this eternally unfolds
itself in the form of their outward appearance.

The two one-sided ways of elevating the spirit to God
thus indicated, accordingly directly exhibit their one-
sidedness in a double form.   The relations which spring
from this call for mention.   What has in general to be
effected is that in the characteristic of the one side,
namely, Being, the other characteristic, namely, the Notion,
should appear, and, conversely, that in this latter the first-
mentioned should be exhibited.   Each determines itself
to its Other, gives itself the characteristic of its Other in

and out of itself. If, accordingly, only the one side were
to determine itself so as to be the other, this determination would, on the one hand, be merely a passing over, in
which the first would lose itself, or, on the other hand,
a manifestation of itself, outside of itself, in which each
would certainly preserve its independent existence, but
would not return into itself, would not be that unity
for itself. If we give to the Notion the concrete signification of God, and to Being the concrete signification of
Nature, and conceived of the self-determination of God
in the form of Nature, as found only in the first of the
connections indicated, this would be the process whereby
God becomes Nature. But if, according to the second of
the connections, Nature is to be taken merely as a manifestation of God, then she, as something in course of
transition, would represent the unity inherent in this only
for a third thing, only for us, and this would not be unity
which is actually present in-and-for-itself, the true unity,
determined beforehand. When we put this thought in
more concrete forms, and conceive of God as the Idea
existing for itself from which we start, and think of Being
as also the totality of Being, as Nature, then the advance
from the Idea to Nature takes (1) the form simply of a
passing over into Nature, in which the Idea is lost and
disappears. (2) In order to bring out more clearly the
meaning of this transition, we may say that this would be
merely an act of remembrance on our part that the simple
result had issued from an Other which had, however, disappeared. So far, again, as the outward form is concerned,
it would be simply we who had brought the semblance or
appearance into relation with its Essence and referred it
back to this. Or, looking at the question from a broader
standpoint, we may say that God had merely created
Nature, not a finite spirit which returns from Nature
back to Him ; that He had an unfruitful love of the world
as of something which was the mere semblance or show
of Himself, and which as such remained an Other in

relation to Him which did not reflect Him, and through which He did not shine as through Himself. And what is the third thing supposed to be ; what are we supposed to be who have brought this show or semblance into relation with its Essence, and referred it back to its central point, and have been the means whereby the Essence first manifested itself and appeared in itself ? What would this third thing be ? What would we be ? We would represent a knowledge whose existence was presupposed in an absolute way, in fact an independent act of a formal universality which embraced everything in itself, and in which that necessarily existing unity which is in-and-for-itself would itself be included as a mere phenomenon or semblance without objectivity.

If we form a more definite conception of the relation which is set forth in this determination, then it will be seen that the elevation to God of determinate Being, of Nature, and of natural Being in general, and, along with this, of our consciousness, the active form of this elevation itself, is simply religion or piety which rises to God in a subjective way only, either simply in the shape of an act of transition whereby we disappear in God, or by setting ourselves over against Him as a semblance or illusion. If the finite were thus to disappear in Him, He would be merely the absolute substance, from which nothing proceeds,. and into which nothing returns to itself, and even to form ideas of or to think of the absolute substance would be already too much, something which would itself have to disappear. If, however, the relation of reflection is still preserved, the elevation of the pious mind to God, in the sense that religion as such, and consequently the subjective for itself, continues to represent what has Being and is independent, then what is primarily independent or self-existent, and the elevation to which constitutes religion, is something produced by religion, something conceived of, postulated, thought or believed, an appearance or semblance merely, not anything truly independent which starts from itself.

It is substance as an idea merely, which does not decide for itself, and which consequently is not the activity which as activity is found only in the subjective elevation as such. It would not in this case be known and recognised as true that God is the Spirit who Himself arouses in men that desire to rise to Him, that religious feeling in which the elevation begins.

If from this one-sidedness there results a broader idea and a further development of what does not, to begin with, get beyond something which has the character of a reflex semblance, and if we thus reach its emancipation, in which it, as being independent and active, would in its turn be defined as not-semblance, then we would attribute to this independent existence merely a relative, and consequently a half connection with its other side, which contained in it itself a non-communicating and incommunicable kernel which had nothing to do with the Other. We would be dealing merely with the superficial form, in which the two sides were apparently related to each other, and which would not imply a relation springing from their essence and established by their essence. Both sides consequently would be wanting in the true, total return of Spirit into itself, and Spirit would thus not search into the deep things of the Godhead. But this return into itself and this searching into the Other are essentially coincident ; for mere immediacy, substantial Being, does not imply anything deep. It is the real return into self which alone makes the depths of God, and it is just the act of searching into the Essence which is return into self.

We may stop here with this preliminary reference to the more concrete sense of the difference indicated, and which we discovered by means of reflection. What had to be called attention to was that the difference is not a superfluous multiplicity ; further, that the division springing from it, and which was, to begin with, of a formal and external character, contains two characteristics—Nature, natural things, and the progress of consciousness to God and from Him back to Being, both of which equally and necessarily belong to one conception, and this quite as much in the course of the subjective procedure of knowledge as when they have an absolutely objective concrete sense, and, regarded each for itself, present a one-sidedness of a most important kind. So far as knowledge is concerned, their integration is found in the totality which the Notion in general represents, and, more strictly speaking, in what was said about it, namely, that its unity as a unity of the two moments is a result representing the most absolute basis and result of the two moments. Without, however, presupposing this totality and its necessity, it will follow from the result of the *one* movement—and since we are beginning we can begin only in a one-sided way from the one—that by its own dialectic nature it forces itself to go over into the other, and passes from itself over into this complete integration. The objective signification of what is, to begin with, a merely subjective conclusion will, however, at once make it evident that the inadequate, finite form of that proof is done away with. Its finitude consists, above all, in this one-sidedness which attaches to its indifference and its separation from the content. When this one-sidedness has been done away with and absorbed, it comes to have the content also in itself in its true form. The process of elevation to God is in itself the abolition of the one-sidedness of subjectivity in general, and, above all, of knowledge.

To the distinction which, regarded from the formal side, appears as a difference in the kinds of the proofs of the existence of God, there has yet to be added the fact that if we look at the proof from the one side according to which we pass from the Being of God to the conception of God, it presents itself under two forms.

The first proof starts from the Being which as something contingent does not support itself, and from this reasons to a true necessary Being in-and-for-itself—this is the proof *ex contingentia mundi.*

The other proof starts from Being in so far as it has a definite character determined in accordance with relations implying an end, and reasons to a wise author of this Being—this is the Teleological Proof of the existence of God.

We have still to deal with the other side, according to which the notion or conception of God is made the starting-point, and from which we reason to its Being— the Ontological Proof. As this is the plan we mean to follow out, there are thus three proofs which we have to consider; and also, as being of no less importance, we have to consider the criticism which has been given of them, and owing to which they have been discarded and forgotten.

TENTH LECTURE

THE proofs we have to deal with, regarded in their first aspect, presuppose the world in general, and, above all, its contingency. The starting-point is constituted by empirical things, and by the Whole composed of these things, namely, the world. The Whole is certainly superior to its parts, the Whole, that is to say defined as the unity which embraces and gives their character to all the parts, as, for instance, even when we speak of the Whole of a house, and still more in the case of that Whole which is a self-existent unity, as the soul is in reference to the living body. By the term world, however, we understand the aggregate of material things, the collection merely of that infinite number of existing things which are actually visible, and each of which is, to begin with, conceived of as existing for itself. The world embraces men equally with natural things. When the world is thus taken as an aggregate, and even as an aggregate merely of natural things, it is not conceived of as Nature, by which we understand something which is in itself a systematic Whole, a system of arrangements and gradations, and particularly of laws. The term world as thus understood expresses the aggregate merely, and suggests that it is based simply on the existing mass of things, and has thus no superiority, no qualitative superiority at least, over material things.

So far as we are concerned, these things further determine themselves in a variety of ways, and chiefly as limited Being, finitude, contingency, and so on. This is the kind of starting-point from which the spirit raises itself to God. It adjudges limited, finite or contingent Being to be untrue Being, above and beyond which true Being exists. It escapes into the region of another, unlimited Being, which represents the Essence as opposed to that unessential, external Being. The world of finitude, of things temporal, of change, of transitoriness, is not the true form of existence, but the Infinite, Eternal, and Unchangeable. And even if what we have called limitless Being, the Infinite, Eternal, and Unchangeable, does not succeed in expressing the absolute fulness of meaning contained in the word God, still God is limitless Being, He is infinite, eternal, and unchangeable, and thus the spirit rises at least to those divine predicates or to those fundamental qualities of His nature which, though abstract, are yet universal, or at least to that universal region, to the pure æther in which God dwells.

This elevation of the soul to God is, speaking generally, that fact in the history of the human spirit which we call religion, but religion in a general sense, that is, in a purely abstract sense, and thus this elevation is the general, but merely the general, basis of religion.

The principle of immediate knowledge does not get beyond this elevation as a fact. It appeals to it, and rests in it as a fact, and asserts that it represents that universal fact in men, and even in all men, which is called the inner revelation of God in the human spirit, or reason. We have already sufficiently examined this principle, and I accordingly refer to it once more only in so far as we here confine our attention to the fact in question. This very fact, the act of elevation to God namely, is as such rather something which is directly of the nature of mediation. It has its beginning and starting-point in finite, contingent existence, in material things, and represents an advance from these to something else. It is consequently mediated by that beginning, and is an elevation to what is infinite and in itself necessary, only inasmuch as it does not stop short at that beginning which is here alone the Immediate (and this an Immediate which afterwards exhibits a merely relative character), but rises to the Infinite by the mediate step of the abandonment and renunciation of such a stand-point. This elevation which is represented by conscious-ness, is consequently in itself mediated knowledge.

With regard to the point from which this elevation starts, we may here further remark that the content is not of a sensuous kind, not an empirical concrete content composed of sensation or perception, nor a concrete content of imagination—the truth rather being that the abstract thought-determinations implied in the ideas of the fini-tude and contingency of the world form the starting-point. The goal at which the elevation arrives is of a similar kind, namely, the infinitude or absolute necessity of God, conceived of not as having a more developed and richer determination, but as being wholly within the limits of these general categories. With regard to this aspect of the question it is necessary to point out that the universality of the fact of this elevation is false so far as its form is concerned. For instance, it can be maintained that even amongst the Greeks the thought of infinity, of inherently existing necessity as representing the ulti-mate principle of all things, was the possession of the philosophers only. Material things did not appear in this general way to the popular conception in the abstract form of material things and as contingent and finite things, but rather in their empirical and concrete shape. So in the same way God was not conceived of under the category of the Infinite, the Eternal, the inherently Necessary, but, on the contrary, in accordance with the definite shapes created by the imagination. Still less is it the case that those nations who occupied a lower stage of culture put their conceptions in any such actually universal forms. These general forms of thought do certainly pass through men's minds, as we say, because men are thinking beings, and when they have received a fixed form in language they are still further developed into the conscious thought upon which the proof proper is based, but even in that case they take, to begin with, the form of characteristics of concrete objects ; they don't require to get a fixed place in consciousness as independent in their own right. It was to the culture of our time that these categories of thought first became familiar, and they are now universal, or at least universally diffused. But those very people who have shared in this culture, and no less those who have been referred to as unpractised in the independent exercise of thought based on general conceptions, have not reached this idea in any immediate way, but, on the contrary, by following the varied course of thought, and by the study of the sense in which words are used. People have essentially learned to think, and have given currency to their thoughts. The culture which is capable of abstract conception is something which has been reached through mediation of an infinitely manifold character. The one fact in this fact of the elevation of Man to God is that it is a mediation.

It is this circumstance, namely, that the elevation of the spirit to God has mediation in itself, which invites to proof, that is, to the explication of the separate moments of this process of the spirit, and to their explication in the form of thought. It is the spirit in its most inward character, that is, in its thought, which produces this elevation, which in its turn represents the course followed by the thought-determinations or characteristic qualities of thought. What is intended to be effected by this process of proof is that this activity of thought should be brought into consciousness, that consciousness should recognise it as representing those moments of thought in a connected form. Against this unfolding of these moments which shows itself in the region of mediation through thought, faith, which wishes to continue to be immediate certainty, protests, and so, too, does the criticism of the Understanding, which is at home in the intricacies of that mediation, and is at home in the latter in order that it may introduce confusion into the elevation itself. So far as faith is concerned, we may say that however many faults Understanding may find with these proofs, and whatever defective points there may be in their manner of unfolding the moments of the elevation of the spirit from the accidental and temporal to the infinite and eternal, the human heart will not allow itself to be deprived of this elevation. In so far as the human heart has been checked in this matter of elevation to God by the Understanding, faith has, on the one hand, appealed to it to hold fast by this elevation, and not to trouble itself with the fault-finding of the Understanding; but it has, on the other hand, told itself not to trouble about proof at all, in order that it may reach what is the surest standing ground, and in the interest of its own simplicity it has ranged itself on the side of the critical Understanding in direct opposition to proof. Faith will not allow itself to be robbed of its right of rising to God, that is, of its witness to the truth, because this is inherently necessary, and is more than any single chance fact connected with Spirit. There are facts, inner experiences in Spirit, and still more are there in the individual spirits—for Spirit does not exist as an abstraction, but in the form of many spirits— facts of an infinitely varied sort, and sometimes of the most opposite and depraved character. In order that this fact may be rightly conceived of as a fact of Spirit as such, and not merely as a fact belonging to the various ephemeral contingent spirits, it is requisite to conceive of it in its necessary character. It is this necessary character which alone vouches for its truth in this contingent and arbitrary sphere. The sphere to which this higher fact belongs is, further, essentially the sphere of abstraction. Not only is it very difficult to have a clear and definite conscious- ness of what abstraction is and what is the nature of its inner connection, but this power of abstraction is itself the real danger, and this is a danger which is unavoidable when abstraction has once appeared, when the believing human spirit has once tasted of the Tree of Knowledge, and thought has begun to spring up within it in the free and independent form which peculiarly belongs to it.

If, accordingly, we look more narrowly at the inner course followed by Spirit in thought and its moments, it will be seen, as has been already observed, that the first starting-point represents a category of thought, namely, that of the contingency of natural things. The first form of the elevation of the spirit to God is represented historically by the so-called Cosmological Proof of the existence of God. It has also been pointed out that on the definiteness of the starting-point depends also the definiteness of the goal which we wish to reach. Natural things might be defined in another way, and in that case the result or the truth would also be differently defined. We might have differences which would appear unimportant to very imperfectly developed thought, but which from that standpoint of thought which we at present occupy would be seen to be the very thing with which we were really concerned and which has to be reckoned with. If things were thus defined in a general way as *existing*, it might be shown that the truth of existence as determinate Being, was Being itself, indeterminate, limitless Being. God would thus be defined as Being—the most abstract of all definitions, and the one with which, as is well known, the Eleatics started. We recall this abstraction most vividly in connection with the distinction already made between thought in its inner and implicit form and the bringing forward of thoughts into consciousness. Who is there who does not use the word Being ? (The weather *is* fine. Where *are* you ? and so on, *ad infinitum*.) And who, in forming conceptions, does not make use of this pure category of thought, though it is concealed in the concrete content (the weather, and so on, *ad infinitum*), of which consciousness in forming any such conceptions is composed, and of which alone, therefore, it has any knowledge ? There is an infinite difference between the possession and employment of the category of thought called Being in this way, and its employment by the Eleatics, who gave it a fixed meaning in itself, and conceived of it as the ultimate principle, as the Absolute,

along with God at least, or apart from any God at all.
Further, when things are defined as finite, Spirit has risen
from them to what is infinite ; and when they are defined
at the same time as real Being, then Spirit has risen to
the Infinite as representing what is ideal or ideal Being.
Or if they are expressly defined as having Being in a
merely immediate way, then Spirit rises from this pure
immediacy, which is a mere semblance of Being, to the
Essence, and regards this as representing the ground or
basis of Being.　It may again rise from them as representing parts, to God as representing the Whole ; or from
them as external and selfless things, to God as representing
the force behind them ; or from them as effects, to their
cause.　All these characteristics are applied to things by
thought, and in the same way the categories of Being, the
Infinite, the Ideal, Essence and Ground, the Whole, Force,
Cause, are used to describe God.　It is implied that they
may be employed to describe Him, yet still as suggesting
that though they may be validly applied to Him, and
though God is really Being, the Infinite, Essence, the
Whole, Force, and so on, they do not, all the same, exhaust
His nature, which is deeper and richer than anything such
determinations can express.　The advance from any such
determination of existence taken as a starting-point and
as representing the finite in general, to its final determination, that is, to the Infinite in thought, deserves the name
Proof exactly in the same way as those proofs to which
the name has been formally given.　In this way the
number of proofs goes far beyond that of those already
mentioned.　From what standpoint are we to regard this
further increase in the number of the proofs which have
thus grown up in what is perhaps for us an unpleasant
way ?　We cannot exactly reject this multiplicity of arguments.　On the contrary, when we have once placed ourselves at the standpoint of those mediations of thought
which are recognised as proofs, we find we have to explain
why in thus adducing them we have confined, and can

confine, ourselves just to the number mentioned, and to
the categories contained in them. In reference to this
new and further extended variety of proofs, we have to
think principally of what was said in connection with
those which appeared at an earlier stage and in a more
limited shape. This multiplicity of starting-points which
thus presents itself is nothing else than that large number
of categories which naturally belong to the logical treatment of the subject. We have merely to indicate the
manner in which they point to this latter. They show
themselves to be nothing but the series of the continuous
determinations which belong to the Notion, and not to any
one notion, but to the Notion in itself. They represent
the development of the Notion till it reaches externali-
sation, the condition in which its elements are mutually
exclusive, though it has really gone deeper into itself.
The one side of this continuous advance is represented
by the finite definiteness of a form of the Notion ; the
other, by its most obvious truth, which is in its turn
simply the truth in a more concrete and deeper form than
that which preceded it. The highest stage in one sphere
is at the same time the beginning of a higher stage. It
is logic which unfolds in its necessity this advance in the
determination of the Notion. Each stage through which
it passes so far involves the elevation of a category of
finitude into its infinitude, and it thus likewise involves
from its starting-point onwards a metaphysical conception of God, and, since this elevation is conceived of in
its necessity, a proof of His Being. Thus also the transition from the one stage to the higher stage presents
itself as a necessary advance in more concrete and deeper
determination, and not only as a series of random conceptions, and so as an advance to perfectly concrete truth,
to the full and perfect manifestation of the Notion, to the
equating or identification of these its manifestations with
itself. Logic is, so far, metaphysical theology, which treats
of the evolution of the Idea of God in the æther of pure

thought, and thus concerns itself peculiarly with this Idea, which is perfectly independent in-and-for-itself.

Such detailed treatment is not the object of these lectures. We wish to confine ourselves here to the *historical* discussion of those characteristics of the Notion the rising from which to the characteristics of the Notion which are its truth, and which may be held to be the characteristics of the Notion of God, is the point to be considered. The reason of the general incompleteness which marks that method of taking up the characteristics of the Notion can only be found in the defective ideas prevalent with regard to the nature of the characteristics of the Notion itself, and of their mutual connection, as well as of the nature of the act of rising from them as finite to the Infinite. The more immediate reason why the characteristic of the contingency of the world and that of the absolutely necessary Essence which corresponds to it appear as the starting-point and as the result of the proof respectively—and this reason is at the same time a relative justification of the preference given to them—is to be looked for in the fact that the category of the relation between contingency and necessity is that in which all the relations of the finitude and the infinitude of Being are resumed and comprised. The most concrete determination of the finitude of Being is contingency, and in the same way the infinitude of Being in its most completely determined form is necessity. Being in its own essentiality is reality, and reality is in itself the general relation between contingency and necessity which finds its complete determination in absolute necessity. Finitude, by being taken up into this thought-determination, has the advantage, so to speak, of being so far prepared by this means as to point in itself to the transition to its truth or necessity. The term contingency, or accident, already suggests a kind of existence whose special character it is to pass away.

Necessity itself, however, has its truth in freedom; with

it we enter into a new sphere, into the region of the Notion itself. This latter accordingly affords another relation for the determination of elevation to God and for the course it follows, a different determination both of the starting-point and the result, and, first of all, the determination of what is conformable to an end, and that of the End. This accordingly becomes the category for a further proof of the existence of God. But the Notion is not something merely submerged in objectivity, as it is when regarded as an end, in which case it is merely the determination of things ; but, on the contrary, it is for itself, and exists independently of objectivity. Regarded in this light, it is itself the starting-point, and its transition has a determination of its own, which has been already referred to. The fact, therefore, that the first Proof, the Cosmological Proof, adopts the category of the relation of contingency and absolute necessity, finds, as has been remarked, its relative justification in this, that this relation is the most individual, most concrete, and, in fact, the ultimate characteristic of reality as such, and accordingly represents and comprises in itself the truth of the more abstract categories of Being taken collectively. The movement of this relation likewise includes the movement of the earlier, more abstract characteristics of finitude to the still more abstract characteristics of infinitude; or rather, it is, in a logically abstract sense, the movement, or procedure of the proof, that is, it is the form of syllogistic reasoning, in all cases only one and the same, which is represented in it.[1]

As is well known, the effect of the criticism directed by Kant against the metaphysical proofs of the existence of God has been that these arguments have been abandoned, and that they are no longer mentioned in any scientific treatise on the subject; in fact, one is almost ashamed to

[1] Lecture X. ends here, and what follows is a fragment found amongst Hegel's papers, and inserted at this point by the German editor.

adduce them at all.   It is allowed, however, that they
may be used in a popular way, and these helps to truth
are universally employed in connection with the instruction of youth, and the edification of those who are grown
up.   So, too, that eloquence which has for its principal
aim to warm the heart and elevate the feelings necessarily
takes and uses them as the inner fundamental and connecting principles of the ideas with which it deals.   With
regard to the so-called Cosmological Proof, Kant ("Critique
of Pure Reason," 2nd edition, p. 643) makes the general
remark that if we presuppose the existence of anything,
we cannot avoid what follows from this, namely, that
something or other exists in a necessary way, and that
this is an absolutely natural conclusion ; and he goes on
further to remark, at p. 651, with regard to the Physico-
theological Proof, that " it ought always to be mentioned
with respect, since it is the oldest, the clearest, and the
one most in harmony with ordinary human reason."   He
declares that " it would not only be a comfortless task, but
an absolutely useless one, to attempt to detract in any way
from the authority of this proof."   He holds, further, that
" reason can never be so far repressed by any doubts suggested by subtle abstract speculation as to be unable to
extricate herself from any such burrowing indecision as
from a dream, by the mere glance which she directs to
the wonders of Nature and the majesty of the universe,
in order thus to go from one form of greatness to another
until the highest of all is reached, and to rise from the
conditioned to the condition, until she arrives at the
supreme and unconditioned Author of all."

If, then, the proof first adduced expresses an unavoidable conclusion from which it is impossible to escape, and
if it would be absolutely useless to seek to detract from
the authority of the second proof, and if reason can never
be so far repressed as to renounce this method of proof
and not to rise through it to the unconditioned Author
of all, it must certainly appear strange that we should

evade the demand referred to, and if all the while reason
be held to be so entirely repressed that it no longer attaches any weight to this proof. But just as it may
appear to be a sin against the good society of the philosophers of our time to continue to mention those proofs,
it equally appears that the philosophy of Kant, and Kant's
refutations of those proofs, are something which we have
long ago done with, and which is therefore not to be mentioned any more.

The fact, however, is that it is Kant's criticism alone
which has done away with these proofs in a scientific way,
and which has itself become the source of the other and
shorter method of rejecting them, that method, namely,
which makes feeling alone the judge of truth, and asserts not only that thought is superfluous, but that it
is damnable. In so far, then, as we are concerned in
getting to know the scientific reasons for which these
proofs have lost their authority, it is Kant's criticism
alone with which we are called to deal. It is, however,
to be noticed, further, that the ordinary proofs which
Kant subjects to criticism, and in particular the Cosmological and Physico-theological Proofs, whose method we
are here considering, contain characteristics of a more
concrete kind than the abstract merely qualitative characteristics of finitude and infinitude. Thus the Cosmological Proof contains the characteristics of contingent
existence and of absolutely necessary Essence. It has
also been observed that even when the antitheses are
expressed by the terms conditioned and unconditioned, or
by accident and substance, they still necessarily have here
this merely qualitative meaning. Here, accordingly, the
really essential point to be dealt with is the formal procedure of the mediation connected with the proof; and,
besides, the content and the dialectic nature of the characteristics themselves are not dealt with in the metaphysical syllogisms referred to, nor in Kant's criticism
either. It is, however, just the mediation of this very

dialectic element which it is necessary to carry through and pass judgment upon. For the rest, the particular mode in which the mediation in those metaphysical lines of argument, as well as that belonging to Kant's estimate of them, is to be conceived of, is, as a whole, the same; and this is true of all the separate proofs of the existence of God, that is, of all those belonging to the class which starts from some given form of existence. And if we here look more closely at the nature of this syllogism of the Understanding, we shall have also settled its character so far as the other proofs are concerned, and in dealing with them we shall have to direct our attention merely to the content of the characteristics in its more definite form.

The consideration of Kant's criticism of the Cosmological Proof comes to be all the more interesting from the fact that, according to Kant, this proof has concealed in it " a whole nest of dialectic assumptions, which, nevertheless, transcendental criticism is able to lay bare and destroy." I shall first restate this proof in the form in which it is usually expressed, which is the one employed by Kant, and which runs thus : If *anything exists*—not merely *exists*, but exists *a contingentia mundi*, is defined as *contingent*—then some absolutely necessary Essence must exist as well. Now I myself at least exist, and therefore an absolutely rational Essence exists. Kant remarks, first of all, that the minor term contains something derived from experience, and that the major term concludes from experience in general that something necessary exists; that consequently the proof is not carried through in an absolutely *à priori* way, a remark which connects itself with what was mentioned before as to the general nature of this style of argument, which takes up merely one aspect of the total true mediation.

The next remark has reference to a point of supreme importance in connection with this style of argument, and which Kant expresses in the following form. The necessary Essence can be characterised as necessary only

in one single mode, that is, in respect of all possible
opposing predicates only by means of one of these, and
consequently there can be only one single conception of
any such thing, namely, that of the most real Essence—
a conception which confessedly forms the subject of the
Ontological Proof, to be dealt with much later on.

It is against this latter more comprehensive characteristic of necessary Essence that Kant first of all directs
his criticism, and which he describes as a mere refinement
of reasoning. The empirical ground of proof above
mentioned cannot tell us what are the attributes of this
necessary Essence. To reach these, reason has absolutely
to part company with experience, and to seek in pure
conceptions what kind of attributes or qualities an
absolutely necessary Essence must possess, and what
thing amongst all possible things has the requisite quali-
fications which should belong to an absolute necessity.
We might attribute to the age the many marks of want
of intellectual training which characterise these expressions, and be willing to admit that anything like this is
not to be found in the scientific and philosophical modes
of statement current in our day. At all events, God‑
would not in these days be any longer qualified as a
thing, nor would we try to seek amongst all possible
things some one thing which should suit the conception
of God. We speak indeed of the qualities or attributes of
this or that man, or of Peruvian bark, and such like ; but
in philosophical statements we do not speak of attributes
in reference to God as a thing. Only we all the more
frequently hear conceptions spoken of simply as abstract
specific forms of thought, so that it is no longer necessary
to indicate what we mean when we ask information regarding the notion or conception of anything, or when, in fact,
we wish to form a conception of any object. It has,
however, quite become a generally accepted principle, or
rather it has come to form part of the belief of this
age, that reason should be reproached with putting its

investigations in the form of pure conceptions, and even that this should be reckoned a crime; in other words, it is blamed for showing itself active in a way different from that of sense-perception, or from that followed by imagination and poetry. In the case of Kant we see, at any rate, in his treatment of the subject, the definite presuppositions from which he starts, and the logical result of the reasoning process he follows, so that any opinion arrived at is expressly reached and proved by means of principles, and it is held that any view must be deduced from principles, and be, in fact, of a philosophical kind. In our day, on the contrary, if we go along the highway of knowledge, we meet with the oracular utterances of feeling, and the assertions of the individual person who has the pretension to speak in the name of all men, and as a consequence of this pretends that he has also a right to impose his assertions upon everybody. There cannot possibly be any kind of precision in the characteristics which spring from such sources of knowledge, nor in the form in which they are expressed, nor can they lay claim to be logical or to be based on principles or grounds.

That part of Kant's criticism referred to suggests the definite thought, first of all, that the proof we are dealing with leads us merely to the idea of a necessary Essence, but that any such characteristic is different from the conception of God, that is, from the characteristic of the most real Essence, and that this latter must be deduced by reason from the former by means of conceptions pure and simple. It will at once be seen that if this proof does not bring us any further than to the idea of an absolutely necessary Essence, the only objection which could be urged against it would be, that the idea of God which is limited to what is implied in this characteristic is at any rate not such a profound idea as we, whose conception of God is more comprehensive, wish for. It is quite possible that individuals and nations belonging to an earlier age, or who, while belonging to our age, are living outside the pale of Christianity and of our civilisation, might have no more profound idea of God than this. For all such, this proof would consequently be sufficient enough. We may, in any case, allow that God and God only is the absolutely necessary Essence, even if this characteristic does not exhaust the Christian idea, which, as a matter of fact, includes in it something more profound than the metaphysical characteristic of so-called natural theology—something more profound, too, than what is found in the conception of God which belongs to immediate knowledge and faith. It is itself questionable if immediate knowledge can even say this much of God, that He is the absolutely necessary Essence; at any rate, if one person can know this much of God immediately, another may equally well not know so much of Him immediately in the absence of any right on the part of any one to expect more of him, for a right implies reasons and proofs, that is, mediations of knowledge, and mediations are excluded from and forbidden to immediate knowledge of this kind.

But if the development of what is contained in the characteristic of absolutely necessary Essence gives us still further characteristics as duly following from it, what objection can there be to accepting these, and to being convinced of their validity ? The ground of proof may be empirical; but if the proof is in itself a properly deduced consequence, and if the existence of a necessary Essence is once for all established by this consequence, reason starting from this basis pursues its investigations by the aid of what are purely conceptions ; but this can be reckoned an unjustifiable act only when the employment of reason in general is considered wrong, and, as a matter of fact, Kant carries the degradation of reason as far as those do who limit all truth to immediate knowledge.

However, the characteristic of the so-called most real Essence is easily deducible from the characteristic of the absolutely necessary Essence, or even from the characteristic of the Infinite, beyond which we have not gone, for all and every limitation contains a reference to an Other, and is consequently opposed to the characteristic of the Absolutely-necessary and Infinite.

The real illusion or fallacy in the mode of inference which is supposed to belong to this proof, is sought for by Kant in the proposition that every purely necessary Essence is at the same time the most real Essence, and he holds that this proposition is the *nervus probandi* of the Cosmological Proof. He seeks, however, to expose the fallacy by pointing out that, since a most real Essence is not one whit different from any other Essence, the proposition permits of being simply inverted, that is, *any*— and by this is meant *the* most real—Essence is absolutely necessary, or, in other words, the most real Essence which as such gets its determinate nature by means of the Notion, must also contain within it the characteristic of absolute necessity. This, however, is just the principle and method of the Ontological Proof of the existence of God, which consists in this, that it starts from the notion or conception, and passes by means of the conception to existence. The Cosmological Proof uses the Ontological as a prop, since it promises to conduct us by a new footpath, and yet after a short detour brings us back to the old one, the existence of which it refused to admit, and which we abandoned for its sake.

It will be seen that the objection does not touch the Cosmological Proof, either in so far as this latter merely attains by itself to the characteristic of something absolutely necessary, or in so far as it advances from this by way of development to the further characteristic of what is most real. So far as this connection between the two characteristics in question is concerned, it being the point against which Kant particularly directs his objections, we can see that it is quite in accordance with the nature of proof that the transition from one already established characteristic to a second, or from a proposition already proved to another, should permit of being clearly exhibited; but we can see, too, that reasoned knowledge cannot go back in the same way from the second to the first, and cannot deduce the second from the first. Euclid first demonstrated the proposition of the known relation between the sides of a right-angled triangle by starting from this definite quality of the triangle, and deducing the relationship of the sides from it. Then the converse proposition was also demonstrated, and ir. this case he started from the fact of this relation, and deduced from it the right-angled character of the triangle, the sides of which had that relation to one another, and yet this was done in such a way that the demonstration of this second proposition presupposed and made use of the first. In another instance this demonstration of the converse proposition is given apagogically by presupposing the first. Thus the proposition, that if in a rectilineal figure the sum of the angles is equal to two right angles, the figure is a triangle, can be easily proved to follow apagogically from the proposition previously demonstrated that in a triangle the three angles together make two right angles. When it is shown that a predicate belongs to an object, we must go further if we are to show that such a predicate belongs to it exclusively, and that it is not merely one of the characteristics of the object which may belong to others as well, but that it is involved in the definition of the object. This proof might be stated in various ways, and is not compelled exactly to follow one single path, namely, that which starts from the conception of the second characteristic. Besides, in dealing with the connection between the so-called most real Essence and the absolutely necessary Essence, it is only one aspect of this latter that we have to take directly into account, and we have nothing at all to do with that aspect in reference to which Kant brings forward the difficulty discovered by him in the Ontological Proof.

The characteristic of absolutely necessary Essence involves the necessity partly of its Being, partly of the
characteristics of its content. If it be asked what is
implied in the further predicate, the all-embracing, unlimited reality, the reply is that this question has no
reference to Being as such, but to what is to be further
distinguished as the characteristic of the content. In the
Cosmological Proof, Being has already a definite existence
of its own, and the question as to how we pass from
absolute necessity to the All-Reality, and back from the
latter to the former, has reference to this content only,
and not to Being. Kant finds the defect of the Ontological Proof in the fact that in connection with its
fundamental characteristic, the All of realities, Being is
likewise conceived of as a reality. In the Cosmological
Proof, however, we have already this Being elsewhere.
Inasmuch as it adds the characteristic of All-Reality
to what is for it absolutely necessary, it does not at all
require that Being should be characterised as reality, and
that it should be comprised in that All-Reality.

Kant in his criticism begins by taking the advance of
the characteristic of the Absolutely-necessary to unlimited
reality only in this sense, since, as was previously indicated, for him the point of this advance is the discovery
of the attributes possessed by the absolutely necessary
Essence, as the Cosmological Proof in itself has made
only one step in advance, namely, to the existence of an
absolutely necessary Essence in general, but cannot tell
us what kind of attributes this Essence possesses. We
must therefore hold that Kant is in error in asserting
that the Cosmological Proof rests on the Ontological, and
we must regard it as a mistake even to maintain that
it requires this latter to complete it, that is, in regard
to what it has in general to accomplish. That more,
however, has to be accomplished than it accomplishes, is
a matter for further consideration, and this further step
is undoubtedly taken in the moment contained in the

Ontological Proof. But it is not the need of thus going further, upon which Kant grounds his objection to this proof. On the contrary, his argument is conducted from points of view which lie wholly within the sphere of this proof, and which do not touch it.

But the objection referred to is not the only one which Kant brings forward against the line of argument fol-. lowed by the Cosmological Proof. He goes on (p. 637) to expose the " further assumptions," a " whole nest " of which, he declares, is concealed in it.

It contains, above all, the transcendental principle according to which we reason from what is contingent to a cause. This principle, however, applies in the world of sense only, and has no meaning whatever outside of it. For the purely intellectual conception of the contingent cannot possibly produce a synthetic proposition such as that of causality, a proposition which has a meaning and a use merely in the world of sense, but which is supposed to help us to get beyond the world of sense. What is maintained here, on the one hand, is the well-known doctrine, which is Kant's main doctrine, of the inadmissibility of getting beyond sense by means of thought, and of the limitation of the use and meaning of the categories of thought to the world of sense. The elucidation of this doctrine does not come within the scope of our present treatment of the subject. What has to be said on this point may be summed up in the following question : If thought cannot pass beyond the world of sense, would it not be necessary, on the other hand, to show first of all how it is conceivable that thought can enter into the world of sense ? The other assertion is that the intellectual conception of the contingent cannot form the basis of a synthetic proposition such as that of causality. As a matter of fact, it is by means of this intellectual category of contingency that the temporal world as present to perception is conceived of ; and by employing this very category which is an intellectual one, thought has already passed beyond the world of sense, and transferred itself to another sphere, without having found it necessary to endeavour to pass beyond the world of sense by using first of all the category of causality. Then, again, this intellectual conception of the contingent is supposed to be incapable of producing a synthetic proposition such as is involved in the idea of causality. As a matter of fact, however, it has to be shown that the finite passes through itself, through what it is meant to be, through its own content, to its Other, to the Infinite itself; and this is what forms the basis of a synthetic proposition according to Kant's use of the term. The nature of the contingent is of a similar kind. It is not necessary to take the category of causality as referring to the Other into which contingency passes over; on the contrary, this Other is, to begin with, the absolute necessity, and is consequently Substance also. The relation of substantiality, however, is itself one of those synthetic relations which Kant refers to as the categories, and this just means that "the purely intellectual characteristic of the contingent"—for the categories are essentially the characteristic qualities of thought—gives rise to the synthetic principle of substantiality, so that if we posit contingency we posit substantiality as well. This principle which expresses an intellectual relation, and is a category, is certainly not employed here in an element which is heterogeneous, namely, in the world of sense, but, on the contrary, in the intellectual world, which is its natural home. If it had no defect otherwise, it might, in fact, be applied with absolute justice in that sphere in which we are concerned with God, who can be conceived of only in thought and in Spirit, and this in opposition to its employment in the sensuous element, which is foreign to it.

The second fundamental fallacy to which Kant directs attention (p. 637) is that contained in arguing from the impossibility of there being an infinite series of successive given causes in the world of sense, to the existence of a first cause. We are not justified in arguing thus on the principles which guide the use of reason even in experience itself, and still less can we extend this fundamental principle beyond experience. It is quite true we cannot within the world of sense and experience reason to the existence of a first cause, for in this world as a finite world there can be only conditioned causes. But just because of this, reason is not only justified in passing into the intelligible sphere, but is forced to do it; or rather, as a matter of fact, it is only in this sphere that reason is at home. It does not pass beyond the world of sense, but because it has this idea of a first cause it simply finds itself in another region, and we can look for a meaning in reason only in so far as it and its idea are thought of as being independent of the world of sense, and as having an independent standing in-and-for-themselves.

The third charge brought by Kant against reason in connection with this proof is that it finds what is a false self-satisfaction, inasmuch as in the matter of the completion of the series of causes it finally casts aside a condition of any kind, while, as a matter of fact, there can be no necessity apart from a condition; and he objects, again, that the fact that we cannot conceive of anything further is held to be a completion of the conception. Now it is certain that if we are dealing with an unconditioned necessity, with an absolutely necessary Essence, we can reach it only in so far as it is conceived of as unconditioned, that is, in so far as the characteristic quality of having conditions has been done away with. But, adds Kant, anything necessary cannot exist apart from conditions. A necessity of this sort which rests on conditions, that is, on conditions external to it, is a merely external, conditioned necessity; while an unconditioned absolute necessity is simply one which contains its conditions within itself, if we must speak of conditions in connection with it. The difficulty here is just the truly dialectic relation above referred to according to which the condition, or whatever other definition may be given of contingent existence or the finite, is something whose very nature it is to rise to the unconditioned, to the infinite, and thus in what is conditioned to do away with what conditions, and in the act of mediating to do away with the mediation. Kant, however, did not penetrate beyond the relations of the Understanding to the conception of this infinite negativity. Continuing this argument, he says (p. 641), we cannot avoid having the thought, and yet we cannot entertain it, that a Being whom we conceive of as the Highest should, as it were, say to Himself: I am from eternity to eternity, besides me there is nothing, unless what exists by my will; but whence then am I? Here everything sinks under us, and floats without support or foothold in the presence merely of speculative reason, while it costs the latter nothing to allow the greatest as well as the smallest perfection to go. But there is one thing which speculative reason must above all else "allow to go," and that is the putting of such a question as, Whence am I? into the mouth of the absolutely necessary and unconditioned. As if that outside of which nothing exists unless through its will, that which is simply infinite, could look beyond itself for an other than itself, and ask about something beyond itself.

In bringing forward these objections, Kant, in short, gives vent to the view which he had, to begin with, in common with Jacobi, and which afterwards came to be the regular beaten track of argument, the view, namely, that where we do not have the fact of being conditioned along with what conditions, it is impossible to form conceptions at all—in other words, that where the rational begins, reason ends.

The fourth error to which Kant draws attention is connected with the ostensible confusion between the logical possibility of the conception of all reality and the transcendental characteristics, which latter will be further dealt with when we come to consider Kant's criticism of the Ontological Proof.

To this criticism Kant adds (p. 642) the "discovery" and "explanation"—made in his peculiar style—of the dialectic illusion which exists in all transcendental proofs of the existence of a necessary Essence, an explanation which contains nothing new ; and then we have in Kant's usual fashion an incessant repetition of what is always one and the same assurance, namely, that we cannot think the Thing-in-itself.

He calls the Cosmological Proof, as he does the Ontological, a transcendental proof, because it is independent of empirical principles ; that is to say, it is supposed to be established, not by reasoning from any particular quality of experience whatsoever, but from pure principles of reason, and even abandons that method of deduction according to which existence is given through empirical consciousness, in order to base itself on what are simply pure conceptions. What better method indeed could philosophical proof adopt than that of basing itself only on pure conceptions ? Kant, on the contrary, in speaking thus, intends to say the very worst he possibly can of this proof. So far, however, as the dialectic illusion is concerned, the discovery of which is here made by Kant, we find it to consist in the fact that while I must indeed allow that existence in general has a necessary element in it, no single thing can, on the other hand, be thought of as necessary in itself, and that I can never complete the act of going back to the conditions of existence without assuming the existence of something necessary while I can at the same time never start from this.

It must in justice be allowed that this remark contains the essential moment on which the whole question turns. What is necessary in itself must show that it has its beginning in itself, and must be conceived of in such a way as to allow of its being proved that its beginning is in itself. This requirement is indeed the only

interesting point, and we must assume that it lay at the
bottom of what was previously referred to, namely, the
trouble Kant took to prove that the Cosmological Proof
rests on the Ontological. The sole question is as to
how we can begin to show that anything starts from
itself, or rather how we can combine the two ideas that
the Infinite starts from an Other, and yet in doing this
starts equally from itself.

As regards the so-called explanation and solution, so
to speak, of this illusion, it will be seen to be of the same
character as the solution which he has given of what he
calls the antinomies of reason.   If I must think (p. 644
of a certain necessary element as belonging to existing
things in general, and yet am not warranted in thinking that anything is necessary in itself, the unavoidable
conclusion is that necessity and contingency cannot apply
to, or have any connection with, the things themselves,
because otherwise we would be landed in a contradiction.
Here we have that tenderness towards things which will
not permit any contradiction to be attached to them,
although even the most superficial experience, equally
with experience of the most thorough kind, everywhere
shows that these things are full of contradictions.   Kant
then goes on to say that neither of these two fundamental principles, of contingency and necessity, is objective ; but that they can in any case be only subjective
principles of reason, implying, on the one hand, that we
cannot stop short unless with an explanation completed
in an *à priori* way, while, on the other hand, any such
complete explanation is not to be looked for, that is, not
in the empirical sphere.   Thus the contradiction is preserved and is left wholly unsolved, while it is at the
same time transferred from things to reason.   If the
circumstance that the contradiction such as it is here
held to be, and such as it actually is, is not directly
solved, implies a defect, then the defect would as a
matter of fact have to be transferred to the so-called

things—which are partly merely empirical and finite, but are also partly that Thing-in-itself which is incapable of manifesting itself—rather than to reason, which, even as understood by Kant, is the faculty which deals with ideas, with the Unconditioned and the Infinite. But in truth reason can in any case bear the weight of the contradiction, and can certainly solve it too; and things, at all events, know how to bear it, or rather, we should say, they are only contradiction in the form of existence; and this is true of that Kantian schema of the Thing-in-itself quite as much as of empirical things, and only in so far as they are rational can they solve it directly within themselves.

In Kant's criticism of the Cosmological Proof those moments are at least discussed on which the point at issue really turns. We have noted two circumstances connected with this criticism : first, that the Cosmological Argument starts from Being as a presupposition, and from this goes on to the content, to the conception of God ; and second, that Kant finds fault with the line of argument on the ground that it rests on the Ontological Proof, *i.e.*, on the Proof in which the conception is presupposed, and in which we advance from this conception to Being. Since, according to the standpoint we at present occupy in conducting our investigation, the conception of God has no further determinate quality than that of the Infinite, it follows that what we are concerned with is, speaking generally, the Being of the Infinite. In accordance with the distinction previously referred to, in the one instance it is Being from which we start, and which has to get a determinate character as the Infinite ; and in the other it is the Infinite from which we start, and which has to get a determinate character as having Being. Further, in the Cosmological Proof finite Being appears as a starting - point adopted empirically. The Proof essentially sets out from experience, as Kant says (p. 633), in order to lay a really firm foundation for itself.

The relation here implied ought more strictly, however, to be referred back to the form of the judgment in general. In every judgment the subject is an idea which has been presupposed, and which is defined in the predicate, that is, an idea which is defined or determined in a general way by thought, which means, again, that the determinations or specific qualities of the content of the subject have to be indicated, even if, as in the case of the material predicates, red, hard, and so on, this general mode of determination, which is, so to speak, the share thought has in the matter, is really nothing more than the empty form of universality. Thus, when it is said that God is infinite, eternal, and so on, God is, to begin with, as a subject simply something hypothetical, existing in idea, and it is only in the predicate that it is first asserted *what* He is. So far as the subject is concerned, we do not know what He is, that is, what content He has, or what is the determinate character of the content, as otherwise it would be superfluous to have the copula "is" and to attach the predicate to it. Then further, since the subject represents the hypothetical element which exists in idea, this presupposition can be taken as signifying what has Being, and as implying that the subject *is*, or, on the other hand, that it is at first only an idea, that instead of being posited by sense-intuition, or sense-perception, it is posited in the sphere of ideas by imagination, by conception, by reason, and that it, in fact, gets such content as it has in the sphere of general ideas.

If we express these two moments in accordance with this more definite form, we shall at once get a more definite idea of the demands which are made upon them. Those moments give rise to the two following propositions—

> *Being* defined, to begin with, as finite,
> is *infinite;* and
> The Infinite is.

For, so far as the first proposition is concerned, it is

evident that it is Being properly so called which is presupposed as a fixed subject, and that it is what must in any view of it *remain*, that is, it is what must have the predicate of the Infinite attached to it. Being in so far as it is, to begin with, characterised as finite, and because the finite and the Infinite are simultaneously conceived of as subjects, represents what is common to both. The real point is not that a transition is made from Being to the Infinite as representing something different from Being, but, on the contrary, that we pass from the finite to the Infinite, and that in this transition Being remains unaltered. It is consequently shown here to be the permanent subject whose first characteristic, namely, finitude, is translated into infinitude. It is almost superfluous to remark that since Being is conceived of as subject and finitude as simply one characteristic, and, in fact, as the subsequent predicate shows, as a purely transitory characteristic, when we are dealing with the proposition taken by itself alone : Being is infinite, or is to be characterised as infinite, we must by the term Being understand Being as such, and not empirical Being, not the moral finite world.

This first proposition is accordingly the proposition of the Cosmological Argument, Being is the subject, and this presupposition whether it is taken as given or deduced, it does not matter how, is in reference to the act of proof as mediation through grounds or reasons in general, the immediate in general. This consciousness that the subject represents what is presupposed in general, is what is alone to be regarded as the important thing in connection with knowledge reached by demonstration. The predicate of the proposition is the content which must be proved to belong to the subject. Here it is the Infinite, which has consequently to be shown to be the predicate of Being and of its content, and as reached by means of mediation.

The second proposition : the Infinite *is*, has the more definitely determinate content as its subject, and here it is Being which has to show itself to be what is mediated. It is this proposition which forms the real point of interest in the Ontological Proof, and has to appear as the result. So far as the demands of the kind of proof sought by the Understanding, and of the mere knowledge of the Understanding, are concerned, the proof of this second proposition as connected with the first proposition of the Cosmological Argument may be dispensed with ; but it is certainly demanded by the requirements of reason in its higher form, though this higher requirement of reason appears in Kant's criticism disguised, so to speak, as a mere piece of chicanery, which has been deduced from some more remote consequence.

The fact, however, that these two propositions are necessary rests on the nature of the Notion, in so far as this latter is conceived of in accordance with its true nature, that is, in a speculative way. Here, however, it is presupposed that this knowledge of the Notion has been got from logic, just as it is presupposed in the same way that logic tells us that a true proof is rendered impossible by the very nature of such propositions as the two referred to. This may, however, be briefly indicated here as well, in accordance with the explanation which has been given regarding the peculiar nature of these judgments, and it is all the more fitting to make this plain at this point, since the current principle of so-called immediate knowledge recognises and takes into consideration just this very proof of the Understanding and no other, a proof which is inadmissible in philosophy. What has to be demonstrated is a proposition, a judgment, in fact, with a subject and predicate. We cannot, to begin with, find any fault with the demand here implied, and it looks as if the whole point turned on the nature of the act of proof. But the very fact that it is a judgment which has to be proved at once renders any true philosophical proof impossible. For it is the subject which is presupposed, and consequently becomes the standard for the predicate the truth of which has to be proved ; and accordingly the essential criterion so far as the proposition is concerned, is merely whether the predicate is adequate to the subject or not, and idea or ordinary thought, on which the presupposition is based, is taken as deciding the truth. But the main and only concern of knowledge, the claims of which have not been satisfied, and which have not even been taken into account, is just to find out whether this very presupposition contained in the subject, and consequently the further specification which it gets through the predicate, is the totality of the proposition and is true.

This is something which reason forces us to, working from within outward, unconsciously as it were. From what has been already adduced, it is evident that an attempt has been made to find what are called several proofs of the existence of God : the one set of which is based on one of the propositions above indicated, that, namely, in which Being is the subject and constitutes the presupposition, and in which the Infinite is a characteristic posited in it by means of mediation ; and the other set of which has for its basis the reverse proposition, by means of which the first of the propositions loses its one-sidedness. Here the defective element, namely, the fact that Being is presupposed, is cancelled, and conversely it is now Being which has to be posited as mediated.

What has to be accomplished by the proof has accordingly been stated in a complete enough way, but still the nature of the proof itself as such has been in consequence not touched upon. For each of the propositions has been stated separately, the proof of it accordingly starts from the presupposition which the subject contains, and which has each time to be shown to be necessary through the other, and not as immediately necessary. Either proposition presupposes the other, and no true beginning can be found for them. For this very reason it appears at first to be a matter of indifference where a beginning is made. Only the starting-point is not a matter of indifference, and the whole point just is to find out why it is not. The question is not as to whether or not we are to begin with one or other of the presuppositions, that is, with the immediate characteristic, the ordinary idea; but rather, what we have got to see is that no beginning can be made with any such presupposition, that is, that it cannot be regarded and treated as forming the basis, the permanent foundation of the proof.

For the statement that the presuppositions belonging to each of the two propositions—of which the one is proved by the other—have to be represented as mediated, when taken in its more obvious sense, deprives them of the essential meaning which belongs to them as immediate characteristics. For the fact that they are posited as mediated implies that their essential character consists in their being transitory rather than permanent subjects. In this way, however, the whole nature of the proof is altered, for it stood in need of having the subject as a fixed basis and standard. If it starts from something which has a transitory character, it loses all support, and cannot, in fact, have any existence at all. If we consider the form of the judgment more closely, it will be seen that what has just been explained is involved in the form itself, and, in fact, the judgment is what it is just owing to its form. It has, that is, for its subject something immediate, something which has Being in general, while as its predicate, which is meant to express what the subject is, it has something universal, namely, thought. The judgment consequently itself signifies that what has Being is not a something having Being, but is a thought.

This will at once become clearer from the example with which we are dealing, and which will better help us to understand, however, why we are limited to what the example directly contains, namely, the first of the two propositions, in which the Infinite is posited as what has been mediated. The express consideration of the other, in which Being appears as a result, will be taken up in a different place.

The major proposition of the Cosmological Proof in the more abstract form in which we took it, contains what is the essential element of the connection of the finite and the Infinite, the thought, namely, that the latter is got by way of hypothesis out of the former. The proposition, " If the finite exists, the Infinite exists also," put in a more definite form is primarily the following: " The Being of the finite is not only its Being, but is also the Being of the Infinite." We have thus reduced it to its simplest form, and have left out of account those developments which might be added to it by means of the still further specified forms of reflection which belong to the Infinite as having its Being conditioned by the finite, or to the Infinite as being presupposed through the finite, or to the relation of causality between finite and Infinite. All these relations are contained in that one simple form. If, in accordance with the definition previously given, we speak of Being in more definite terms as the subject of the judgment, the proposition will run thus: " Being is to be defined not as finite only but also as infinite." The real point is the demonstration of this connection. This, as was shown above, springs from the conception of the finite, and this speculative way of dealing with the nature of the finite, with the mediation out of which the Infinite proceeds, is the pivot round which the whole question, namely, as to the knowledge of God and the philosophical understanding of Him, turns. The essential point, however, in this mediation is, that the Being of the finite is not the affirmative, but that, on the contrary, the Infinite is posited and mediated by the abrogation of this Being of the finite.

The essential and formal defect in the Cosmological Proof consists in the fact that finite Being is not only taken directly as the beginning and starting-point, but is regarded as something true, something affirmative, with an existence of its own. All those forms of reflection referred to, such as the presupposed, the conditioned, causality, have this in common, that what forms the presupposition, the condition, the effect, are taken as affirmative, and the connection is not conceived of as a transition, which it essentially is. What the study of the finite from a speculative point of view really yields, is not merely the thought, that if the finite exists, the Infinite exists too, not that Being is to be defined as not merely finite, but that it is further to be defined as infinite. If the finite were this affirmative, the major proposition would be the proposition—finite Being as finite is infinite, for it would be its permanent finitude which the Infinite included in itself. Those characteristics such as presupposition, condition, causality, when taken together, give a still greater stability to the affirmative show or appearance of the Being of the finite, and are for this very reason only finite, that is, untrue relations, relations of what is untrue. To get to know that this is their nature is what alone constitutes the logical interest attaching to them, though their dialectic in accordance with their special characteristics takes in each case a special form, which is, however, based on the general dialectic of the finite already referred to. The proposition which ought to constitute the major proposition of the syllogism must accordingly take the following form rather : the Being of the finite is not its own Being, but is, on the contrary, the Being of its Other, namely, the Infinite. Or to put it otherwise, Being which is characterised as finite possesses this characteristic only in the sense that it cannot exist independently in relation to the Infinite, but is, on the contrary, ideal merely, a moment of the Infinite. Consequently the minor proposition : the finite *is*—disappears in any affirmative sense, and if we may still say it exists, we mean that its existence is merely an appearance or phenomenal existence. It is just the fact that the finite world is merely a manifestation or appearance which constitutes the absolute power of the Infinite.

The form taken by the syllogism of the Understanding

has no place for the dialectic character which thus marks
the finite, nor has it any way of expressing it. It is not
in a position to express the rational element in it; and
since religious elevation is the rational element itself, it
cannot find satisfaction in that form of the Understanding,
for there is more in it than this form can express. It is
accordingly in itself of the greatest importance that Kant
should have deprived the so-called proofs of the existence
of God of the regard they enjoyed, even though he had
done no more than create a prejudice against them by
showing their insufficiency. Only, his criticism of these
proofs is insufficient in itself; and besides, he failed to
recognise the deeper basis upon which these proofs rest,
and so was unable to do justice to their true elements.
It was he who at the same time began the complete
maiming of reason, which has since his day been content
to be nothing more than the source of purely immediate
knowledge.

So far we have been dealing with the elucidation
of the conception which constitutes the logical element
in the first characteristic of religion, and have been regarding it, on the one hand, from the side from which it
was viewed in metaphysics in its earlier phase; while, on
the other hand, we have been looking at the outward
form in which it was put. But this is not sufficient if
we are to get a real knowledge of the speculative conception of this characteristic. Still, one part of this knowledge has already been indicated, that, namely, which
has reference to the passing over of finite Being into
infinite Being, and we have now to indicate briefly the
other part, the detailed elucidation of which will be de-
ferred till we come to deal with another form of religion
to be taken up subsequently. This is just what appeared
previously in the form taken by the proposition: the
Infinite *is,* and in which consequently Being is defined
in general as what is mediated. The proof has to de-
monstrate this mediation. It already follows from the

foregoing remarks that the two propositions cannot be separated from each other. The very fact that the form of the syllogism belonging to the Understanding is abandoned so far as the one is concerned, implies that the separation of the two has been abandoned also. The moment which has still to be dealt with is accordingly already contained in the given development of the dialectic of the finite.

If, however, in showing how the finite passes over into the Infinite, we have made it appear as if the finite were taken as the starting-point for the Infinite, so, too, the other proposition, which is merely the converse proposition or transition, seems to be necessarily defined as a passing over from the Infinite to the finite, or, in other words, has to take on the form of the proposition : " The Infinite is finite." In this equation the proposition : the Infinite *is*, would not contain the entire characteristic which has to be dealt with here. This difference disappears, however, when we consider that Being, since it is the Immediate, is directly differentiated from the characteristic of the Infinite, and is, as a direct consequence of this, characterised simply as finite. The logical nature which thus belongs to Being or immediacy in general is, however, presupposed as given by logic. This characteristic of the finitude of Being, however, comes directly into view in the connection in which Being here stands. For the Infinite, in resolving to become Being, determines itself to what is other than itself; but then the Other of the Infinite is just the finite.

If, further, as was previously indicated, the subject appears in the judgment as something presupposed, what has Being in fact, while the predicate is something universal, namely, thought, then in the proposition, " The Infinite *is*," a proposition which is at the same time a judgment, the determination seems rather to be reversed, since the predicate expressly involves Being, while the subject, the Infinite namely, exists in thought only, though certainly in objective thought. Still we might remember the common idea that Being itself is only a thought, chiefly in so far as it is regarded in this abstract and logical way, and all the more if the Infinite, too, is only a thought, for in this case its predicate also could not possibly be anything else but a subjective thought. In any case, the predicate regarded from the point of view of its form in the judgment is the Universal and is thought, while considered according to its content or determinateness it is Being, and taken in a more definite sense it is immediate and also finite or particular Being. If, however, it is meant by this, that Being, because it has been thought, is therefore no longer Being as such, then this is simply an absurd idealism which maintains that if anything is thought it therefore ceases to be, or even that what is cannot be thought, and that therefore only nothing is thinkable. Still the idealism which enters into that aspect of the entire conception or notion to be considered here will be discussed later on when we enter on the explanation already indicated. The point, however, to which attention should really be directed is, that it is just the judgment indicated which, owing to the antithesis of its content and its form, contains in it that counter-stroke which expresses the nature of the absolute union in one of the two previously separated sides, and which is the nature of the Notion itself.

Put shortly, what we have so far learned regarding the Infinite is, that it is the affirmation of the self-annulling finite, the negation of the negation, what is mediated, but mediated by the annulling of the mediation. This already means that the Infinite is simple reference to self, that abstract equality with self which is called Being. Or, it is the self-annulling mediation, while the Immediate is just the mediation absorbed and annulled, in other words, that into which the self-annulling mediation passes, that which it becomes by annulling itself.

It is just in consequence of this that this affirmation,

this thing which is equal to itself in one, is thus immediate and equal to itself only when it is simply the negation of the negation, that is, it itself contains the negation, the finite, but as an appearance or semblance which annuls itself and is preserved in something higher. Or, since the immediacy which it comes to be by this act—that abstract equality with itself into which it passes over and which is Being—is only the moment of the Infinite conceived of in a one-sided way, and the affirmative as representing it appears only as this entire process, and is therefore finite, it follows that the Infinite, in determining itself in the form of Being, determines itself as finitude. But finitude and this immediate Being are consequently just the negation which negates itself. This apparent end, the passing of the living dialectic into the dead repose of the result, is itself only the beginning again of this living dialectic.

This is the Notion, the logical and rational element in the first abstract characteristic of God and religion. The side represented by the latter is expressed by that moment of the Notion which starts from immediate Being, and which is absorbed in and taken up into the Infinite. The objective side, however, as such is contained in the self-unfolding of the Infinite into Being and finitude, which, just because of this, is merely momentary and transitory—transitory merely, in virtue of the infinitude whose manifestation it merely is, and which represents the force in it. The so-called Cosmological Proof is of use solely in connection with the effort to bring into consciousness what the inner life, the pure rational element of the inner movement, really is, and which, regarded in its subjective aspect, is called religious elevation. If this movement, when it appears in that form of the Understanding in which we have seen it, is not conceived of and understood as it is in-and-for-itself, still the substantial element which forms its basis does not lose anything in consequence. It is this substantial element which penetrates the imperfection of the form and exercises its power; or rather, we might say, it is itself the real and substantial force. The religious elevation of the soul to God consequently recognises itself in that expression of the truth, imperfect as it is, and is aware of its inner and true meaning, and so protects itself against the syllogism of the Understanding and its methods which stunt this true meaning. That is why, as Kant says (in the place already referred to, p. 632), "this method of proof undoubtedly most readily carries persuasion with it, not only for the ordinary understanding, but for the speculative understanding too; and it obviously contains, too, the main lines on which all the proofs of natural theology are based, and which have at all times been followed, and will be still further followed, however much people may try to trick them out and conceal them under all sorts of fancy embellishments;" and, I add, it is possible by following the Understanding entirely to miss the meaning of the substantial element contained in these great fundamental lines of argument, and to imagine they have been formally refuted by the critical understanding, or, it may be, in virtue of the want of understanding as well as the want of reason characteristic of so-called immediate knowledge, politely to throw these arguments on one side unrefuted or to ignore them.

ELEVENTH LECTURE

HAVING given this explanation regarding the general scope of the characteristics of the content with which we are dealing, we shall now consider the course followed by the act of elevation first mentioned, in that particular form in which it is at present before us. This course consists simply in reasoning from the contingency of the world to an absolutely necessary Essence belonging to it. If we look at this syllogism as expressed in a formal way and at its particular elements, we find that it runs thus: The contingent does not rest upon itself, but, speaking generally, rests upon the presupposition of something which is in itself absolutely necessary, and which we call its essence, ground, or cause. But the world is contingent, the single things in it are contingent, and it as representing the whole is the aggregate of these; therefore the world presupposes the existence of something absolutely necessary in itself.

The determination from which this conclusion starts is the contingency of material things. If we take these things according as we find them in sensation and in ordinary thought, and if we compare the various processes which go on in the human mind, then we have a right to assert it to be a fact of experience that material things taken by themselves are regarded as contingent. Individual things do not come out of themselves, and do not pass away of themselves; being contingent, they are destined to drop away, and this is not something which happens to them in an accidental way merely, but is what constitutes their nature. Even if the course they follow is one which develops within themselves and is guided by rule and law, still it goes on till it reaches what is their end, or rather, it does nothing but lead up to their end; and so, too, their existence is interfered with in all kinds of ways by other things, and is brought to an end by external causes. If they are regarded as conditioned, then we can see that their conditions are things which exist independently outside of them, and which may correspond to them or not, and by which they are temporarily supported, or, it may be, are not. To begin with, they are seen to be co-ordinated in space without being ranged together in accordance with any other relation naturally belonging to them. The most heterogeneous elements are found side by side, and they can be separated without any kind of derangement being caused in the existence either of the one thing or the other. In the same way they succeed one another outwardly in time. They are, in fact, finite; and however independent they may seem, they are essentially devoid of independence, owing to the limits attaching to their finitude. They *are*; they are in a real sense, but their reality has the value of something which is merely a possibility; they are, and can therefore equally well either be or not be.

Their existence reveals the presence not only of connections between conditions, that is, the points of dependence owing to which they come to be characterised as contingent, but also the connections of cause and effect, the regular rules which govern the course they follow both inwardly and outwardly—laws, in fact. These elements of dependence, this conformity to law, raises them above the category of contingency into the region of necessity, and thus necessity is found within that sphere which we thought of as occupied by what was contingent. Contingency claims things in virtue of their isolation, and therefore they may either exist or not exist; but then, as governed by law, they are the opposite of what is contingent, they are not isolated, but are qualified, limited, related, in fact, to one another. They do

not, however, fare any the better because of the presence
of this antithesis in their nature. Their isolation gives
them a semblance of independence; but the connection
in which they stand with other things—with each other,
that is—directly expresses the fact that these single
things are not independent, shows that they are conditioned and are affected by other things, and are, in
fact, necessarily conditioned by other things, and not by
themselves. These necessary elements, these laws, would
themselves consequently constitute the independent element. Anything which exists essentially in connection
with something else has its essential character and stability not in itself, but in this connection. It is the
connection upon which these are dependent. But these
connections, when defined as causes and effects, the condition and the fact of being conditioned, and so on,
have themselves a limited character, and are themselves
contingent in relation to each other in the sense that
any one of them may equally well exist or not exist, and
may just as easily be disturbed by circumstances—that is,
be interfered with by things which are themselves contingent, and have their active working and value destroyed,
as the separate things over which they have no advantage
in the matter of contingency. Those connections, on the
other hand, to which necessity must be attributed, those
laws, are not in any sense what we call things, but are
rather abstractions. If the connection of necessity thus
manifests itself in the region of contingent things in
laws, and chiefly in the relations of cause and effect, this
necessity itself takes the form of something conditioned,
or limited—appears, in fact, as an outward necessity. It
is itself relegated to the class of categories applying to
things, both in virtue of their isolation, that is, their
externality, and conversely in virtue of their being conditioned, of their limitation and dependence. In the
connection expressed by causes and effects we get not
only the satisfaction which is wanting in the empty un-

related isolation of things, which are just for this reason called contingent; but the indefinite abstraction which attaches to the expression "things," the element of variableness in them, disappears in this relation of necessity in which things become causes, original facts, substances that are active and indeterminate. But in the connections which hold good in this sphere the causes are themselves finite; beginning as causes, their Being is isolated, and therefore contingent; or it is not isolated, and in that case they are effects, and are consequently not independent, but posited through an Other. The various series of causes and effects are partly contingent relatively to each other, and are partly themselves continued into the so-called Infinite, and thus contain in their content nothing but those situations and forms of existence of which each is finite in itself; and what ought to give stability to the connection of the series, the Infinite namely, is not only something above and beyond this world, but is a mere negative, the very meaning of which is relative merely, and is conditioned by what is to be negated by it, and is consequently for this very reason not negated.

Spirit, however, raises itself above this crowd of things contingent, above the merely outward and relative necessity involved in them, above the Infinite, which is a mere negative, and reaches a necessity which does not any longer go beyond itself, but is in-and-for-itself, included within itself, and is determined as complete in itself, while all other determinations are posited by it and are dependent upon it.

These may be in the form of ideas of an accidental or of a more concentrated kind, the essential moments of thought belonging to the inner life of the human spirit, to the reason which does not fully attain in a methodical and formal way the consciousness of its inner process, and still less gets so far as to be able to investigate those thought-determinations through which it passes, or the connections they involve. We have now got to see, how-ever, if thought, which in the process of reasoning pro-ceeds in a formal and methodical way, rightly conceives of and expresses the course followed in the elevation of the soul to God, which, so far, we have assumed to be a fact, and which we have been accustomed to deal with only in connection with the few fundamental characteristics belonging to it. Conversely, again, we have to find out whether those thoughts and the connection between them can be shown to be justified, and have their reality proved, by an examination of the thoughts in themselves, for it is only in this way that the elevation of the soul to God really ceases to be a supposition, and that the unstable element in any right conception of it disappears. We must, however, decline to enter upon this examination here, seeing that if it were demanded on its own account we should have to go on to the ultimate analysis of thought. It has to be carried out in a thorough way in logic, the science of thought; for I identify logic with metaphysic, since the latter, too, is really nothing but an attempt to deal with some concrete content, such as God, the world, the soul, but in such a way that these objects have to be conceived of as noumena, that is, we have to deal with the element of thought in them. At this point it will be preferable to take up the logical results merely, rather than the formal development. An investigation of the proofs of the existence of God cannot be undertaken independently at all, if it is required to have philosophical and scientific completeness. Science is the developed con-nection of the Idea in its totality. In so far as any indi-vidual object is lifted out of that totality, which must be the goal of the scientific development of the Idea, as representing the only method of exhibiting its truth, limits must be set to the investigation undertaken, and these it must presuppose to be definitely fixed, as is the case in other instances of scientific inquiry. Still the investigation may come to have an appearance of independence, owing

to the fact that the unexplained presuppositions, which
are what constitutes the limits of what is dealt with, and
which analysis reaches in the course of its progress, are
in themselves in harmony with consciousness. Every
work contains such ultimate ideas, or fundamental principles, upon which either consciously or unconsciously the
content is based. There is in it a circumscribed horizon
of thoughts which are no further analysed, the horizon of
which rests upon the culture it may be of a period, of a
nation, or of some scientific circle, and beyond which
there is no need to go. In fact it would be prejudicial
to what is called popular comprehension to attempt to
extend this horizon beyond the limits of ordinary ideas
by analysing these, and so to make it include speculative
or philosophical conceptions.

Still, since the subject of these lectures belongs in
itself essentially to the domain of philosophy, we cannot
dispense with abstract conceptions. We have, however,
already mentioned those which belong to this first
standpoint, and we have only to range them together
in a definite way in order to reach the speculative
element; for, speaking generally, to deal with anything
in a speculative or philosophical way simply means to
bring into connection the thoughts which we already
have.

The thoughts, therefore, which have been already indicated, consist, first of all, of the following main characteristics : a thing, a law, &c., is contingent in virtue of
its isolation ; the fact of its existence or non-existence
does not bring about any derangement or alteration so
far as other things are concerned. Then the fact that it
is quite as little kept in existence by them, and that
any stability it gets owing to them is wholly insufficient,
gives them that very insufficient semblance of independence which is just what constitutes their contingency.
The idea of necessity as applied to any existing thing, on
the other hand, requires that it should stand in some

connection with other things, so that regarded in any
of its aspects it is seen to be completely determined
by other existing things, in the form of conditions or
causes, and cannot be separated from them or come into
being of itself, nor can there be any condition, cause, or
fact of connection by means of which it can be so separated, nor any such instance of connection as can contradict the other which qualifies the thing.   In accordance
with this description we place the contingency of a thing
in its isolation, in the want of perfect connection with
other things.   This is the first point.

Conversely, again, since an existing thing thus stands
in a relation of perfect connection, it is in all its aspects
conditioned and dependent, is in fact perfectly wanting
in independence.   It is, on the other hand, in necessity
alone that we find the independence of a thing.   What
is necessary must be.   This fact that it *must be*, expresses its independence by suggesting that what is
necessary is, *because* it is.   This is the other point.

We thus see that the necessity of anything requires
two sorts of opposed characteristics : on the one hand, its
independence, in which, however, it is isolated, and which
makes its existence or non-existence a matter of indifference ; and, on the other, its being based upon and
contained in a complete relation to everything else
whereby it is surrounded, and by the connection involved in which, it is kept in existence ; this means that
it is not independent.   The necessary element is a recognised fact quite as much as the contingent element.
Regarded from the point of view of the first of these
ideas, everything exists in an orderly connection.   The
contingent is separated from the necessary, and points
beyond it to a necessary something, which, however,
when we look at it more closely, is itself included in
contingency, just because, being posited by another, it is
dependent.   When, however, it is taken out of any such
connection it is isolated, and is consequently directly

contingent. The distinctions drawn are accordingly merely imaginary.

Since it is not our intention to examine further the nature of these thoughts, and since we wish in the meantime to leave the antithesis of necessity and contingency out of account, we shall confine ourselves to what is suggested by the idea we have given of them, namely, that neither of the determinations is sufficient to express necessity, but that for this both are required—independence, so that the necessary may not be mediated by an Other ; and also the mediation of this independence in connection with the Other. They thus contradict each other, but since they both belong to the one necessity they must not contradict each other in the unity in which they are joined together in it. Our view of the matter renders it necessary that the thoughts which are united in this necessity should be brought into connection in our minds. In this unity the mediation with an Other will thus itself partake of independence, and this, as a reference to self, will have the mediation with an Other within itself. In this determination, however, both can be united only in such a way that the mediation with an Other is at the same time a mediation with self, that is, their union must imply that the mediation with an Other abolishes itself, and becomes a mediation with self. Thus the unity with self is not a unity which is abstract identity, such as we saw in the form of the isolation in which the thing is related only to itself, and in which its contingency lies. The one-sidedness, on account of which alone it is in contradiction with the equally one-sided mediation by an Other, is done away with, and these untruths have thus disappeared. The unity thus characterised is the true unity, and when truly known is the speculative or philosophical unity. Necessity as thus defined, since it unites in itself these opposite characteristics, is seen to be something more than a simple idea or a simple determinateness ; and further, the dis-

appearance of the opposite characteristics in something
higher is not merely our act, or a matter with which
we only have to do, in the sense that we only bring it
about, but expresses the very nature and action of these
characteristics themselves, since they are united in one
characteristic. So, too, these two moments of necessity,
namely, that its mediation with an Other is in itself, and
that it does away with this mediation and posits itself by
its own act because of this very unity, are not separate
acts. In the mediation with an Other it relates itself to
itself, that is, the Other through which it mediates itself
with itself is itself. Thus as an Other it is negated ; it
is itself the Other, but only momentarily—momentarily
without, however, introducing the quality of time into
the notion, a quality which first appears when the notion
comes to have a definite existence. This Other-Being or
otherness is essentially something which disappears in
something higher, and it is in determinate existence also
that it appears as a real Other. But the absolute necessity is the necessity which is adequate to its notion or
conception.

TWELFTH LECTURE

In the previous Lecture the notion or conception of absolute necessity was explained—of *absolute* necessity, I repeat. Very often absolute means nothing more than abstract, and very frequently, too, it is imagined that when the word absolute is used everything is said that is necessary, and that no further definition can or ought to be given. As a matter of fact it is just with this definition that we are chiefly concerned. Absolute necessity is abstract, the abstract pure and simple, inasmuch as it depends on itself and does not subsist in or from or through an Other. But we have seen that it is not only adequate to its notion or conception, whatever that notion be, so that we were able to compare this notion and its external existence; but that it represents this very adequacy itself. Thus what might be taken as the external aspect is contained in itself, so that this very fact that it depends on itself, this identity or reference to self which constitutes the isolation of things in virtue of which they are contingent, is a form of independence which again is really a want of independence. Possibility is an abstraction of the same kind. A thing is possible if it does not contradict itself, that is, it is what is merely identical with itself, something in which there is no kind of identity with an Other, while, on the other hand, it has not its Other within itself. Contingency and possibility differ only in this, that the contingent has in addition a definite existence. The possible has only the possibility of existence. But the contingent itself has an existence which has absolutely no value beyond being a possibility; it is, but quite as much it is not. In the case of con-

tingency, the nature of determinate Being or existence
belonging to it is, as has been already remarked, so far
evident that it is seen at the same time to have the
character of something which is virtually a nullity, and
consequently the transition to its Other, to the Necessary,
is already expressed in that existence itself. It is an
instance of the same thing as we have in abstract identity,
which is a simple reference to self; it is known as a possibility, and being a possibility it is recognised that it
is not yet anything. The fact that something is possible
does not really imply anything. Identity is characterised
as sterility, and that is what it really is.

What is wanting in this characteristic finds its comple-
ment, as we have seen, in the characteristic which is its
antithesis. Necessity is not abstract, but truly absolute,
solely in virtue of the fact that it contains the connection
with an Other in itself, that it is self-differentiation, but
a differentiation which has disappeared in something
higher and is ideal. It consequently contains what
belongs to necessity in general, but it is distinguished
from this latter as being external and finite, and as
involving a connection having reference to something
else which remains Being and has the value of Being,
and so is merely dependence. It goes by the name of
necessity too, inasmuch as mediation is in general essential to necessity. The connection of its Other with
something else, which is what constitutes it, does not get
support from the ends for which it exists. Absolute
necessity, on the other hand, transforms any such relation
to an Other into a relation to itself, and consequently
produces what is really inner harmony with itself.

Spirit rises above contingency and external necessity,
just because these thoughts are in themselves insufficient
and unsatisfying. It finds satisfaction in the thought of
absolute necessity, because this latter represents something at peace with itself. Its result *as* result, however,
is—it is so, it is simply necessary. Thus all aspiration,

all effort, all longing after an Other, have passed away,
for in it the Other has disappeared, there is no finitude
in it, it is absolutely complete in itself, it is infinite and
present in itself, there is nothing outside of it. It has in
it no limit, for its nature is to be with itself, or at home
with itself. It is not the act of rising to this necessity
on the part of Spirit which in itself produces satisfaction.
The satisfaction has reference to the goal Spirit tries to
reach, and the satisfaction is in proportion to its ability
to reach this goal.

If we pause for a moment to consider this subjective
satisfaction, we find that it reminds us of what the Greeks
found in the idea of subjection to necessity. That Man
should yield to inevitable destiny was the advice of the
wise, and this was in particular the truth expressed by
the tragic chorus, and we admire the repose of their
heroes and the calmness with which they freely and
undauntedly accept the lot which destiny has assigned
to them. This necessity, and the aims of their own wills
which are annihilated by it, the compulsory force of this
destiny and freedom, appear as the opposing elements,
and seem to leave no room for reconciliation nor for any
kind of satisfaction. In fact the play of this antique
necessity is shrouded in a sadness which is neither
driven away by defiance nor disfigured by any feeling of
bitterness, and all lamentation is rather suppressed by
silence than stilled by the healing of the wounded heart.
The element of satisfaction found by Spirit in the thought
of necessity is to be sought for in this alone, that Spirit
simply abides by that abstract result of necessity expressed in the words, " it is so," a result brought about
by Spirit within itself. In this pure *is* there is no
longer any content ; all ends, all interests, all wishes,
even the concrete feeling of life itself, have disappeared
and vanished in it. Spirit produces this abstract result
in itself just because it has given up this particular content of its will, the very substance of its life, and has

renounced everything. It thus transforms into freedom the compulsion exercised upon it by fatality. For this force or compulsion can lay hold of it only by seizing on those sides of its nature which in its concrete existence have an inner and an outer determinate Being. As connected with external existence, Man is under the influence of external force in the shape of other men, of circumstances, and so on; but external existence has its roots in what is inward, in his impulses, interests, and aims; they are the bonds, morally justifiable and morally ordained, or, it may be, not justifiable, which bring him into subjection to force. But the roots belong to his inner life, they are his; he can tear them out of his heart; his will, his freedom represent that power of abstraction from everything whereby the heart can make itself the grave of the heart. When the heart thus inwardly renounces itself, it leaves to force nothing upon which it can lay hold. What is crushed by force is a form of existence which is devoid of heart, an externality in which force can no longer affect Man: he is outside of the sphere in which force can strike.

It has been previously remarked that the result, it *is* so, is the result of the necessity, to which Man clings; and he abides by it as a result, that is, in the sense that it is he who produces this abstract Being. This is the other moment of necessity, mediation through the negation of otherness. This Other is the determinate in general, which we have seen in the form of inner existence, the giving up of concrete aims and interests; for they are not only the ties which bind Man to externality, and consequently bring him into subjection to it, but they themselves represent the particular element, and are external to what is most inward, the self-thinking pure universality, the pure relation of freedom to itself. It is the strength of this freedom that it can in this abstract way comprise within itself and put within itself that particular element which is outside of itself, and can thus make it into something external in which it can no longer be disturbed. The reason why we men are unhappy, or unsatisfied, or simply fretful, is because of the division within us, that is, because of the contradiction represented by the fact that these impulses, aims, and interests, or simply these demands, wishes, and reflections are in us, and that at the same time our existence has in it what is the Other, the antithesis of these. This disunion or unrest in us can be removed in a twofold manner. On the one hand, our outward existence, our condition, the circumstances which affect us and in which our interests in general are involved, may be brought into harmony with the roots of their interests in ourselves, a harmony which is experienced in the form of happiness and satisfaction. On the other hand, in the event of there being a disunion between the two, and consequently in the event of unhappiness, instead of satisfaction there is a natural repose of the heart, or, where the injury goes deeper and affects an energetic will and its just claims, the heroic strength of the will produces at the same time a contentment by taking kindly to the actual state of things and by submitting to what actually is, and this is a yielding in which the mind does not in a one-sided way let go its hold on what is external, circumstances, or the actual condition of things, because they have been overcome and are overpowered, but which gives up by an act of its own will its inner determinateness and allows it to go. This freedom of abstraction is not without an element of pain; but the pain is brought down to the level of natural pain, and has not in it the pain of penitence, the pain attaching to the rebellious sense of wrong-doing, just as it has no consolation or hope. But then it is not in need of consolation, for consolation presupposes a claim which is still maintained and asserted and does not in one way really satisfy, while looked at in another way, it seeks a compensation, and in the act of hoping, a desire for something has been kept in reserve.

But it is just here that we find that moment of sadness already referred to, and which diffuses itself over this act, whereby necessity is transfigured and becomes freedom. The freedom here is the result of mediation through the negation of things finite. As abstract Being, the satisfaction gained is empty reference to self, the inner unsubstantial solitude of self-consciousness.

This defect lies in the determinate character of the result as well as of the starting-point. It is the same in both of these, that is to say, it is just the indeterminateness of Being. The same defect which has been noted as present in the form taken by the process of necessity, as this process exists in the region of the volition of subjective Spirit, will be found, too, in the process when it is an objective content for the thinking consciousness. The defect, however, does not lie in the nature of the process itself ; and we have now to consider that process in the theoretical form, which is the point we have specially to deal with.

THIRTEENTH LECTURE

THE general form of the process has been already referred to as consisting of a mediation with self which contains the moment of mediation in such a way that the Other is posited as something negated or ideal. This process has likewise been described, so far as its more definite moments are concerned, as it presents itself in the form of Man's elevation to God by the path of religion. We have now to compare the explanation given of the act whereby Spirit raises itself to God with that to be found in the formal expression which is called a proof.

The difference between them seems slight, but it is important, and supplies the reason why proof of this kind has been represented as inadequate and has generally been abandoned. *Because* what is material is contingent, *therefore* there exists an absolutely necessary Essence ; this is the simple fashion in which the connection of ideas is put. Since mention is here made of an Essence, and since we have spoken only of absolute necessity, this necessity may certainly be hypostatised in this way ; but the Essence is still indeterminate, and is not a subject or anything living, and still less is it Spirit. We shall, however, afterwards discuss the Essence as such in so far as it contains a determinate quality which has any interest in the present connection.

What is of primary importance is the relation indicated in the proposition : *because* the One, the contingent, exists, is, *therefore* the Other, the Absolutely-necessary, is, or exists. Here there are two forms of Being in connection, one form of Being connected with another form of Being, a connection which we have seen in the shape of

281

external necessity. It is, however, this very external necessity which is recognised to be a form of dependence in which the result depends on the starting-point, but which, in fact, by sinking to a state of contingency, is recognised to be unsatisfying. It is against it, accordingly, that the protests have been directed which have been advanced against this method of proof.

It contains, that is to say, the relation according to which the one characteristic, that of absolutely necessary Being, is mediated by the Other, by means of the characteristic of contingent Being, whereby the former is put in a dependent relation, in the relation, in fact, of what is conditioned to its condition. This was the main objection which, speaking generally, Jacobi brought against the knowledge of God, namely, that to know or to comprehend means merely "to deduce anything from its more immediate causes, or to look at its immediate conditions as a series" (*Letters on the Doctrine of Spinoza*, p. 419); "to comprehend the Unconditioned therefore means to make it into something conditioned or to make it an effect." The latter category, however, according to which the Absolutely-necessary is taken as an effect, can be at once discounted, since the relation it implies is in too direct contradiction to the characteristic with which we are dealing, namely, the Absolutely-necessary. The relation of the condition, which is also that of the ground, is, however, of a more outward character, and can more easily find favour. In any case it is present in the proposition : because the contingent exists, therefore the Absolutely-necessary exists.

While it must be granted that this defect exists, it is, on the other hand, to be observed that no *objective* significance is given to a relation like this implying conditionateness and dependence. This relation is present only in an absolutely subjective sense. The proposition does not state, and is not meant to state, that the Absolutely-necessary has conditions, and is in fact conditioned

by the contingent world—quite the contrary. The entire
development of the connection is seen only in the act
of proof. It is only our knowledge of the Absolutely-
necessary which is conditioned by that starting-point.
The Absolutely-necessary does not exist in virtue of the
fact that it raises itself out of the world of contingency,
and requires this world as its starting-point and presupposition, in order that by starting from it it may thus
first reach its Being. It cannot be the Absolutely-
necessary, it cannot be God who has to be thought of
thus as something mediated by an Other, as something
dependent and conditioned. It is the content of the
proof itself which corrects the defect which is visible
only in its form. We are thus in presence of a distinction and a difference between the form and the nature of
the content, and the form is more certainly seen to contain the defective element, from the very fact that the
content is the Absolutely-necessary. This content is not
itself devoid of form, as was evident from the nature of
its determination. Its own form as being the form of
the True is itself true, and the form which differs from
it is for that reason the Untrue.

If we take what we have in general designated Form,
in its more concrete signification, namely, as knowledge,
we find ourselves amongst the well-known and favourite
categories of finite knowledge, which as being subjective
is defined generally as finite, while the course followed by
the movement of knowledge belonging to it is defined as
a finite act. Here accordingly the same element of inadequacy appears only in another shape. Knowledge is
a finite act, and any such act cannot involve the comprehension of the Absolutely-necessary, of the Infinite.
Knowledge demands, in short, that it should have the
content in itself and should follow it. The knowledge
which has an absolutely necessary, infinite content must
itself be absolutely necessary and infinite. We thus find
ourselves in the best position for wrestling once more

with the antithesis whose affirmative and subsidiary help given by what was more of the nature of immediate knowledge, faith, feeling, and such like, we dealt with in the first Lectures. We must for the present leave the Form in this shape alone, but later on we shall have some reflections to make on the categories belonging to it. We have in the meantime to deal with the Form in the more definite shape in which it appears in the proof which forms the subject of discussion.

If we call to mind the formal syllogism previously dealt with, it will be seen that one part of the first proposition, the major proposition that is, runs thus—*If* the contingent exists; and this is expressed in a more direct way in the other proposition—There *is* a contingent world. While in the former of these propositions the characteristic of contingency is posited essentially in its connection with the Absolutely-necessary, it is nevertheless stated to be at the same time something contingent which has Being. It is in the second proposition, or in this characteristic of the existent as it appears in the first, that the defect lies, and this in fact means that it is directly self-contradictory, and shows itself to be in its very nature an untrue one-sidedness. The contingent, the finite is expressed in terms of what has Being; but it is, on the contrary, characteristic of the finite that it should have an end and drop away, that it should be a kind of Being which has the value of what is merely a possibility and which may either be or not be.

This fundamental error is found in the form of the connection, which is that of an ordinary syllogism. A syllogism of this kind has a permanent immediate element in its premises, it is based on presuppositions which are stated to be not only what is primary, but to be the permanent primary existent element with which the Other is in general so closely connected as some kind of consequence, something conditioned, and so on, that the two characteristics thus linked together constitute a relation

which is external and finite, in which each of the two
sides is in a relation of reference to the other. It constitutes one of the characteristics of these two sides, but
it has at the same time a substantial existence of its
own outside of the relation between them. The characteristic which the two different elements taken together
constitute, and which is in itself simply one, is the
Absolutely-necessary. Its name at once declares it to
be the Only-one, what truly is, the only reality. We
have seen how its notion is the mediation which returns
into itself, the mediation which is merely a mediation
with itself by means of the Other which is distinguished
from it, and which is taken up into the One, the Absolutely-necessary, negated as something having Being, and
preserved merely as something ideal. Outside of this
absolute, inherent unity, however, the two sides of the
relation are in this kind of syllogism kept also externally
apart from each other as things which have Being; the
contingent *is*. This proposition is inherently self-contradictory, and is likewise in contradiction with the result,
the absolute necessity, which is not merely placed on one
side, but, on the contrary, is the whole of Being.

If therefore we begin with the contingent, we must
not set out from it as if it were something which is to
remain fixed in such a way that it continues to be in the
further development of the argument something which
has Being. This is its one-sided determinateness. On
the contrary, it is to be posited with its completely determinate character, which implies that non-Being may
quite as well be attributed to it, and that it consequently
enters into the result as something which passes away.
Not because the contingent is, but, on the contrary,
because it is non-Being, merely phenomenal, because its
Being is not true reality, the absolute necessity is. This
latter is its Being and Truth.

This moment of the Negative is not found in the form
taken by the syllogism of the Understanding, and this is

why it is defective when it appears in this region which is that of the living reason of Spirit, in the region, that is, in which absolute necessity itself is considered as the true result, as something which does indeed mediate itself through an Other, but mediates itself with itself by absorbing this Other. Thus the course followed by that knowledge of necessity is different from the process which necessity is. Such a course is therefore not to be considered as simply necessary true movement, but rather as finite activity. It is not infinite knowledge, it has not the infinite for its content and for the basis of its activity, for the infinite appears only as this mediation with self through the negation of the negative.

The defect which has been pointed out as existing in this form of the process of reasoning, means, as has been indicated, that the elevation of Spirit to God has not been correctly explained in that proof of the existence of God which it constitutes. If we compare the two we see that this act of elevation is undoubtedly also an act whereby Spirit goes beyond worldly existence, as well as beyond what is merely temporal, changeable, and transitory. The world-element, it is true, is declared to be actual existence, and we start from it ; but since, as was remarked, it is defined as the temporal, the contingent, the changeable and transitory, its Being is not satisfying for truth, it is not the truly affirmative, it is defined as what annuls and negates itself. It does not persistently retain its characteristic, *to be ;* on the contrary, a Being is attributed to it which has no more value than non-Being whose characteristic contains in itself its non-Being, its Other, and consequently its contradiction, its disintegration and dissolution. But even if it seem to be the case, or may even actually be the case, that so far as faith is concerned this contingent Being as something present to consciousness remains standing on one side confronting the other side, the Eternal, the Necessary in-and-for-itself, in the form of a world above which is

heaven, still the real point is not the fact that a double
world has been actually conceived of, but the value
which is to be attached to such a conception. This
value is expressed when it is said that the one world is
the world of appearance or illusion, and the other the
world of truth. When the former is abandoned, and we
pass over to the other only in the sense that the world
of appearance still remains present here, the connection
between them as it presents itself to the religious man
does not mean that that world is anything more than
merely the point of departure, or that it is permanently
fixed as a ground or basis to which Being, or the power
of acting as a basis or condition, could be attributed.
Satisfaction, everything in the way of a foundation or
first principle is, on the contrary, found to exist in the
eternal world as something which is independent in-and-
for-itself. As opposed to this, in the form taken by the
syllogism, the Being of both is expressed in a similar
way—both in the one proposition of the connection : If
a contingent world exists, an Absolutely-necessary exists
too ; as also in the other in which it is stated as a presupposition that a contingent world does exist ; and
further, in the third and concluding proposition : Therefore an Absolutely-necessary exists.

A few remarks may be further added regarding these
propositions thus definitely expressed. And first of all
in connection with the last of them, the way in which
the two contrasted characteristics are linked together,
must at once strike us : *Therefore* the Absolutely-necessary exists. Therefore expresses mediation through an
Other, and yet it is immediacy, and directly absorbs the
former of these characteristics, which, as has been indicated, is just what supplies the reason why such knowledge regarding whatever is its object is declared to be
inadmissible. The abolition of mediation through an
Other exists, however, potentially only. The syllogism,
on the other hand, as exhibited in detail, gives full

expression to this. Truth is a force of such a character that it is present even in what is false, and it only requires correct observation and attention in order to discover the True in the False itself, or rather actually to see it there. The True is here mediation with self by the negation of the Other and of the mediation through the Other. The negation, both of mediation through an Other, as well as of the abstract immediacy which is devoid of mediation, is present in the "therefore" above referred to.

Further, if the one proposition is : The contingent *is*, and the other : The necessary in-and-for-itself *is*, this essentially suggests that the Being of the contingent has an absolutely different value from necessary Being in-and-for-itself. Still Being is what is common to both, and it is the one characteristic in both propositions. In accordance with this the transition does not take the form of a passing from one form of Being to another, but from one characteristic of thought to another. Being purifies itself from the predicate of contingency, which is inadequate to express its nature. Being is simple self-identity or equality with self. Contingency, on the other hand, is Being which is absolutely unlike itself, which contradicts itself, and it is only in the Absolutely-necessary that it is once more restored to this condition of self-identity. It is accordingly here that the course thus followed by the act of elevation to God, or this aspect of the act of proof, differs more definitely from the others referred to, in this, namely, that in the former of the two methods of procedure the characteristic which has to be proved, or is supposed to result from the proof, is not Being. Being is rather what the two aspects have permanently in common and which is continued from the one into the other. In the other method of procedure, on the contrary, the transition has to be made from the notion or conception of God to His Being. This transition seems more difficult than that from a determinateness of content in general, what

we are accustomed to call a notion or conception, to
another conception, and to what is more homogeneous,
therefore, than the transition from the notion to Being is
apt to appear.

The idea which lies at the basis of this is that Being
is not itself a conception or thought. The proper place
to consider it, in this antithesis in which it is exhibited
as independent and isolated, will be when we come to
deal with the proof referred to. Here, however, we have
not, to begin with, to take it abstractly and independently.
The fact that it is the element common to the two characteristics, the contingent and the Absolutely-necessary, suggests a comparison and an external separation between
it and them, while at first it is in inseparable union with
each, with contingent Being and absolutely necessary
Being. In this way we shall once more take up the
form of the proof already referred to, and bring out still
more definitely the difference in the contradiction which
it undergoes, regarded from the two opposite sides, the
philosophical side, and that of the abstract understanding.

The proposition indicated expresses the following connection—

Because contingent Being exists, therefore absolutely
necessary Being exists.

If we take this connection in its simple sense without
characterising it more definitely by means of the category
of a ground, or reason, or the like, its meaning is merely
this—

Contingent Being is *at the same time* the Being of an
Other, that of the absolutely necessary Being.

This phrase "at the same time" seems to imply a contradiction, over against which the two contrasted propositions are placed as solutions, of which the one is—

The Being of the contingent is not its own Being, but
merely the Being of an Other, and in a definite sense it is
the Being of its own Other, the Absolutely-necessary. And
the other—

The Being of the contingent is merely its own Being, and is not the Being of an Other, of the Absolutely-necessary.

It has been shown that the first of these propositions has the true meaning, which was also the meaning expressed by the idea contained in the transition. We shall take up further on the speculative or philosophical connection which is itself immanent in those determinations of thought which constitute contingency.

The other proposition, however, is the proposition of the Understanding in which thinkers of modern times have so firmly intrenched themselves. What can be more reasonable than to hold that anything, any form of existence, and so, too, the contingent, since it *is*, is its own Being, is in fact just the definite Being which it is, and not rather an other kind of Being! The contingent is in this way retained on its own account separately from the Absolutely-necessary.

It is still easier to employ the characteristics finite and Infinite in order to express these two characteristics above mentioned, and thus to take the finite for itself, as isolated from its other, the Infinite. There is therefore, it is said, no bridge, no passage from finite Being to infinite Being. The finite is related only to itself, and not to its Other. The distinction which was made between knowledge as form and knowledge as content, is an empty one. This very difference between the two was rightly made the basis of syllogisms, syllogisms which start with the hypothesis that knowledge is finite, and for this reason conclude that this knowledge cannot know the Infinite because it has not the power of comprehending it. Conversely it is concluded that if knowledge did comprehend the Infinite it would necessarily be infinite itself; but it is admittedly not infinite, therefore it has not the power of knowing the Infinite. Its action is defined just as its content is. Finite knowledge and infinite knowledge yield the same kind of relation as is yielded by the

finite and the Infinite in general. The only difference is
that infinite knowledge is in a relation of stronger repul-
sion towards its opposite than the naked Infinite, and
points more directly to the separation of the two sides
of the antithesis, so that one only remains, namely, finite
knowledge. In this way all relation based on mediation
disappears, every kind of relation, that is, in which the
finite and the Infinite as such, and so, too, the contingent
and the Absolutely-necessary, might have stood to each
other. The form of finite and Infinite is the one which
has come to be most in vogue in connection with this
way of looking at the question. That form is more abstract, and accordingly seems more comprehensive, than
the first-mentioned.

The finite in general and finite knowledge have thus
necessity directly ascribed to them over and above contingency. This necessity takes the form of continuous
advance in the series of causes and effects, conditions and
things conditioned, and was formerly described as external
necessity, and was included in the finite as forming a
part of it. It can be understood, indeed, only in reference to knowledge, but when included in the finite it is
put in contrast with the Infinite without risk of the mis-
apprehension which might arise through the employment
of the category of the Absolutely-necessary.

If, accordingly, we keep to this expression, then the
relation of finitude and infinitude at which we stop short
will be that of their absence of relation, their absence of
reference. We have reached the position that the finite
as a whole and finite knowledge are incapable of grasping
the Infinite in general, as well as the Infinite in the form
it takes as absolute necessity, and also of comprehending
the Infinite by the aid of the conceptions of contingency
and finitude from which finite knowledge starts. Finite
knowledge is accordingly finite just because it is based
on finite conceptions; and the finite, including also finite
knowledge, stands in relation to itself only, does not go

beyond itself, because it is its own Being, and not in any sense the Being of an Other, and, least of all, the Being of its own Other. This is the proposition upon which so much reliance is placed. It supplies no way of passing from the finite to the Infinite, nor from the contingent to the Absolutely-necessary, nor from effects to an absolutely first non-finite cause. A gulf is simply fixed between them.

FOURTEENTH LECTURE

THIS dogmatic view of the absolute separation between the finite and the Infinite has to do with Logic. It involves an opinion regarding the nature of the conceptions of the finite and the Infinite which is treated of in Logic. Here we shall confine ourselves chiefly to those characteristics which we have partly dealt with in the preceding Lectures, but which are also found in our own consciousness. The characteristics which belong to the nature of the conceptions themselves, and which have been exhibited in the *Logic* in their own pure determinateness and in that of their connection, must show themselves and be present in our ordinary consciousness as well.

When, therefore, it is said that the Being of the finite is only its own Being, and is in no sense the Being of an Other, it is thereby declared that there is no possible way of passing from the finite to the Infinite, and therefore no mediation between them, neither in themselves nor in and for knowledge, so that, although the finite is mediated through the Infinite, still the converse is not true, which is just the real point of interest. Appeal is thus already made to the fact that the Spirit of Man rises out of the contingent, the temporal, the finite, to God as representing the Absolutely-necessary, the Eternal, the Infinite, to the fact that the so-called gulf does not exist for Spirit, and that it really accomplishes the transition, and that the heart of Man, spite of the Understanding which asserts the existence of this absolute separation, will not admit that there is any such gulf, but, on the contrary, actually makes the transition from the finite to the Infinite in the act of rising to God.

The ready reply to this, however, is that if you grant
the fact of this rising to God, there is certainly an act of
transition on the part of Spirit, but not of Spirit in itself,
not a transition in the conceptions, or indeed in any
sense of the conceptions themselves; and the reason of
this just is that in the conception as here understood,
the Being of the finite is its own Being and not the
Being of an Other.   When we thus regard finite Being
as standing in relation to itself only, it is merely for itself,
and is not Being for an Other.   It is consequently taken
out of the region of change, is unchangeable and absolute.
This is how the matter stands with these so-called conceptions.   Those, however, who assert the impossibility
of any such transition will not admit that the finite is
absolute, unchangeable, imperishable, and eternal.   If
the error involved in taking the finite as absolute were
merely an error of the Schools, an illogical result the
blame of which is to be put on the Understanding; if it
were to be regarded, in fact, as belonging to those abstractions of an extreme kind with which we have got to do
here, then we might very well ask if an error of this sort
really mattered much since we might certainly regard
these abstractions as of no account compared with the
fulness of spiritual life found in religion, which, moreover, constitutes the great and really living interest of
Spirit.   But that it is exclusively the finite which constitutes the true interest amongst these so-called great
and living interests, is only too evident from the attention paid to religion itself, in connection with which, and as
a consequence of the fundamental principle referred to an
amount of study has been bestowed on the history of the
finite materials of the subject, on the history of external
events and opinions far beyond that given to the infinite
element, which has been confessedly reduced to a minimum.
It is by the employment of thoughts and of these abstract
categories of finite and Infinite that the renunciation of
the knowledge of truth is supposed to be justified, and

as a matter of fact it is in the region of pure thought that all these interests of Spirit have free play, in order that they may there have their real nature decided, for thoughts constitute the really inner substantiality of the concrete reality of Spirit.

But suppose we leave this conception of the Understanding, and its assertion that the Being of the finite is only its own Being, and not the Being of an Other, not transition itself, and take up the further idea which emphasises the element of knowledge. If it is agreed that Spirit does actually make this transition, then the fact of this transition is not a fact of knowledge, but of Spirit in general, and in a definite sense of faith. It has been sufficiently proved that this act of elevation to God, whether seen in feeling or in faith, or however you choose to define the mode of its spiritual existence, takes place in the inmost part of Spirit, in the region of thought. Religion as representing what concerns the innermost part of Man's nature has its centre and the root of its movement in thought. God in His Essence is thought, the act of thought itself, just as the ordinary representation of Him and the shape given to Him in the mind, as well as the form and mode in which religion appears, are defined as feeling, intuition, faith, and so on. Knowledge, however, does nothing beyond bringing this inward element into consciousness on its own account, beyond forming a conception of that pulsation of thought in terms of thought. In this, knowledge may appear one-sided, and it may appear all the more as if feeling, intuition, and faith essentially belonged to religion, and were more closely connected with God than His thinking notion and His notion as expressed in thought; but this inner element is present here, and thought just consists in getting a knowledge of it, and rational knowledge in general just means that we know a thing in its essential determinateness.

To have rational knowledge or cognition, to compre-

hend or grasp in thought, are terms which, like
" immediate " and " faith," belong to present-day culture. They have the authority of a preconceived idea
which has a twofold character. On the one hand, there
is the fact that they are absolutely familiar, and are consequently final categories regarding whose signification
and verification there is no need to inquire further. On
the other hand, there is the fact that the inability of
reason to comprehend and know the True and the Infinite
is something settled quite as much as their general meaning is. The words, to know or cognise, to comprehend
or grasp in thought, have the value of a magical formula.
It never occurs to those under the influence of this preconceived idea to ask what the expressions to know, to
grasp in thought, mean, or to get a clear idea of them,
and yet that would be the sole and only point of importance if we were to say something that was really
pertinent regarding the main question. In any such
investigation it would be evident of itself that knowledge
merely expresses the fact of the transition which Spirit
itself makes, and in so far as knowledge is true knowledge or comprehension it is a consciousness of the necessity which is contained in the transition itself, and is
nothing save the act of forming a conception of this
characteristic which is immanent and present in it.

But if, so far as the fact of the transition from the
finite to the Infinite is concerned, it is replied that this
transition takes place in the spirit, or in faith, feeling,
and the like, such an answer would not be the whole
answer, which rather essentially takes the following form.
Religious belief, or feeling, inner revelation, means that
we have an immediate knowledge of God which is not
reached by mediation. It means that the transition does
not consist of an essential connection between the two
sides, but is made in the form of a leap from one to the
other. What we would call a transition is broken up
in this way into two separate acts which are outwardly

opposed, and follow each other in succession of time only, and are related to each other by being compared or re-called. The finite and the Infinite simply keep in this condition of separation, and this being presupposed, Spirit occupies itself with the finite in a particular way ; and in occupying itself with the Infinite in the way of feeling, faith, knowledge, it performs a separate, immedi-ate and simple action—not an act of transition. Just as the finite and the Infinite are without relation to each other, so, too, the acts of Spirit by which it fills itself with these characteristics, and fills itself either with the one or the other, have no relation to each other. Even if they happen to exist contemporaneously, so that the finite is found in consciousness along with the Infinite, they are merely mixed together. They are two inde-pendent forms of activity which do not enter into any relation of mediation with each other.

The repetition which is involved in this conception of the ordinary division of the finite and the Infinite has already been referred to—that separation by which the finite is put on one side in an independent form, and the Infinite on the other in contrast with it, while the former is not the less asserted in this way to be absolute. This is the dualism which, put in a more definite form, is Manicheism. But even those who maintain the existence of such a relation will not admit that the finite is abso-lute, and yet they cannot escape the conclusion which does not merely flow from the statement referred to, but is just this very statement itself, that the finite has no connection with the Infinite, that there is no possible way of passing from the one to the other, but that the one is absolutely distinct from the other. But even if a relation is conceived of as actually existing, it is, owing to the admitted incompatibility between them, a relation of a merely negative kind. The Infinite is thought of as the True and the only Affirmative, that is, the abstract Affirmative, so that its relation to the finite is that of a force in which the finite is annihilated. The finite, in order to be, must keep out of the way of the Infinite, must flee from it. If it comes into contact with it, it can only perish. As regards the subjective existence of these characteristics with which we are dealing, as represented, namely, by finite and infinite knowledge, we find that the one side, that of infinitude, is the immediate knowledge of Man by God. The entire other side, again, is Man in general; it is he who is the finite about which we are chiefly concerned, and it is just this knowledge of God on his part, whether it is called immediate or not, which is his Being, his finite knowledge, and the transition from it to the Infinite. If, accordingly, the manner in which Spirit deals with the finite, and that in which it deals with the Infinite, are supposed to represent two different forms of activity, then the latter form of activity as representing the elevation of Spirit to God would not be the immanent transition referred to; and when Spirit occupied itself with the finite it would in turn do this in an absolute way, and be entirely confined to the finite as such. This point would allow of being dealt with at great length, but it may be sufficient here to remember that, although the finite is the object and the end dealt with by this side, it can occupy itself with it in a true way, whether in the form of cognition, knowledge, opinion, or in a practical and moral fashion, only in so far as the finite is not taken for itself, but is known, recognised, and its existence affirmed in connection with the relation in which it stands to the Infinite, to the Infinite in it, in so far, in fact, as it is an object and an end in connection with this latter category. It is well enough known what place is given to the religious element both in the case of individuals and even in religions themselves, and how this religious element in the form of devotion, contrition of heart and spirit, and the giving of offerings, comes to be regarded as a matter apart with which we can occupy ourselves and then have done with; while the secular life, the sphere of finitude, exists alongside of it, and gives itself up to the pursuit of its own ends, and is left to its own interests without any influence being exercised upon it by the Infinite, the Eternal, and the True—that is, without there being any passing over into the Infinite within the sphere of the finite, without the finite coming to truth and morality by the mediation of the Infinite, and so, too, without the Infinite being brought into the region of present reality through the mediation of the finite. We do not require here to enter upon the consideration of the lame conclusion that the one who has knowledge, namely, Man, must be absolute in order to comprehend the Absolute, because the same thing applies to faith or immediate knowledge as being also an inner act of comprehension, if not of the absolute Spirit of God, at all events of the Infinite. If this knowledge is so afraid of the concrete element in its object, then this object must at least have some meaning for it. It is really the non-concrete which has few characteristics or none at all, that is the abstract, the negative, what is least of all, the Infinite in short.

But then it is just by means of this miserable abstraction of the Infinite that ordinary thought repels the attempt to comprehend the Infinite, and for the simple reason that the present and actual Man, the human spirit, human reason, is definitely opposed to the Infinite in the form of a fixed abstraction of the finite. Ordinary thought would more readily allow that the human spirit, thought, or reason, can comprehend the Absolutely-necessary, for this latter is thus directly declared and stated to be the negative as opposed to its Other, namely, the contingent, which has on its part a necessity too, external necessity that is. What accordingly can be clearer than that Man, who moreover *is*, that is to say, is something positive or affirmative, cannot comprehend his negative ? And conversely, is it not still more clear that since his Being, his affirmation, is finitude, and therefore negation, it cannot comprehend infinitude, which, as opposed to finitude, is equally negation but in the reverse way, since it is Being, affirmation in contrast with the characteristic attached to finitude? What then can be clearer than that finitude comes to Man from both sides? He can comprehend a few feet of space, yet outside of this volume there lies the infinitude of space. He possesses a span of infinite time, which in the same way shrinks up into a moment as compared with this infinite time, just as his volume of space shrinks up into a point. But considered apart from this outward finitude which characterises him in contrast with those infinite externalities, he is intelligence, is able to perceive, to form ideas, to know, to have cognition of things. The object on which he exercises his intelligence is the world, this aggregate of infinite particular things. How small is the number of these known by individual men—it is not Man who knows but the individual—as compared with the infinite mass which actually exists. In order clearly to realise the paltry nature of human knowledge, we have only to remember a fact which cannot be denied, and which we are accustomed to describe as divine Omniscience, and to put it in the fashion in which it is expressed by the organist in L——, in a funeral sermon reported in "The Courses of Life on Ascending Lines" (Part II., Supplement B.)—to mention once more a work marked by humour of the highest kind : " Neighbour Brise was speaking to me yesterday about the greatness of the good God, and the idea came into my head that the good God knew how to name every sparrow, every goldfinch, every wren, every mite, every midge, just as you call the people in the village, Schmied's Gregory, Briefen's Peter, Heifried's Hans. Just think how the good God can call to every one of these midges which are so like each other that you would swear they were all sisters and brothers—just think of it ! " But as compared with practical finitude the theoretical element

at least appears great and wide ; and yet how thoroughly
we realise what human limitation is, when these aims,
and plans, and wishes, and all that so long as it is in the
mind has no limits, are brought into contact with the
reality for which they are intended. All that wide
extent of practical imagination, all that endeavour, that
aspiration, reveals its narrowness by the very fact that it
is only endeavour, only aspiration. It is this finitude
with which the attempt to form a conception of the Infinite, to comprehend it, is confronted. The critical Understanding which holds by this principle, supposed to be so
convincing, has really not got beyond the stage of culture
occupied by that organist in L——, has in fact not even
attained to it. The organist used the pictorial idea
referred to in the simplicity of his heart, in order to
bring the idea of the greatness of God's love before a
peasant community. The critical Understanding, on the
other hand, employs finite things in order to bring objection against God's love and God's greatness, that is to say,
against God's presence in the human spirit. This Understanding keeps firmly in its mind the midge of finitude,
that proposition already considered—the finite *is,* a proposition the falseness of which is directly evident, for
the finite is something the essential character and nature
of which consist just in this that it passes away, that it
is not, so that it is impossible to think of the finite or
form an idea of it apart from the determination of Not-
Being, which is involved in the thought of what is
transient. Who has got the length of saying, the finite
passes away? If the idea of Now is inserted between
the finite and its passing away, and if in this way a kind
of permanence is supposed to be given to Being—" the
finite passes away, but it is now "—then this Now itself
is something which not only passes away, but has itself
actually passed away, since it is. The very fact that I
have this consciousness of the Now, and have put it into
words, shows that it is no longer Now, but something

different. It lasts, it is true, but not as this particular Now, and Now can only mean this actual Now, in this particular moment, something without length, a mere point. It continues, in fact, only as being the negation of this particular Now, as the negation of the finite, and consequently as the Infinite, the Universal. The Universal is already infinite. That respect for the Infinite which keeps the Understanding from finding the Infinite in every Universal ought to be called a silly respect. The Infinite is lofty and majestic, but to place its grandeur and majesty in that countless swarm of midges, and to find the infinitude of knowledge in the knowledge of those countless midges, that is, of the individual midges, is a proof of the impotence, not of faith, of Spirit, or of reason, but of the Understanding to conceive of the finite as a nullity, and of its Being as something which has equally the value and signification which belong to Not-Being.

Spirit is immortal; it is eternal; and it is immortal and eternal in virtue of the fact that it is infinite, that it has no such spatial finitude as we associate with the body when we speak of it being five feet in height, two feet in breadth and thickness, that it is not the Now of time, that the content of its knowledge does not consist of these countless midges, that its volition and freedom have not to do with the infinite mass of existing obstacles, nor of the aims and activities which such resisting obstacles and hindrances have to encounter. The infinitude of Spirit is its inwardness, in an abstract sense its pure inwardness, and this is its thought, and this abstract thought is a real, present infinitude, while its concrete inwardness consists in the fact that this thought is Spirit.

Thus, after starting with the absolute separation of the two sides, we have come back to their connection, and it makes no difference whether this connection is represented as existing in the subjective or objective sphere. The only question is as to whether it has been correctly conceived of. In so far as it is represented as merely subjective, as a proof only for us, it is of course granted that it is not objective and has not been correctly conceived of in-and-for-itself. But, then, what is incorrect in it is not to be looked for in the fact that there is no such connection at all, that is to say, that there is no such thing as the elevation of Spirit to God.

The real point, therefore, would be the consideration of this connection in its determinateness. The consideration of it in this way is a matter at once of the deepest and most elevated kind, and just because of this it is the most difficult of tasks. You cannot carry it on by means of finite categories; that is, the modes of thought which we employ in ordinary life and in dealing with contingent things, as well as those we are accustomed to in the sciences, don't suffice for it. The latter have their foundation, their logic, in connections which belong to what is finite, such as cause and effect; their laws, their descriptive terms, their modes of arguing, are purely relations belonging to what is conditioned, and which lose their significance in the heights where the Infinite is. They must indeed be employed, but at the same time they have always to be referred back to their proper sphere and have their meaning rectified. The fact of the fellowship of God and Man with each other involves a fellowship of Spirit with Spirit. It involves the most important questions. It is a fellowship, and this very circumstance involves the difficulty of at once maintaining the fact of difference and of defining it in such a way as to preserve the fact of fellowship. That Man knows God implies, in accordance with the essential idea of communion or fellowship, that there is a community of knowledge; that is to say, Man knows God only in so far as God Himself knows Himself in Man. This knowledge is God's self-consciousness, but it is at the same time a knowledge of God on the part of Man, and this knowledge of God by Man is a knowledge of Man by God. The Spirit of Man, whereby he knows God, is simply the Spirit of God Himself. It is at this stage that the questions regarding the freedom of Man, the union of his individual consciousness and knowledge with the knowledge which brings him into fellowship with God, and the knowledge of God in him, come to be discussed. This wealth of relationship which exists between the human spirit and God is not, however, our subject. We have to take up this relationship only in its most abstract aspect, that is to say, in the form of the connection of the finite with the Infinite. However strong the contrast between the poverty of this connection and the wealth of the content referred to may seem, still the logical relation is at the same time also the basis of the movement of that fulness of content.

FIFTEENTH LECTURE

THE connection between these forms of thought referred to which constitutes the entire content of the Proof under discussion, has already been examined in the foregoing Lectures. That this connection does not correspond to the results supposed to be reached in the Proof, is a point to be thoroughly discussed afterwards. The peculiarly speculative aspect of the connection, however, still remains to be considered, and we have here to indicate, without entering upon this logical examination in detail, what characteristic of this connection has reference to this speculative aspect. The moment to which attention has mainly to be directed in reference to this connection, is the fact that it is a transition, that is to say, the point of departure has here the characteristic quality of something negative, has the character of contingent Being, of what is a phenomenon or an appearance only, which has its truth in the Absolutely-necessary, in the truly affirmative element in this latter. As regards, first of all, the former of these characteristics, the negative moment namely, if we are to get a philosophical grasp of it, all that is necessary is that it be not taken as representing mere Nothing. It does not exist in any such abstract form, but, on the contrary, is merely a moment in the contingency of the world. There ought accordingly to be no difficulty in not taking the negative as abstract Nothing. The popular idea of contingency, limitation, finitude, phenomenon, involves the idea of definite Being, of definite existence, but at the same time it substantially involves negation. Ordinary thought is more concrete and true than the Understanding which abstracts, and which when

it hears of a negative too easily makes Nothing out
of it, pure Nothing, Nothing as such, and gives up all
thought of its being in any way connected with existence
in so far as existence is defined as contingent, phenomenal, and so on. Reflective analysis points to the two
moments which exist in a content of this kind—namely,
an affirmative, definite Being, existence as one particular
form of Being; but a moment also which involves the
quality of finality, mortality, limits, and so on, in the
form of negation. Thought, if it is to form a conception
of the contingent, cannot allow these moments to be
separated into a Nothing for itself and a Being for itself.
For they do not exist in this form in the contingent;
on the contrary, it comprises both in itself. They are
therefore not to be taken as existing each by itself in
connection with one another, nor is the contingent to be
taken just as it is, as representing the connection between
them. This then is the speculative determination. It
remains true to the content of ordinary thought or conception, while, on the contrary, this content escapes
abstract thought which asserts the independence of the
two moments. It has resolved into its parts the contingent, which is the object of the Understanding.

The contingent accordingly, as thus defined, represents
what is a contradiction in itself. What thus resolves
itself becomes in consequence just exactly what it became in the hands of the Understanding. But resolution is of two sorts. The resolution effected by the
Understanding results simply in the disappearance of the
object, of the concrete union; while in the other kind of
resolution the object is preserved. Still this preservation
does not help it much, or not at all, for in being thus
preserved it is defined as a contradiction, and contradiction dissolves itself; what contradicts itself is Nothing.
However correct this may be, it is at the same time
incorrect. Contradiction and Nothing are at all events
distinct from one another. Contradiction is concrete, it

at least has a content, it at least contains things which
contradict themselves ; it at least gives expression to them,
it declares what it is a contradiction of: Nothing, on the
contrary, does not express anything at all, it is devoid of
content, it is the absolutely empty.   This concrete quality
of the one and the absolutely abstract quality of the other
constitute a very important difference.   Further, Nothing
is in no sense contradiction.   Nothing does not contradict itself, it is identical with itself ; it accordingly fulfils
perfectly the conditions of the logical proposition that a
thing should not contradict itself—or if this proposition is
expressed thus, Nothing ought to contradict itself, this is
an ought which has no result, for Nothing does not do what
it ought, that is, it does not contradict itself.   If, however, it is put in the way of a thesis thus—Nothing
which exists contradicts itself, then it is plainly correct,
for the subject of this proposition is a Nothing which at
the same time *is*, but Nothing itself as such is merely
simple, the one characteristic which is equivalent to
itself, which does not contradict itself.

Thus, the cancelling or solution of the contradiction
in Nothing, as given by the Understanding, moves *in
vacuo*, or, more accurately, in contradiction itself, which
in virtue of a solution of this kind declares itself in fact
to be still in existence, to be unsolved.   The reason why
the contradiction is still uncancelled is just that the
content, the contingent, is first posited only in its negation in itself, and not yet in the affirmation which must
be contained in this cancelling since it is not abstract
Nothing.   Even the contingent is certainly, to begin with,
as it presents itself to the ordinary thought, an affirmative.   It represents definite Being, existence ; it is the
world, affirmation, Reality, or however you like to term it,
and it is this enough and to spare ; but as such it is not
yet posited in its solution, not given in the explication
of its content and substance, and it is just this content
which is meant to lead to its truth, namely, the Abso-

lutely-necessary. It is the contingent itself in which, as was said, the finitude, the limitation of the world has been indicated in order that it may itself directly point to its solution, that is, in accordance with the negative side already indicated. And further, the analysis or resolution of this contingent which is posited as already resolved in the contradiction, is seen to be the affirmative which is contained in it. This resolution has been already referred to. It was got and adopted from the idea formed by the human mind as representing the transition of Spirit from the contingent to the Absolutely-necessary, which in accordance with this would itself be this very affirmative, the resolution of that first and merely negative resolution. So, too, to indicate the speculative element in this final and most inner point would simply mean to put in a completely connected form the thoughts which are already contained in the conception we are dealing with, namely, in that first resolution. The Understanding which conceived of it merely as contradiction which resolves itself into Nothing, takes up only one of the two moments contained in it, and leaves the other alone.

As a matter of fact the concrete result in its unfolded shape, that is, its speculative form, has been already brought under our notice, and that long ago, namely, in the definition which was given of absolute necessity. In that connection, however, an external kind of reflection and style of argument was employed in reference to the moments which belong to this necessity or from which it results. What we have got to do here is merely to call attention to those moments which are found in what we have seen to be the contradiction which is the resolution of the contingent. In absolute necessity what we found first of all was the moment of mediation, and, to begin with, of mediation through an Other. The analysis of the contingent directly shows that the moments of this mediation are Being in general, or material existence, and

the negation of this, whereby it is degraded to the state
of something which has a semblance of Being, something
which is virtually a nullity. Each moment is not isolated
and taken by itself, but is thought of as attaching to the
one characteristic, namely, to the contingent, and as existing purely in relation to the Other, as having any meaning only in this relation. This one characteristic, which
holds them together, is what mediates them. In it, it is
true, the one exists by means of the other ; but then each
can exist for itself outside of their connection, and each
ought, in fact, to exist for itself, Being for itself and
negation for itself. If, however, we call the former
Being as it appears in the more concrete shape in which
we have it here, namely, as material existence, we practically grant that this material existence is not for itself, is
not absolute or eternal, but is, on the contrary, virtually
a nullity which has indeed a Being, but not an independent Being, a Being-for-self, for it is just this Being
possessed by it which is characterised as something contingent. Since, accordingly, in the case of contingency
each of the two characteristics exists only in relation to
the other, this mediation between them appears to be
contingent itself, to be merely isolated, and to be found
only in this particular place. The unsatisfactory thing
is that the characteristics can be taken for themselves,
that is to say, as they themselves are as such, and as
related only to themselves, and therefore immediately and
thus as not mediated in themselves. Mediation is consequently something which happens to them in a merely
outward way, and is itself contingent ; that is, the peculiar inner necessity of contingency is not demonstrated.

This reflection consequently leads up to the necessity
of the starting-point in itself which we took as something
given, as a starting-point in fact. It leads up not to the
transition from the contingent to the necessary, but to
the transition which is implicitly contained in the contingent itself, to the transition from one of each of the

moments which constitute the contingent, to its Other. This would bring us back to the analysis of the first abstract, logical moments, and it is sufficient here to regard contingency as the act of transition in itself, as its cancelling of itself or annulling of itself, as this is ordinarily conceived of.

In the resolution of contingency just described, there is at the same time indicated the second moment, that of absolute necessity, that is, the moment of mediation with self. The moments of contingency are, to begin with, in a relation of antithesis to each other, and each is posited as mediated by its antithesis or Other. In the unity of the two, however, each is something negated, and their difference is consequently done away with, and although we still speak of one of the two, it is no longer related to something different from it, but to itself; we have thus mediation with self.

The speculative way of looking at this accordingly implies that the contingent is known in itself in so far as it is resolved into its parts, and this resolution at first takes the form of an external analysis of this characteristic. It is, however, not merely this, but is really the resolution of that characteristic in itself. The contingent is by its very nature that which resolves itself, disintegrates itself, it is transition in itself. But, in the second place, this resolution is not the abstraction of Nothing, but is rather affirmation within the resolution, that affirmation which we call absolute necessity. It is thus that we form a philosophical conception of this transition. The result is shown to be immanent in the contingent, *i.e.*, it is the very nature of the contingent to revert back to its truth, and the elevation of our spirit to God—in so far as we have provisionally no further definition of God than the description of Him as Absolute Being, or because we for the present rest satisfied with it—is the course of development followed by this movement of the Thing or true fact. It is this Thing or true fact in-and-for-itself which is the impelling power in us, and which gives the impulse to this movement.

It has been already remarked that for the consciousness to which the determinations of thought do not present themselves in this pure speculative form, and consequently not in their self-solution and self-movement, but which represents them to itself by general ideas, the transition is rendered more easy by the fact that the thing from which we start, namely, the contingent, already means something which resolves itself, which passes over into its Other. In this way the connection between that from which the start is made and the point ultimately reached, is made absolutely clear. This starting-point is consequently the one which is most advantageous for consciousness, and the one which is most in accordance with an end. It is the instinct of thought which implicitly makes this transition, which is the essential fact or Thing, but at the same time this instinct brings it into consciousness in the form of a determination of thought, of such a kind that it appears easy for it to represent it as a general idea merely, that is, in the form of abstract identity. When the world, in fact, is defined as the contingent, this means that reference is made to its Not-Being, while it is hinted that its truth is its Other or antithesis.

The transition is rendered intelligible by the fact that it is not only implicitly contained in the starting-point, but that this latter directly suggests the transition, that is, this characteristic is also posited and is therefore in it. In this way its determinate existence is something given for consciousness, which makes use of ordinary ideas just in so far as it has to do with immediate existence, which is here a determination or quality of thought. Equally intelligible is the result, the Absolutely-necessary; it contains mediation, and it is just this understanding of the connection in general which passes for being the easiest possible, a connection which in a finite way is taken as the connection of the one with an Other, but which, on the other hand, carries its corrective with it in so far as this connection issues in an insufficient end. A connection of this kind, owing to the fact that the law which governs it constantly requires that it should repeat itself in the matter which composes it, always lead up to an Other, that is, to a negative, while the affirmative which reappears in this act of development is simply something which issues from itself, and thus the one as well as the Other finds no rest, and no satisfaction. The Absolutely-necessary, again, since regarded from one point of view it itself produces that connection, is something which can also break off the connection, bring back into itself this going out of itself and secure the final result. The Absolutely-necessary *is, because it is;* thus that Other and the act of going out towards that Other are set aside, and by this unconscious inconsequence satisfaction is secured.

SIXTEENTH LECTURE

THE foregoing Lectures have dealt with the dialectical element, with the absolute fluidity, of the characteristics that enter into the movement which represents this first form of the elevation of the spirit to God. We have now further to deal with the result in itself as defined in accordance with the standpoint adopted.

This result is the absolutely necessary Essence. The meaning of a result is known to consist simply in this, that in it the determination of the mediation, and consequently of the result, has been absorbed in something higher. The mediation was the self-annulling of the mediation. Essence means what is as yet absolutely abstract self-identity; it is not subject, and still less is it Spirit. The entire determination is found in absolute necessity, which in its character as Being is at the same time what has immediate Being, and which, as a matter of fact, implicitly determines itself as subject, but at first in the purely superficial form of something having Being, in the form of the Absolutely-necessary.

The fact that this determination is not adequate to express our idea of God is a defect which we may in the meantime leave alone, inasmuch as it has been already indicated that the other proofs bring with them further and more concrete determinations. There are, however, religious and philosophical systems whose defectiveness consists just in this, that they have not got beyond the characteristic of absolute necessity. The consideration of the more concrete forms in which this principle has embodied itself in religion, belongs to the philosophy of religion and to the history of religion. Regarding the subject in this aspect, it may here be merely remarked that in general those religions which have this determinateness as their basis have, so far as the inner logical development of concrete Spirit is concerned, richer and more varied elements than any which the abstract principle at first brings with it. In the sphere of phenomena and in consciousness the other moments of the Idea in its full and completed form, are superadded in a way which is inconsistent with that abstract principle. It is, however, essential to find out whether these additions in the way of definite form belong merely to imagination, and whether the concrete in its inner nature does not get beyond that abstraction—so that, as in the Oriental and particularly in the Indian mythology, the infinite realm of divine persons who are brought in not only as forces in general, but as self-conscious, willing figures, continues to be devoid of Spirit—or whether, on the other hand, spite of that one necessity, the higher spiritual principle emerges in these persons, and whether, in consequence, spiritual freedom comes to view in their worshippers. Thus in the religion of the Greeks we see absolute necessity in the form of Fate occupying the place of what is supreme and ultimate, and it is only in subordination to this necessity that we have the joyous company of the concrete and living Gods. These are also conceived of as spiritual and conscious, and in the above-mentioned and in other mythologies are multiplied so as to make a still larger crowd of heroes, nymphs of the sea, of the rivers, and so on, muses, fauns, &c., and are connected with the ordinary external life of the world and its contingent things, partly as chorus and accompaniment in the form of a further particularisation of one of the divine supreme deities, partly as figures of minor importance. Here necessity constitutes the abstract force which is above all the particular spiritual, moral, and natural forces. These latter, however, partly possess the character of non-spiritual, merely natural force, which remains completely under the power of necessity, while their personalities are merely personifications; and yet, although they may not exactly deserve to be called persons, they also partly contain the higher characteristic of subjective inherent freedom. In this way they occupy a position above that of their mistress, namely, necessity, to which only the limited element in this deeper principle is subordinate, a principle which has elsewhere to await its purification from this finitude in the region of which it at first appears, and has to manifest itself independently in its infinite freedom.

The logical working out of the category of absolute necessity is to be looked for in systems which start from abstract thoughts. This application in detail of the category has reference to the relation between this principle and the manifoldness of the natural and spiritual world. If absolute necessity thus forms the basis as representing what is alone true and truly real, in what relation do material things stand to it? These things are not only natural things, but also include Spirit, the spiritual individuality with all its conceptions, interests, and aims. This relation has, however, been already defined in connection with the principle referred to. They are contingent things. Further, they are distinct from absolute necessity itself; but they have no independent Being as against it, and neither has it, consequently, as against them. There is only one Being, and this belongs to necessity, and things by their very nature form part of it. What we have defined as absolute necessity has to be more definitely hypostatised in the form of universal Being or Substance, while, in its character as a result, it is a self-mediated unity in virtue of the abrogation of mediation. It is thus simple Being, and is what alone represents the subsisting element of things. When our attention was previously called to necessity in the form of Greek Fate, it was thought of as characterless or indeterminate force; but Being itself has already come down from the abstraction referred to, to the level of the things

above which it ought to be. Still, if Essence or Substance itself were merely an abstraction, things would
have an independent existence of concrete individuality
outside of it. It must at the same time be characterised
as the force of these things, the negative principle which
makes its validity felt in them, and by means of which
they represent what is perishing and transitory and has
merely a phenomenal existence. We have seen how this
negative element represents the peculiar nature of contingent things. They have thus this force within themselves, and do not represent manifestation in general, but
the manifestation of necessity. This necessity contains
things, or rather it contains them in their stage of mediation. It is not, however, mediated by something other
than itself, but it is the direct mediation of itself with
itself. It is the variable element or alternation of its
absolute unity whereby it determines itself as mediation,
that is, as external necessity, a relation of an Other to
an Other, that is, whereby it spreads itself out into infinite multiplicity, into the absolutely conditioned world,
but in such a way that it degrades external mediation,
the contingent world to the condition of a world of
appearance, and in this nullity comes into harmony with
itself, posits itself as equal to itself, and does this in the
world as representing its force. Everything is thus included in it, and it is immediately present in everything.
It is the Being, as it also is the changeable and variable
element of the world.

The determination of necessity as unfolded in the
philosophical conception of it, is, speaking generally, the
standpoint which we are in the habit of calling Pantheism, and sometimes in a more developed and definite form,
sometimes in a more superficial form, it is what expresses
the relation indicated. The very fact of the interest
which this name has again awakened in modern times,
and still more the interest of the principle itself, render
it necessary that we should direct our attention to it.

The misunderstanding which prevails with regard to Pantheism ought not to be allowed to pass without being mentioned and corrected; and after that we shall have to consider in this connection the place of the principle in the higher totality, in the true Idea of God. Since at a previous stage the consideration of the religious form taken by the principle was dispensed with, we may, by way of bringing a picture of it before the mind, take the Hindu religion as representing Pantheism in its most developed form. With this development there is bound up at the same time the fact that the absolute Substance, the sole and only One, is represented in the form of thought as distinguished from the accidental world, as existing. Religion in itself essentially involves the relation of Man to God, and still less when it appears in the form of Pantheism does it leave the one Essence in that condition of objectivity in which metaphysic imagines it has left it as an object while preserving its special character. We have to call attention first of all to the remarkable character of this attempt to bring Substance under the conditions of subjectivity. Self-conscious thought does not only make that abstraction of Substance, but is the very act of abstraction itself. It is just that simple unity as existing for itself which is called Substance. This thought is thus conceived of as the force which creates and preserves the world, and which also alters and changes its existence as this appears in particular forms. This thought is termed Brāhma. It exists as the natural self-consciousness of the Brahmans, and as the self-consciousness of others who put under restraint and kill their consciousness in its manifold forms, their sensations, their material and spiritual interests, and all the active life connected with them, and reduce it to the perfect simplicity and emptiness of that substantial unity. Thus this thought, this abstraction of men in themselves, is held to be the force of the world. The universal force takes particular forms in gods, who are nevertheless transitory and temporary; or, what comes to the same thing, all life, whether in the form of spiritual or natural individuality, is torn away from the finitude of its perfectly conditioned connection—all understanding in this latter being destroyed—and is elevated into the form of divine existence.

As we were reminded, the principle of individualisation appears in this Pantheism in its several religious shapes, in a form inconsistent with the force of substantial unity. Individuality, it is true, does not exactly get the length of being personality, but the force unfolds itself in a sufficiently wild way as an illogical transition into its opposite. We find ourselves in a region of unbridled madness in which the present in its most ordinary form is directly elevated to the rank of something divine, and Substance is conceived of as existing in finite shapes, while the shapes assumed have a volatile character and directly melt away.

The Oriental theory of the universe is in general represented by this idea of sublimity which puts all individualisation into special shapes, and infinitely extends all particular forms of existence and particular interests. It beholds the One in all things, and consequently clothes this purely abstract One in all the glory and splendour of the natural and spiritual universe. The souls of the Eastern Poets dive into this ocean and drown in it all the necessities, the aims, the cares of this petty circumscribed life, and revel in the enjoyment of this freedom, upon which they lavish by way of ornament and adornment all the beauty of the world.

It will be already clear from this picture, and this is a point upon which I have elsewhere explained my views, that the expression Pantheism, or rather the German expression in which it appears in a somewhat transposed form, that God is the One and All, or everything—τὸ ἐν καὶ πᾶν—leads to the false idea that in pantheistic religion or in philosophy, everything (*Alles*),

that is, every existing thing in its finitude and particularity, is held to be possessed of Being as God or as
a god, and that the finite is deified as having Being.
It could only be a narrow and ordinary or rather a
scholastic kind of mind which would expect this to be
the case, and which, being perfectly unconcerned about
what actually is, sticks to one category, and to the category, in fact, of finite particularisation, and accordingly
conceives of the manifoldness which it finds mentioned,
as a permanent, existing, substantial particularisation.
There can be no mistake but that the essential and
Christian definition of freedom or individuality, which as
free is infinite in itself and is personality, has misled the
Understanding into conceiving of the particularisation of
finitude under the category of an existing unchangeable
atom, and into overlooking the moment of the negative
which is involved in force and in the general system to
which it belongs. It imagines Pantheism as saying that
all, that is, all things in their existing isolation, are God,
since it takes the $\pi \hat{a} \nu$ in this definite category as referring
to all and every individual thing. Such an absurd idea
has never come into anybody's head outside of the ranks
of these opponents of Pantheism. This latter represents
a view which is, on the contrary, quite the opposite of
that which they associate with it. The finite, the contingent is *not* something which subsists for itself. In
the affirmative sense it is only a manifestation, a revelation of the One, only an appearance of it which is itself
merely contingency. The fact is that it is the negative
aspect, the disappearance in the one force, the ideality
of what has Being as a momentary standpoint in the
force, which is the predominant aspect. In opposition to
this the Understanding holds that these things exist for
themselves and have their essence in themselves, and are
thus in and in accordance with this finite essentiality,
supposed to be divine or even to be God. They cannot
free themselves from the absoluteness of their finitude,

and this finitude is not thought of as something which disappears and is absorbed in this unity with the Divine, but is still preserved by them in it as existing. On the other hand, since the finite is, as they say, robbed of its infinitude by Pantheism, the finite has in consequence no longer any Being at all.

It is preferable to use the expression, " the philosophical systems of substantiality," and not to speak of systems of Pantheism, because of the false idea associated with this term. We may take the Eleatic system in general as representing these in ancient times, and the Spinozistic as their modern representative. These systems of substantiality are, as we have seen, more logical than the religions corresponding to them, since they keep within the sphere of metaphysical abstraction. The one aspect of the defect which attaches to them is represented by the one-sidedness referred to as existing in the idea formed by the Understanding of the course taken by the spirit's elevation to God. That is to say, they start from actual existence, treat it as a nullity, and recognise the Absolute One as the truth of this existence. They start with a presupposition, they negate it in the absolute unity, but they don't get out of this unity back to the presupposition. They don't think of the world, which is considered to be merely comprised within an abstraction of contingency, of the many and so on, as produced out of Substance. Everything passes into this unity as into a kind of eternal night, while this unity is not characterised as a principle which moves itself to its manifestation, or produces it, " as the unmoved which moves," according to the profound expression of Aristotle.

(*a.*) In these systems the Absolute, or God, is defined as the One, Being, the Being in all existence, the absolute Substance, the Essence which is necessary not through an Other, but in-and-for-itself, the *Causa Sui*, the cause of itself, and consequently its own effect, that is, the mediation which cancels itself. The unity implied in this latter characteristic belongs to an infinitely deeper and more developed form of thought than the abstract unity of Being, or the One. This conception has been sufficiently explained. *Causa Sui* is a very striking expression for that unity, and we may accordingly give some further attention to its elucidation. The relation of cause and effect belongs to the moment of mediation through an Other already referred to, and which we saw in necessity, and is its definite form. Anything is completely mediated by an Other in so far as this Other is its cause. This is the original thing or fact as absolutely immediate and independent; the effect, on the other hand, is what is posited merely, dependent, and so forth. In the antithesis of Being and Nothing, One and Many, and so on, the characteristics are found existing in such a way as to imply that they are matched with each other in their relation, and yet that they have, as unrelated, a valid independent existence besides. The Positive, the Whole, and so on, is, it is true, related to the Negative, to the parts, and this relation forms part of its essential meaning; but the Positive as well as the Negative, the Whole, the parts, and so on, have in addition an independent existence outside of this relation. But cause and effect have a meaning simply and solely in virtue of their relation. The meaning of the cause does not extend beyond the fact that it has an effect. The stone which falls has the effect of producing an impression on the object upon which it falls. Looked at apart from this effect which it has as a heavy body, it is physically separate and distinct from other equally heavy bodies. Or, to put it otherwise, since it is a cause while it continues to produce this impression, if we, for example, imagine its effect to be transitory, then when it strikes against another body it ceases so far to be a cause, and outside of this relation it is just a stone, which it was before. This idea haunts the popular mind chiefly in so far as it characterises the thing as the original fact and as continuing to exist outside of that effect it produces. Apart from that effect which it has produced, the stone is undoubtedly a stone, only it is not a cause. It is a cause only in connection with its effect, or, to introduce the note of time, during its effect.

Cause and effect are thus, speaking generally, inseparable. Each has meaning and existence only in so far as it stands in this relation to the other, and yet they are supposed to be absolutely different. We cling with equal firmness to the idea that the cause is not the effect and the effect is not the cause, and the Understanding holds obstinately to this fact of the independent being of these two categories and of the absence of relation between them.

When, however, we have come to see that the cause is inseparable from the effect, and that it has any meaning only as being in the latter, then it follows that the cause itself is mediated by the effect; it is only in and through the effect that it is cause. This, however, means nothing more than that the cause is the cause of itself, and not of an Other. For this which is supposed to be an Other is of such a kind that the cause is first a cause in it, and therefore in it simply reaches itself, and in it affects only itself.

Jacobi has some reflections on this Spinozistic category, the *Causa Sui* ("Letters on the Doctrine of Spinoza," 2nd ed., p. 416), and I refer to his criticisms upon it just because they afford us an example of how Jacobi, the pioneer of the party of immediate knowledge or faith, who is so much given to rejecting the Understanding in his consideration of thought, does not get beyond the mere Understanding. I pass over what he says in the passage referred to regarding the distinction between the category of ground and consequence, and that of cause and effect, and the fact that in his later controversial essays he imagines he has found in this difference a true description and definition of the nature of God. I merely indicate the more immediate conclusion referred to by him, namely, that from the interchange of the two "it may be successfully inferred that things can originate without originating, and alter without undergoing alteration, and can be before and after each other without being before and after." Such conclusions are too absurd to require any further comment. The contradiction to which the Understanding reduces a principle is an ultimate one; it is simply the limit of the horizon of thought beyond which it is not possible to go, but in presence of which we must turn back. We have, however, seen how the solution of this contradiction is reached, and we shall apply it to the contradiction in the form in which it here appears and is here stated, or rather we shall simply briefly indicate the estimate to be formed of the above assertion. The conclusion referred to, that things may originate without originating, and alter without undergoing alteration, is manifestly absurd. We can see that it expresses the idea of self-mediation through an Other, of mediation as self-annulling mediation, but likewise that this mediation is directly abandoned. The abstract expression, Things, does its part in bringing the finite before the mind. The finite is a form of limited Being to which only one of two opposite qualities attaches, and which does not remain with itself in the Other, but simply perishes. But then the Infinite is this mediation with self through the Other, and without repeating the exposition of this conception, we may take an example from the sphere of natural things without going at all to that of spiritual existence, namely, life as a whole. What is well known to us as its self-preservation is "successfully" expressed in terms of thought as the infinite relation in virtue of which the living individual of whose process of self-preservation we alone speak here, without paying attention to its other characteristics, continually produces itself in its existence. This existence is not identical Being, Being in a state of repose, but, on the contrary, represents

origination, alteration, mediation with an Other, though
it is a mediation which returns to itself.   The living
force of what has life consists in making life originate,
and the living already is; and so we may indeed say—
though it is certainly a bold expression—that such and
such a thing originates without originating.   It undergoes alteration; every pulsation is an alteration not only
in all the pulse-veins, but in all the parts of its entire
constitution.   In all this change it remains the same
individual, and it remains such only in so far as it is
this inherently self-altering active force.   We may thus
say of it that it alters without undergoing alteration,
and finally—though we cannot certainly say that of the
things—that it previously exists without existing previously, just as we have seen with regard to the cause
that it exists previously, is the original cause, while at
the same time previously, before its effect, it is not a
cause, and so on.   It is, however, tedious, and would
even be an endless task to follow up and arrange the
expressions in which the Understanding presents its finite
categories and seeks to give them the character of something permanent.

This annihilation of the category of causality as used
by the Understanding takes place in connection with
the conception which is expressed by the term *Causa Sui.*
Jacobi, without recognising in it this negation of the
finite relation, the speculative element, that is, despatches
it simply in a psychological, or, if you like, in a prag-
matical fashion.   He declares that "it is difficult to
conclude from the apodictic proposition, everything *must*
have a cause, that it is possible everything *may not*
have a cause.   Therefore it is that the *Causa Sui* has
been invented."   It is certainly difficult for the Understanding not only to have to abandon its apodictic proposition, but to have to assume another possibility
which, moreover, has a wrong look in connection with
the expression referred to.   But it is not hard for

reason, which, on the contrary, in its character as the free, and especially as the religious human spirit, abandons such a finite relation as this of mediation with an Other, and knows how to solve in thought the contradiction which comes to consciousness in thought.

Dialectic development, such as has been here given, does not, however, belong to the systems of simple substantiality,~to pantheistic systems. They do not get beyond Being or Substance, a form which we shall take up later on. This category, taken in itself, is the basis of all religions and philosophies. In all these God is Absolute Being, an Essence, which exists absolutely in-and-for-itself, and does not exist through an Other, but represents independence pure and simple.

(b.) Categories like these, which are of so abstract a character, do not apply very widely, and are very unsatisfactory. Aristotle ("Metaphysics," i. 5) says of Xenophanes, that "he was the first to unify (ἐνίσας), he did not advance anything of a definite nature, and so gazing into the whole Heavens—into space (ins Blaue), as we say—said, the One is God." The Eleatics, who followed him, showed more definitely that the many and the characteristics which rest on multiplicity lead to contradiction and resolve themselves into nothing; and Spinoza, in particular, showed that all that is finite disappears in the unity of Substance, and thus there is no longer left any further, concrete, fruitful determination for this Substance itself. Development has to do only with the form of the starting-points which finds itself in presence of subjective reflection, and with that of its dialectic, by means of which it brings back into that universality the particular and finite, which appear in an independent way. It is true that in Parmenides this One is defined as thought, or that which thinks, what has Being; and so, too, in Spinoza, Substance is defined as the unity of Being (of extension) and thought. Only, one cannot therefore say that this Being or Substance is hereby posited as something which thinks, that is, as activity which determines itself in itself. On the contrary, the unity of Being and thought continues to be conceived of as the One, the Unmoved, the Stolid. There is an outward distinction into attributes and modes, movement and will, a distinction effected by the Understanding. The One is not unfolded as self-developing necessity, not, in accordance with what is indicated by its notion, as the process which mediates the necessity with itself and within itself. If the principle of movement is here wanting, it is certainly found in more concrete principles in the flux of Heraclitus, in number too, and so on; but, on the one hand, the unity of Being, the divine self-equality, is not preserved, and, on the other, a principle of this kind stands in exactly the same relation to the ordinary existing world as the Being, the One, or the Substance referred to.

(c.) Besides this One there is, however, the actual contingent world, Being with the quality of the Negative, the realm of limitations and things finite, and in this connection it makes no difference whether this realm is conceived of as a realm of external existence, of semblance or illusion, or, according to the definition of superficial Idealism, as a merely subjective world, a world of consciousness. This manifoldness with its infinite developments is, to begin with, separated from that Substance, and we have to find out in what relation it stands to this One. On the one hand, this definite existence of the world is merely taken for granted. Spinoza, whose system is the most fully developed, starts from definitions, that is, from the actual characteristics of thought and of ordinary ideas in general. The starting-points of consciousness are presupposed. On the other hand, the Understanding forms this accidental world into a system in accordance with the relations or categories of external necessity. Parmenides gives the beginnings of a system of the phenomenal world at the head of which the goddess Necessity is placed. Spinoza did not construct any philosophy of Nature, but treated of the other part of concrete philosophy, namely, a system of ethics. This system of ethics was from one point of view to be logically connected with the principle of absolute Substance, at least in a general way, because Man's highest characteristic, his tendency to seek after God, is the pure love of God, according to Spinoza's expression, *sub specie æterni.* Only, the principles which underlie his philosophical treatment of the subject, the content, the starting-points, have no connection with the Substance itself. All systematic detailed treatment of the phenomenal world, however logical it may be in itself, when it follows the ordinary procedure, and starts with what is perceived by the senses, becomes an ordinary science in which what is recognised as the Absolute itself, the One, Substance, is not supposed to be living, is not the moving principle, the method, for it is devoid of definite character. There is nothing left of it for the phenomenal world, unless that this natural and spiritual world in general is wholly abstract, is a phenomenal world, a world of appearance, or else that the Being of the world in its affirmative form is Being, the One, Substance, while the particularisation in virtue of which Being is a world, evolution, emanation, is a falling of Substance out of itself into finitude, which is an absolutely inconceivable mode of existence. It is further implied that in Substance itself there is no principle involving the characteristic of being creative; and thirdly, that it is likewise abstract force, the positing of finitude as something negative, the disappearance of the finite.

(Concluded 19th August 1829.)

AMPLIFICATION OF THE TELEOLOGICAL PROOF IN THE LECTURES ON THE PHILOSOPHY OF RELIGION DELIVERED IN THE SUMMER OF 1831.

KANT has criticised this proof too, as well as the other proofs of the existence of God, and it was chiefly owing to him that they were discredited, so that it is now scarcely considered worth while to look at them closely. And yet Kant says of this proof that it deserves to be always regarded with respect. When, however, he adds that the teleological proof is the oldest, he is wrong. The first determination of God is that of force or power, and the next in order is that of wisdom. This is the proof we meet with first amongst the Greeks also, and it is stated by Socrates (Xenophon, *Memor.*, at the end of Book First). Socrates takes conformity to an end, especially in the form of the Good, as his fundamental principle. The reason why he is in prison, he declares, is that the Athenians consider it to be good. This proof accordingly coincides historically with the development of freedom.

We have already considered the transition from the religion of power to the religion of spirituality in general. We have already had in the intermediate stages also the very same mediation which we recognise as present in the religion of beauty, but broken up and as yet devoid of any spiritual character. But since with that transition to the religion of spirituality there is added another and essential determination, we have first to bring out its meaning in an abstract way, and direct attention to it.

Here we have the determination of freedom as such, of
an activity as freedom, a working in accordance with
freedom, no longer an unhindered working in accordance
with power, but a working in accordance with ends.
Freedom is self-determination, and what is active has
self-determination implicitly as its end in so far as it
spontaneously determines itself within itself. Power is
simply the act of self-projection, and implies that there
is an unreconciled element in what is projected; and
though this is implicitly an image or picture of the
power, still it is not expressly felt in consciousness that
what creates simply preserves and produces itself in its
creation in suchwise that the characteristics of the
Divine itself appear in the creature. God is here conceived of as possessed of the characteristic of wisdom, of
activity in accordance with an end. Power is good and
righteous, but action in accordance with an end is what
first constitutes this characteristic of rationality, according
to which nothing comes out of the act but what had been
already previously determined upon, that is, this identity
of the creating power with itself.

The difference which exists among the proofs of the
existence of God consists simply in the difference of
their determination. There is in them a mediation, a
starting-point, and a point at which we arrive. In the
Teleological and Physico-theological Proofs both points
possess in common the characteristic of conformity to an
end. We start from a form of Being which is actually
characterised as in conformity with an end, and what is
thereby mediated is the idea of God as positing and
working out an end. Being, considered as the immediate
from which we start in the Cosmological Proof, is, to
begin with, a manifold, contingent Being. In accordance
with this, God is defined as necessity which has Being
in-and-for-itself, the force or power which is above the
contingent. The higher determination accordingly is,
that conformity to an end is present in Being. The

rational element already finds expression in the end in the form of a free self-determination and carrying out of this content, so that this content which at first in its character as an end is inward, is realised, and the reality corresponds to the notion or end.

A thing is good in so far as it fulfils its destiny or end, and this means that the reality is adequate to the notion or destined character. In the world we perceive a harmonious working of external things, of things which exist in a relation of indifference to each other, which come into existence accidentally so far as other things are concerned, and have no essential reference to one another. Still, although things thus exist apart from each other, there is evidence of a unity in virtue of which there is an absolute conformity amongst them. Kant states this in a detailed way, as follows. The present world reveals to us an inexhaustible scene of manifold life, of order, conformity to ends, and so on. This determination in accordance with an end is seen specially in what has life, both as it is in itself and in its relation to things outside of it. Man, the animal, is something inherently manifold, has certain members, entrails, &c., and although these appear to exist alongside of each other, still the general determination in accordance with an end is present through them all and maintains them. The one exists only through the other and for the other, and all the members and component parts of men are simply means for the self-preservation of the individual which is here the end. Man, all that has life in fact, has many needs : air, nourishment, light, &c., are necessary for his sustenance. All this actually exists on its own account, and the capacity of making it minister to an end is external to it. Animals, flesh, air, and so on, which are required by Man, do not in themselves declare that they are ends, and yet the one is simply a means for the other. There is here an inner connection which is necessary, but which does not exist as such. This inner connection is not

made by the objects themselves, but is produced by something else, as these things themselves are. The conformity
to an end does not produce itself spontaneously; the
active working in accordance with an end is outside of
the things, and this harmony which implicitly exists and
posits itself, is the force which presides over these objects,
which destines them to stand to each other in the relation
of things whose existence is determined by an end. The
world is thus no longer an aggregate of contingent things,
but a collection of relations in conformity with an end,
which, however, attach themselves to things from without.
This relation of ends must have a cause, a cause full of
power and wisdom.

This activity in accordance with an end, this cause, is
God.

Kant remarks that this proof is the clearest of all, and
can be understood by the ordinary man. It is owing to it
that Nature first acquires an interest; it gives life to the
knowledge of Nature, just as it has its origin in Nature.
This is in a general form the Teleological Proof.

Kant's criticism is accordingly as follows. This proof,
he says, is defective above all, because it takes into consideration merely the form of things. Reference to an
end applies only to the determination of form. Each
thing preserves itself, and is therefore not merely a
means for others, but is an end itself. The quality in
virtue of which a thing can be a means has reference to
its form merely, and not to its matter. The conclusion,
therefore, does not carry us further than the fact, that
there is a forming cause; but we do not prove by this
that matter also has been produced by it. The proof,
says Kant, does not therefore adequately express the idea
of God as the creator of matter and not merely of form.

Form contains the characteristics which are mutually
related; but matter is to be thought of as without form,
and consequently as without relation. This proof therefore stops short at a demiurge, a constructor of matter,

and does not get the length of a creator. So far as this criticism is concerned, we may undoubtedly say that all relation is form, and this implies that form is separated from matter. We can see that God's activity would in this way be a finite one. When *we* produce anything technical we must take the material for it from the outside. Activity is thus limited and finite. Matter is thus thought of as permanently existing for itself, as eternal. That, in virtue of which things are brought into connection with each other, represents the qualities, the form, not the permanent existence of things as such. The subsistence or permanent existence of things is their matter. It is, to begin with, undoubtedly correct that the relations of things are included within their form ; but the question is, Is this distinction, this separation between form and matter admissible, and can we thus put each specially by itself ? It has been shown, on the contrary, in the *Logic* (*Encyclop. Phil.*, § 129), that formless matter is a nonentity, a pure abstraction of the Understanding, which we may certainly construct, but which ought not to be given out to be anything true. The matter which is opposed to God as something unalterable is simply a product of reflection, or, to put it otherwise, this identity of formlessness, this continuous unity of matter is itself one of the specific qualities of form. We must therefore recognise the truth that matter which is thus placed on one side by itself, belongs itself to the other side, to form. But then the form is also identical with itself, relates itself to itself, and in virtue of this has just the very quality which is distinguished from it as matter. The activity of God Himself, His simple unity with Himself, the form, is matter. This remaining equal to self, this subsistence is present in the form in such a way that the latter relates itself to itself, and that is its subsistence, which is just what matter is. Thus the one does not exist apart from the other ; on the contrary, they are both the same.

Kant goes on to say, further, that the syllogism starts from the fact of the order and conformity to an end observable in the world. We find there arrangements in accordance with an end. It is this reference of things to an end, not found in the things themselves, which accordingly serves for the starting-point. We have in this way a third thing, a cause, posited. From the fact of arrangement in accordance with an end, we reason to the existence of its author, who has established the teleology of the relations. We cannot therefore infer the existence of anything more than what, so far as content is concerned, is actually given in presently existing things, and is in conformity with the starting-point. The teleological arrangement strikes us as wonderfully grand, as one of supreme excellence and wisdom ; but a wisdom which is very great and worthy of admiration is not yet absolute wisdom. It is an extraordinary power which is recognised as present here, but it is not yet Almighty Power. This, says Kant, is a leap which we are not justified in taking, and so we take refuge in the Ontological Proof, and this starts from the conception of the most real Essence. The mere sense-perception, however, from which we start in the Teleological Proof, does not bring us so far as this totality. It must certainly be granted that the starting-point has a smaller content than what we arrive at. In the world there is merely relative and not absolute wisdom. We must look at this more closely. We have here a syllogism. We reason from the one to the other. We start with the peculiar constitution of the world, and from this go on to conclude the existence of an active force, of something that binds together things which exist apart from each other ; this represents their inner nature, their potentiality, and is not present in them in an immediate way. The form of the reasoning process here produces the false impression that God has a basis from which we start. God appears as something conditioned. The arrangement of things in accordance with an end is the condition, and the existence of God is apparently asserted to be something mediated or conditioned. This is an objection upon which Jacobi laid special stress. We try, he says, to reach the unconditioned through the conditions. But, as we have already seen, this merely seems to be the case, and this false impression disappears of itself when we reach the real meaning of the result. So far as this meaning is concerned, it will be allowed that the process is merely the course followed by subjective knowledge. This mediation does not attach to God Himself. He is certainly the Unconditioned, infinite activity which determines itself in accordance with ends, and which has arranged the world on a teleological plan. We do not imagine, when we speak of that process of knowledge, that these conditions from which we start precede that infinite activity. On the contrary, this represents the process of subjective knowledge only, and the result we reach is that it is God who has established these teleological arrangements, and that therefore they represent something established in the first instance by Him, and are not to be regarded as something fundamental. The ground or principle from which we start disappears in what is characterised as the true principle. This is the meaning of the conclusion, that what conditions is itself in turn explained to be the conditioned. The result declares that to posit as the foundation what is itself conditioned would be to introduce a defective element. This procedure accordingly, both actually and as regards its end, is not merely subjective, not something which goes on merely in thought; on the contrary, this defective side is itself removed by means of the result. The objective thus asserts its presence in this form of knowledge. There is not only an affirmative transition here, but there is also a negative moment in it, which is not, however, posited in the form of the syllogism. There is therefore a mediation which is the negation of the first immediacy. The course followed by

Spirit is, it is true, a transition to the activity which is in-and-for-itself and posits ends, but, it is involved in the course thus followed, that the actual existence of this teleological arrangement is not held to represent Being in-and-for-itself. This is found only in reason, the activity of eternal reason. That other Being is not true Being, but only an appearance or semblance of this activity.

In dealing with the determination of ends, we must further distinguish between Form and Content. If we consider form pure and simple, we have Being in accordance with an end which is finite, and, so far as form is concerned, its finitude consists in the fact that the end and means, or the material in which the end is realised, are different. This is finitude. We thus use a certain material in order to carry out our ends, since the activity and the material are different. The finitude of form is what constitutes the finitude of Being in accordance with an end. The truth of this relation, however, is not anything of this kind. On the contrary, the truth is in the teleological activity which is means and matter in itself, a teleological activity which accomplishes its ends through itself. This is what is meant by the infinite activity of the end. The end accomplishes itself, realises itself through its own activity, and thus comes into harmony with itself in the process of realising itself. The finitude of the end consists, as we saw, in the separableness of means and material. Viewed thus, the end represents what is as yet a technical mode of action. The truth of the determination of the end consists in the fact that the end has within itself its means, as also the material in which it realises itself. Regarded in this aspect, the end is true so far as the form is concerned, for objective truth consists simply in the correspondence between the notion and reality. The end is true only when what uses the means, and the means, as well as the reality, are identical with the end. The end thus presents itself as something which possesses reality in itself, and is not something subjective, one-sided, the moments of which exist outside of it. This is the truth of the end, while the teleological relation seen in finitude represents, on the contrary, something untrue. It is necessary to remark here that teleological activity as representing a relation thus defined in accordance with its truth, exists in the form of something higher, which is, however, at the same time present, and which we can certainly speak of as the Infinite, since it is a teleological activity which has both material and means in itself. Regarded from another point of view, however, it is finite as well. Teleological determination in this its true form, which is the form we require it to have, is found actually existing, though only in one of its aspects, in what has life, in what is organic. Life as the subject is the soul. This latter is the end, that is, it posits itself, realises itself, and thus the product is the same as the thing that produces. What has life is, however, an organism; the organs are the means. The living soul has a body in itself, and it is only in union with this that it constitutes a whole, something real. The organs are the means of life, and these very means, the organs themselves, are also the element in which life realises and maintains itself, they are material also. This is self-preservation. What has life preserves itself; it is beginning and end; the product is at the same time what begins. The living as such is constantly in a state of activity. The feeling of need is the beginning of activity, and impels to the satisfaction of the need, and this satisfaction, again, is the beginning of a new need. The living exists only in so far as it is constantly a product. This gives us the truth of the end so far as form is concerned. The organs of the living being are means, but they are equally the end; in exercising their activity they produce themselves only. Each organ maintains the other, and in this way maintains itself. This activity constitutes an end, a soul, which is present in every point of the organism. Every part of

the body experiences sensation; the soul is in it. Here
we have teleological activity in its true form. But the
living subject is also something thoroughly finite. The
teleological activity presents here the character of something which is formally true, but which is not complete.
The living being produces itself; it has the material of
production in itself. Each organ excretes animal lymph
which is made use of by other organs in order to repro-
duce themselves. The living being has the material in
itself, only this is merely an abstract process. Finitude
shows itself in this, that while the organs draw their
nourishment from themselves they employ material for
this taken from the outside. Everything organic is related to inorganic Nature, which has a definite independent existence. Regarded in one aspect, the organism is
infinite since it represents a circle of pure return into
self; but it is at the same time in a state of tension relatively to external inorganic Nature, and has its needs.
Here the means come from the outside. Man requires
air, light, water; he also feeds on other living things, on
animals which he in this way reduces to the state of inorganic Nature, to means. It is this relation particularly
which leads to the idea of a higher unity representing
that harmony in which the means correspond to the end.
This harmony is not found in the subject itself, and yet
it has in it the harmony which constitutes organic life,
as we have seen. The whole construction of the organs,
of the nerve and blood system, of the entrails, lungs,
liver, stomach, and so on, presents a remarkable agreement. But does not this harmony itself demand something else outside of the subject? We may let this
question alone at present; for if we get a grip of the
notion of organism such as has been given, then this
development of teleological determination is itself a necessary consequence of the living nature of the subject in
general. If we do not get a grip of that notion, then
the living being will not be the concrete unity referred

to. In order to understand what life is, recourse is accordingly had to external mechanical modes of conception as illustrated by the action of the blood, and to chemical conceptions as seen in analysis of foods. It is not, however, possible by such processes to discover what life itself is. It is necessary to suppose the existence of some third thing which has brought these processes into existence. As a matter of fact, however, it is just the subject which is this unity, this harmony of the organism. Still this unity involves the relation of the living subject to external Nature, which is thought of as having a merely indifferent and accidental connection with the subject.

The conditions involved in this relation do not form the sole basis of the development of what has life ; still, if the living being did not find these conditions ready to hand, it could not possibly exist. The observation of this fact directly produces the feeling that there must exist something higher which has introduced this harmony. It at once awakens sympathetic attention and admiration in men. Every animal has its own narrow range of means of sustenance, and indeed many animals are limited to a single source of sustenance, human nature having in this respect also the most general character. This fact accordingly, that there exists for every animal this outward particular condition, rouses in Man that feeling of astonishment which passes over into a sense of exalted reverence for that third something which has brought about this unity. This represents Man's elevation to the thought of that higher existence which produces the conditions necessary for the accomplishment of its end. The subject secures its own preservation, and the act whereby it does this is, further, in all living things an unconscious one, is what in animals we term instinct. The one gets its means of sustenance by force, the other produces it with the help of art. This it is which we term the wisdom of God in Nature, in which we meet with that infinitely manifold arrangement in respect of the various activities and conditions necessary to the existence of all particular things. When we consider all those particular forms in which the living being shows its activity, we find that they are contingent, so to speak; that they have not been produced by the subject itself, and necessitate the existence of a cause outside of them. The fact of life merely involves self-preservation in general; but living beings differ from one another in an infinite variety of ways, and this variety is the work of something other than themselves. The question is simply this, How does inorganic Nature pass over into organic Nature, and how is it possible for it to serve as a means for what is organic? We are here met by a peculiar conception of the way in which these two come together. Animals are inorganic as contrasted with men, and plants are inorganic as contrasted with animals. But Nature, which is in itself inorganic, as represented, for instance, by the sun, the moon, and in general by what appears in the form of means and material, is in the first instance immediate, and exists previous to the organic. Regarded in this way, the relation is one in which the inorganic is independent, while, on the other hand, the organic is what is dependent. The former, the so-called immediate, is the unconditioned. Inorganic Nature appears complete in itself; plants, animals, men, approach it in the first instance from the outside. The earth might have continued to exist without vegetation, the vegetable kingdom without animals, the animal kingdom without men. These various forms of existence thus seem to be independent and to be there for themselves. We are in the habit of referring to this as a matter of experience. Thus there are mountains without any vegetation, without animals and men. The moon has no atmosphere, there does not go on in it any meteorological process such as supplies the conditions necessary for vegetation. It thus exists without having any vegetative nature, and so on.

Inorganic existence of this kind appears as independent, and Man is related to it in an external way. The idea thus arises that Nature is in itself a producing force which creates blindly, and out of which vegetation comes. From this latter in turn comes what is animal, and then finally Man possessed of conscious thought. We can undoubtedly assert that Nature produces stages of which the one is always the condition of that which follows. But then, since organic life and Man thus appear on the scene in an accidental way, the question arises whether or not Man will get what is necessary. According to the idea referred to, this is equally a matter of chance, since here there is no unity having a valid existence on its own account. Aristotle gave expression to the same idea. Nature is constantly producing living things, and the point is whether or not these will be able to exist. Whether or not any of the things thus produced will be able to maintain itself, is a pure matter of accident. Nature has already made an endless number of attempts, and has produced a host of monstrosities; myriads of beings of various forms have issued from her which were not, however, able to continue in existence, and besides, she did not concern herself at all with the disappearance of such forms of life. By way of proving this assertion, people are in the habit of directing attention specially to the remains of monsters which are still to be found here and there. These species disappeared, it is asserted, because the conditions necessary to their existence had ceased. Regarded in this fashion, the harmony which exists between the organic and the inorganic is held to be accidental. There is here no necessity to begin and ask about a unity. The presence of design is itself affirmed to be accidental. Now, here is what is really involved in this conception. What, speaking generally, we call inorganic Nature as such is thought of as having an independent existence, while the organic is attached to it in an external fashion, so that it is a mere matter of chance whether or not the organic finds the conditions of existence in what confronts it. So far as the form of what essentially constitutes the conception is concerned, we have to remark that inorganic Nature is what comes first, is what is immediate. It was in harmony with the childlike ideas of the Mosaic age that the heavens and the earth, light, and so on, should have been thought of as created first, while the organic appeared later in point of time. The question is this : Is that the true definition or essential nature of the notion of the inorganic, and do living things and Man represent what is dependent ?   Philosophy, on the other hand, explains the truth involved in the definition of the notion ; and apart from this, Man is certain that he is related to the rest of Nature as an end, and that Nature is meant to be a means so far as he is concerned, and that this represents the relation in which the inorganic in general stands to the organic.   The organic is in its formal aspect, and by its very nature, something which exists in accordance with an end.   It is means and end, and is therefore something infinite in itself.   It is an end which returns back into itself ; and even regarded as something dependent on what is outside of it, it has the character of an end, and consequently it represents what is truly first in comparison with what has been termed the immediate, in comparison, that is, with Nature.   This immediacy is merely one-sided determination, and ought to be brought down to the level of something that is merely posited.   This is the true relation.   Man is not an accident added on to what is first ; but, on the contrary, the organic is itself what is first.   The inorganic has in it merely the semblance of Being.   This relation is logically developed in Science itself.

This relation, however, still involves an element of separation, as seen in the fact that the organic, regarded from one side, is related outwardly to inorganic Nature, which is not posited as existing in the organic itself. The living being develops out of the germ, and the development is the action of the limbs, the internal organs, and so on; the soul is the unity which brings this about. The truth, however, of organic and inorganic Nature here also is simply the essential relation between the two, their unity and inseparability. This unity is a third something which is neither the one nor the other. It is not found in immediate existence. The absolute determination which brings both, the organic as well as the inorganic, into unity, namely, the subject, is the organic; while the other appears as object, but changes itself into the predicate of the organic, into something which is held to belong to it. This is the reciprocal element in this relation. Both are put into one, and in this one each is something dependent and conditioned. We might call this third something, the thought to which consciousness raises itself, God, using the word in a general sense. It falls, however, very far short of the Notion of God. Taken in this sense, it represents the activity of production, which is a judgment whereby both sides are produced together. In the one Notion they harmonise and exist for one another. The thought to which we rise, namely, that the truth of the relation of ends is this third something, is thus absolutely correct, taking that third thing in the sense in which it has just been defined. Taken thus, however, it is defined in a formal way, and the definition rests, in fact, on something whose truth it is. It is itself living activity; but this is not yet Spirit, rational action. The correspondence between the Notion as representing the organic, and reality as representing the inorganic, simply expresses the essence of life itself. It is involved in a more definite form in what the ancients called the νοῦς. The world is a harmonious whole, an organic life which is determined in accordance with ends. It was this which the ancients held to be νοῦς, and, taken in a more extended signification, this life was also called the world-soul, the λόγος. All that is posited here is simply the fact of life, and it is not implied that the world-soul is distinguished as Spirit from this active life belonging to it. The soul is simply the living element in the organic; it is not something apart from the body, something material, but is rather the life-force which penetrates the body. Plato accordingly called God an immortal ζῶον, that is, an eternally living being. He did not get beyond the category of life. When we grasp the fact of life in its true nature, it is seen to be one principle, one organic life of the universe, one living system. All that is, simply constitutes the organs of the one subject. The planets which revolve round the sun are simply the giant members of this one system. Regarded in this fashion, the universe is not an aggregate of many accidents existing in a relation of indifference, but is a system endowed with life. With this thought we have not, however, yet reached the essential characteristic of Spirit.

We have considered the formal aspect of the relation of ends. The other aspect is that of the content. The question here may take any of the following forms: What are the essential characteristics of the end, or what is the content of the end which is being realised, or how are these ends constituted in respect of what is called wisdom? So far as the content is concerned, the starting-point is the same as that of experience. We start, that is, from immediate Being. The study of ends in the form in which we actually meet with them, has, when pursued from this side, contributed more than anything else to the neglect of the teleological proof, so much so indeed that this latter has come to be regarded with disdain. We are in the habit of speaking of the wise arrangements of Nature. The various and manifold kinds of animals are, as regards the real nature of the life they have, finite. The external means necessary for this life actually exist; life in its various forms is the end.　If accordingly we ask what the substance of this end is, it is seen to be nothing else save the preservation of these insects, of these animals, &c.　We may indeed find pleasure in contemplating their life; but the necessity of their nature and destiny is of an absolutely insignificant kind, or, to put it otherwise, is an absolutely insignificant conception.　When we say, God has made things thus, we are making a pious observation, we are rising to God; but when we think of God we have the idea of an absolute, infinite end, and these petty ends present a sharp contrast to what we recognise as His actual nature.　If we now consider what goes on in higher spheres of existence, and look at human ends, which we may regard as relatively the highest of all, we see that they are for the most part frustrated and disappear, leaving no permanent result.　In Nature millions of seeds perish just when they begin to exist, and without ever being able to develop the life-force in them.　The life of the largest portion of living things is based on the destruction of other living things; and the same holds good of higher ends.　If we traverse the domain of morality, and go on even to its highest stage, namely, civil life, and then consider whether the ends here are realised or not, we shall find, indeed, that much is attained, but that still more is rendered abortive, and destroyed by the passions and wickedness of men; and this is true of the greatest and most exalted ends.　We see the earth covered with ruins, with remains of the splendid edifices and works left by the finest nations whose ends we recognise as having a substantial value.　Great natural objects and human works do indeed endure and defy time, but all that splendid national life has irrecoverably perished.　We thus see how, on the one hand, petty, subordinate, even despicable designs are fulfilled; and, on the other, how those which are recognised as having substantial value are frustrated.　We are here certainly forced to rise to the thought of a higher determination and a higher end, when we thus lament the misfortune which has befallen so much that is of high value, and mourn its disappearance. We must regard all those ends, however much they interest us, as finite and subordinate, and ascribe to their finitude the destruction which overtakes them. But this universal end is not discoverable in experience, and thus the general character of the transition is altered, for the transition means that we start from something given, that we reason syllogistically from what we find in experience. But then what we find present in experience is characterised by limitation. The supreme end is the Good, the general final-end of the world. Reason has to regard this end as the absolute final-end of the world, and must look upon it as being based purely on the essential nature of reason, beyond which Spirit cannot go. Reason in the form of thought is, however, recognised as being the source of this end. The next step accordingly is that this end should show that it is accomplished in the world. But the Good is what has a determinate character in-and-for-itself by means of reason; and to this, Nature stands opposed, partly as physical Nature which follows its own course and its own laws, and partly as the natural element in Man, his particular ends which are opposed to the Good. If we go by what our senses show us, we find much that is good in the world, but also an infinite quantity of evil, and we would just have to reckon up the amount of evil, and the amount of good which does not attain realisation, in order to discover which preponderates. The Good, however, is something absolutely substantial; it belongs to the very essence of its nature that it should be realised. But it is something which merely *ought* to be real, for it cannot reveal itself in experience. It stops short with being something which ought to exist, something which is a postulate. But since the Good has not itself the power thus to realise itself, it is necessary to postulate a third thing through which the final-end of the world will be realised. This is an absolute postulate. Moral good belongs essentially to Man ; but since his power is finite, and since the realisation of the Good in him is limited owing to the natural element attaching to him, since, in fact, he is himself the enemy of the Good, it is not within his power to realise it. The existence of God is here conceived of simply as a postulate, as something that should be, and which should have for Man subjective certainty, because the Good represents what is ultimate in his reason. But this certainty is merely subjective; it remains merely a belief, an ideal, and it cannot be shown that it actually exists. Aye, if the Good is to be really moral and present, then we should have to go the length of requiring and presupposing the perpetual existence of the discord, for moral Good can only exist and can only *be* in so far as it is in conflict with evil. It would thus be necessary to postulate the perpetual existence of the enemy, of what is opposed to the Good. If, then, we turn to the content, we find it to be limited ; and if we go on to the supreme end, we find ourselves in another region, where we start from what is inward, not from what is actually present and supplied by experience. If, on the other hand, we start from experience, the Good, the final-end is something subjective merely, and in this case the contradiction between Man's finite life and the Good would have to exist always.

AMPLIFICATION OF THE TELEOLOGICAL AND ONTOLOGICAL PROOFS GIVEN IN THE LECTURES ON THE PHILOSOPHY OF RELIGION FOR THE YEAR 1827.

AMONGST the proofs of the existence of God, the Cosmological occupies the first place. Only in it is the affirmative, absolute Being, the Infinite, defined not merely as infinite in general, but, in contrast to the characteristic of contingency, as absolutely necessary. The True is the absolutely necessary Essence, and not merely Being or Essence.

This category already involves other characteristics. In fact, these proofs might be multiplied by dozens; each stage of the logical Idea may contribute its quota. The characteristic of absolute necessity is involved in the course of thought described.

The absolutely necessary Essence, taken in a general, abstract sense, is Being not as immediate, but as reflected into itself. We have defined Essence as the non-finite, the negation of that negative we term the finite. That to which we make the transition is thus not abstract Being, barren Being, but Being which is the negation of the negation.

It involves in it the element of difference, the difference which carries itself back into simplicity. In this Infinite, this absolute Being or Essence, there is thus involved the determination of difference, negation of the negation, but difference as it relates itself to itself. But determination of this kind is what we call self-determina-

tion.   Negation is determination or specification, negation
of determination is itself an act of determination.   To
posit a difference, is just to posit a determination.   Where
there is no negation, there is no difference, no determination.

In this unity, in this absolute Being, there is thus
involved determination in general, and it is indeed *in it*
since it is self-determination.   It is thus defined as
determination which is in itself and does not come from
without.   This unrest is involved in its very nature as
the negation of the negation, and this unrest determines
itself more definitely as activity.   This determination of
Essence in itself is Necessity in itself, the positing of
determination, of difference, and the cancelling and absorption of it in such a way that the one is action, and this
self-determination thus reached remains in simple relation
to itself.

Finite Being does not continue to be an Other ; there
is no gulf between the Infinite and the finite.   The
finite is something which cancels itself, loses itself in
something higher, so that its truth is the Infinite, what
has Being in-and-for-itself.   Finite, contingent Being is
something which implicitly negates itself, but this negation which it undergoes is just the Affirmative, a transition to affirmation, and this affirmation is the absolutely
necessary Essence.

Another form of the argument, the basis of which is
constituted by the same characteristic, and which is the
same in respect of the characteristic of the form, though
the content is greater, is seen in the Physico-theological
or Teleological Proof.   Here, too, we have finite Being
on one side ; but it is not determined merely abstractly
as Being only, but as something which has in it a determination with a richer content, that of something living.
Life taken in its more specific sense implies that there
are ends in Nature, and that there is an arrangement in
conformity with these ends, which is, at the same time,

not produced by these ends, so that the orderly arrangement is there independently for itself, and though from a different point of view it may be characterised as an end also, still what is thus actually given shows itself to be in conformity with these ends.

The physico-theological method of regarding the world can be merely the study of outward teleological arrangement, and so this way of looking at things has fallen into discredit, and justly too; for here we have to do merely with finite ends, which require means, as, for instance, the fact that Man requires this or that for his animal life. This might be further specified. If we regard these ends as something primary, and hold that there exist means for the satisfaction of these ends, and that it is God who permits these means to exist for the sake of such ends, then we very soon come to see that this method of regarding things is inadequate to express what God is.

These ends, in so far as they appear in definite special forms, are seen to be essentially unimportant, so that we cannot possibly hold them in high esteem, and cannot conceive that they represent something which is the direct object of the will and wisdom of God. All this has been summed up in one of Goethe's *Xenien*. There some one is represented as praising God the Creator, on the ground that He created the cork tree in order that we might have stoppers.

We may remark in reference to the Kantian philosophy that Kant, in his " Critique of Judgment," adduced the important conception of *inner* ends, that is, the conception of life-force. This is Aristotle's conception, namely, that every living thing is an end which has its means in itself, its members, its organisation; and the process of these members constitutes the end, that is to say, the movement of life.

This is infinite, not finite conformity to an end, in which end and means are not outside themselves. The means produces the end, and the end the means. The world is living, it contains the movement of life and the realm of living things. What has not life—inorganic Nature, the sun, the stars—stands in an essential and direct relation to what has life, and to Man in so far as he in a measure belongs to living Nature, and partly because he sets particular ends before himself. This finite conformity to an end is found in Man.

That is the characteristic note of life in general, and at the same time of life as it actually is, life as seen in the world. This, it is true, is life in itself, inner conformity to an end; but it means that each kind or species of life represents a very narrow sphere, and has a very limited nature.

The real advance accordingly is from this finite mode of life to absolute, universal conformity to an end, to the thought that this world is a κόσμος, a system, in which everything has an essential relation to everything else, and nothing is isolated; something which is regularly arranged in itself, in which everything has its place, is closely connected with the whole, subsists through the whole, and thus takes an active part in the production, in the life of the whole.

The main point thus is that a transition is made from finite life to one universal life, to one end which is articulated into particular ends, in such a way that in this particularisation things are in a condition of harmony and of reciprocal essential relation.

God is defined, to begin with, as the absolutely necessary Essence; but this definition, as Kant has already observed, falls very far short of expressing the conception of God. God alone is the absolute necessity, but this definition does not exhaust the conception of God; the definition in which He is described as the universal life-force, the one universal life, is both higher and deeper.

Since life is essentially subjectivity, something living, this universal life is subjective, the νοῦς, a soul. Thus the idea of the soul is involved in the universal life, the characteristic of the one all-disposing, all-ruling, organising νοῦς.

As regards the formal element here, we have to note the very same thing as we found in connection with the previous proofs. We have here once more the transition of the Understanding; *because* there are arrangements, ends of a like kind, there is a wisdom which disposes and orders everything. But the act of rising to this thought involves at the same time the negative moment, which is the main point, namely, that this life, these ends as they actually are, and as existing in their immediate finite form, do not represent what is true. On the contrary, it is this one life movement, this one νοῦς, which is what is true.

There are not two things; there is indeed a starting-point, but the mediation is of such a character that in the transition what is the first does not continue to be the basis, the condition. On the contrary, its untruth, its negation, is involved in this transition; the negation of the negative, finite element in it, the negation of the particularity of life. This negative is negated, and in this act of elevation, finite particularity disappears. As representing truth, the object of consciousness is the system of one life movement, the νοῦς of one life movement, the soul, the Universal Soul.

Here it happens again that this definition: God is the one universal active force of life, the soul which produces, posits, organises a κόσμος, is a conception which does not yet suffice to express the conception of God. It is essentially involved in the conception of God that He is Spirit.

We have still to consider the third, essential and absolute form from this point of view. In the transition just referred to, the content was life, the finite life movement, immediate life which actually exists. Here in the third form the content which forms the basis is

Spirit. Put in the form of a syllogism, it runs thus: Because finite minds exist or are,—and it is Being which here constitutes the starting-point,—therefore the absolute Mind or Spirit exists or is.

But this "because," this merely affirmative relation, is defective in this respect, that the finite minds would require to be thought of as the basis, and God would be a consequence of the existence of finite minds. The true form is: There are finite minds, but the finite has no truth, the truth of the finite spirit is the absolute Spirit.

The finitude of finite minds is no true Being; it is by its very nature dialectic, which implies that it abrogates itself, negates itself, and the negation of this finitude is affirmation as infinitude, as something universal in-and-for-itself. This is the highest form of the transition; for the transition is here Spirit itself.

There are in this connection two characteristics, Being and God. In so far as we start from Being, this latter, looked at as it first shows itself, is directly finite. Since these characteristics exist, we could equally as well begin from God and go on to Being, though, when we say we could, we must remember that we cannot speak of what we can do in connection with the conception of God, because He is absolute necessity.

This starting-point when it thus appears in finite form does not yet involve Being; for a God who is not, is something finite, and is not truly God. The finitude of this relation consists in the fact that it is subjective, that it is this general conception in fact. God has existence, but He has only this purely finite existence in our idea of Him.

This is one-sided; we have introduced into this content, namely, God, the taint of that one-sidedness, that finitude, which is termed the idea of God. The main point is that the idea should get rid of this defect whereby it is something merely represented in the mind, something subjective, and that this content should have attached to it the determination of Being.

We have to consider this second mediation as it appears in this finite form, or form of the Understanding, in the shape of the Ontological Proof. This proof starts from the Notion or conception of God, and goes from this to Being. We do not find this transition amongst the ancients, for instance in Greek philosophy, nor was it made in the Christian Church till after a long time. It was one of the great scholastic philosophers, Anselm, Archbishop of Canterbury, that profound, philosophical thinker, who first grasped this idea.

We have the idea of God ; but He is not merely an idea, He is. How are we to make this transition ? How are we to get to see that God is not merely something subjective in us ? How is this determination of Being to be mediated with God ?

The Kantian criticism was directed against this so-called Ontological Proof too, and with triumphant success, so to speak, in its day. It is still held at the present day that these proofs have been refuted as being worthless efforts on the part of the Understanding. We have, however, already recognised the fact that the act whereby these higher thoughts are here reached is the act of Spirit, the act peculiarly belonging to thinking Spirit, which Man will not renounce the right to exercise ; and so, too, this proof is an act of the same sort.

The ancients did not know of this transition ; for, in order to arrive at it, it is necessary that Spirit should go down into itself as deeply as possible. Spirit, when once it has arrived at its highest form of freedom, namely, subjectivity, first conceives this thought of God as subjective, and reaches first this antithesis of subjectivity and objectivity.

Anselm expressed the nature of this transition in the following fashion. The idea of God is that He is absolutely perfect. If accordingly we think of God only as idea, then we find that what is merely subjective, and merely represented in the form of an idea, is defective, and not perfect; for that is the more perfect which is not merely represented as an idea, but also *is*, really is. Therefore, since God is what is most perfect, He is not idea merely, but, on the contrary, He is possessed of actuality or reality.

The later, broader, and more rational form which represents the development of this thought of Anselm asserts that the conception or Notion of God implies that He is the Substance of all realities, the most real Essence. But Being also is reality, therefore Being belongs to Him.

It has been urged against this that Being is no reality, that it does not belong to the reality of a notion. Reality in a notion or conception implies determinate content in a notion, but Being adds nothing to the notion or to the content of the notion. Kant has put it in the following plausible form: I form an idea of a hundred thalers; but the notion or conception, the determinateness of the content is the same whether I form an idea of them, or whether I actually possess them.

As against the first proposition that Being ought to follow from the Notion in general, it has been urged that Notion and Being are different from each other: the Notion thus exists for itself, while Being is different. Being must come to the Notion from the outside, from elsewhere. Being is not involved in the Notion. This can be put in a very plausible way by the aid of the hundred thalers.

In ordinary life an idea of a hundred thalers is called a notion or conception. That is not a notion at all in which you may have any kind of determination of content. It is certainly true that Being may not belong to an abstract sense-idea such as blue, or to any determinateness of the Understanding which happens to be in my mind; but then this ought not to be called a notion.

The Notion, and still more the absolute Notion, the Notion in-and-for-itself, the Notion of God, is to be taken for itself, and this Notion contains Being as a determinate characteristic. Being is a form of the determinateness of the Notion. This may easily be shown to be the case in two ways.

First of all, the Notion is essentially the Universal which determines itself, which particularises itself; it is what has the active power of differentiation, of particularising and determining itself, of positing a finitude, and of negating this its own finitude, and of being through the negation of this finitude identical with itself.

This is the Notion in general. This is just what the Notion of God, the absolute Notion, God, really is. God as Spirit or as love means that God particularises Himself, begets the Son, creates the world, an Other of Himself, and possesses Himself, is identical with Himself, in this Other.

In the Notion in general, and still more in the Idea, what, in fact, we see is, that through the negation of the particularisation, the positing of which is at the same time the work of the activity which He Himself is, He is identical with Himself, relates Himself to Himself.

The primary question is, What is Being? what is this attribute, this determinateness, namely, reality? Being is nothing but the unutterable, the inconceivable; it is not that concrete something which the Notion is, but merely the abstraction of reference to self. We may say, it is immediacy, Being is the Immediate in general, and conversely the Immediate is Being, it is in relation to itself, that is, the mediation is negated.

This determination, namely, reference to self, or immediacy, accordingly directly exists for itself in the Notion in general, and it is involved in the absolute Notion, in the Notion of God, that He is reference to self. This abstract reference to self is directly found in the Notion itself.

The Notion is what has life, what is self-mediating; and so Being, too, is one of its characteristics. Being is different from the Notion to this extent, that Being is not the entire Notion, but is only one of its characteristics, merely that simple aspect of the Notion in virtue of which it is at home with itself, is self-identity.

Being is the determination which is found in the Notion as something different from the Notion, because the Notion is the whole of which Being is only one determination. The other point is that the Notion contains this determination in itself, this latter is one of its determinations; but Being is also different from the Notion, because the Notion is the totality. In so far as they are different, mediation forms a necessary element in their union.

They are not immediately identical; all immediacy is true and real only in so far as it is mediation within self, and conversely all mediation, in so far as it is immediacy in itself, has reference to self. The Notion is different from Being, and the peculiar quality of the difference lies in this that the Notion absorbs and abolishes it.

The Notion is the totality, represented by the movement, the process, whereby it makes itself objective. The Notion as such, as distinct from Being, is something purely subjective, and that implies a defect. The Notion, however, is all that is deepest and highest. The very idea of the Notion implies that it has to do away with this defect of subjectivity, with this distinction between itself and Being, and has to objectify itself. It is itself the act of producing itself as something which has Being, as something objective.

Whenever we think of the Notion, we must give up the idea that it is something which *we* only possess, and construct within ourselves. The Notion is the Soul, the final-end of an object, of what has life; what we call Soul is the Notion, and in Spirit, in consciousness, the

Notion as such attains to existence as a free Notion existing in its subjectivity as distinct from its reality as such.

The sun, the animal *is* the Notion merely, but has not the Notion; for them the Notion has not become objective. It is in consciousness and not in the sun that we find that division which is called I, the existing Notion, the Notion in its subjective reality, and I, this Notion, am the subjective.

No man, however, is content with his mere self-hood. The Ego is active, and this activity shows itself in objectifying self, in giving to it reality, definite existence. In its more extended and concrete signification, this activity of the Notion is impulse. All sense of satisfaction arises through this process whereby subjectivity is done away with, and what is inward and subjective is posited as at the same time outward, objective, and real, that process by which the unity of the merely subjective and merely objective is brought about, and the two are stripped of their one-sidedness.

There is nothing so well illustrated by all that goes on in the world as the abolition of the antithesis of subjective and objective, whereby the unity of the two is effected.

The thought of Anselm, therefore, so far as its content is concerned, is the truer and more necessary thought; but the form of the proof deduced from it is certainly defective in the same way as the modes of mediation previously referred to. This unity of Notion and Being is hypothetical, and its defect consists just in the very fact of its being hypothetical.

What is presupposed is that the pure Notion, the Notion in-and-for-itself, the Notion of God, *is*, involves Being also.

If we compare this content with faith or immediate knowledge, we shall find that the content is the same as that of Anselm's presupposition.

When the matter is regarded from this standpoint of immediate knowledge, what is said is this. It is a fact of consciousness that I have the idea of God, and along with this idea, Being must be given, so that Being is bound up with the content of the idea. If it is said that we believe it, that we know it immediately, then the unity of the idea and Being is expressed in the form of the presupposition just exactly as it is in Anselm's argument, and we have not got one bit further. This is the presupposition we everywhere meet with in Spinoza too. He defines the Absolute Cause, Substance, as that which cannot be thought of as not existing, the conception of which involves existence; that is, the idea of God is directly bound up with Being.

This inseparableness of Notion and Being is found in an absolute form only in the case of God. The finitude of things consists in the fact that the Notion, and the determinate form of the Notion, and the Being of the Notion, are essentially different. The finite is what does not correspond to its notion or rather to *the* Notion.

We have the notion of Soul; the reality, the Being is represented by the corporeal form. Man is mortal; we express this truth also by saying, Soul and body can part. There we have the fact of separation, but in the pure Notion we have the inseparableness referred to.

When we say that every impulse is an example of the Notion which realises itself, we are saying what is formally correct; the impulse which has received satisfaction is undoubtedly infinite so far as the form is concerned. But the impulse has a content, and so far as the determinate character of its content is concerned, it is finite and limited; in this respect it does not correspond to the Notion, to the pure Notion.

This is the explanation of what is involved in the standpoint of the knowledge of the Notion. What was considered last was the knowledge of God, the certainty of the existence of God in general. The essential thought in this connection is the following. When we have knowledge of an object, the object is before us; we are directly related to it. But this immediacy involves mediation, what was called the act of rising to God, the fact that the human spirit comes to consider the finite as non-existent.

By means of this negation Man's spirit raises itself to God, brings itself into harmony with God. The conclusion : I know that God is, is the simple relation which has originated in this negation.

AMPLIFICATION OF THE ONTOLOGICAL PROOF IN THE LECTURES ON THE PHILOSOPHY OF RELIGION FOR THE YEAR 1831.

In the sphere of revealed religion what we have first to consider is the abstract Notion or conception of God. This free, pure revealed Notion is what forms the basis. The manifestation of the Notion, its Being for an Other, is its existence, and the region in which this existence shows itself is the finite spirit. This is the second point —finite Spirit and finite consciousness are concrete. The chief thing in this religion is to attain to a knowledge of the process whereby God manifests Himself in the finite spirit, and is identical with Himself in it. The third point is the identity of the Notion and existence. Identity here is, strictly speaking, an awkward expression, for what we have in God is essentially life.

In the forms hitherto treated of we advanced from what was lower to what was higher, and took as the starting-point one definite form of existence regarded in its different aspects. Being was first taken in its most comprehensive aspect as contingent Being, in the Cosmological Proof. The truth of contingent Being is Being necessary in-and-for-itself. Existence was then further conceived of as involving relations of ends, and this supplied us with the Teleological Proof. Here there is an advance, a beginning from existence as actually given and present. These proofs consequently form part of the finite determination of God. The Notion of God is that of something boundless, not boundless in the bad sense, but rather as representing what has at the same time the most determinate character possible, pure self-determination. These first proofs belong to the domain of finite connection, of finite determination, since we start with what is given. Here, on the other hand, the starting-point is the free, pure Notion, and it is accordingly at this stage that we meet with the Ontological Proof of the existence of God. It constitutes the abstract metaphysical basis of this stage. It was first discovered in Christendom by Anselm of Canterbury. It was then further developed by all the later philosophers, by Descartes, Leibnitz, and Wolff, yet always along with the other proofs, though it alone is the true one. The Ontological Proof starts from the Notion. The Notion is considered to be something subjective, and is defined as something opposed to the object and to reality. Here it constitutes the starting-point, and what we have got to do is to show that Being, too, belongs to this Notion. The exact method of procedure is as follows. The Notion of God is first of all described, and it is shown that He cannot be conceived of unless as including Being in Himself. In so far as Being is separated from the Notion, God exists in a merely subjective way in our thought. As thus subjective He is imperfect, and imperfection belongs only to finite Spirit. It has to be shown that it is not only our notion which exists, but that He exists independent of our thinking. Anselm states the proof in the following simple form : God is what is most perfect, beyond which nothing can be thought of as existing; if God is merely an idea, then He is not what is most perfect. This, however, is in contradiction with the first statement; for we consider that as perfect which is not merely an idea, but which is also possessed of Being. If God is merely subjective, we could bring forward something higher which would be possessed of Being as well. This is further developed as follows. We begin with what is most perfect, and this is defined as the most real Essence, as the Substance.

of all realities. This has been termed possibility. The Notion as subjective, since it is distinguished from Being, is merely what is possible, or at all events it ought to be what is possible. According to the old Logic, possibility exists only where it can be shown that no contradiction exists. Realities are, in accordance with this idea, to be considered as existing in God only in their affirmative aspect, as limitless, and in such a way that negation is supposed to be eliminated. But it is easy to prove that in this case all that is left is the abstraction of something which is one with itself. For when we speak of realities we mean to imply that they represent different characteristics, such as wisdom, righteousness, almighty power, omniscience. These characteristics are attributes which may easily be shown to be in contradiction with each other. Goodness is not righteousness; absolute power is in contradiction with wisdom; for this latter presupposes final-ends. Power, on the other hand, means the limitlessness of negation and production. If, as is demanded, the Notion is not to contradict itself, all determinateness must be dropped, for every judgment or difference advances to the state of opposition. God is the Substance of all realities, it is said, and since one of these is Being, Being is consequently united with the Notion. This proof maintained itself until recent times, and we find it worked out particularly in Mendelssohn's "Morning Hours." Spinoza defines the Notion or conception of God by saying that it is that which cannot be conceived of apart from Being. The finite is something whose existence does not correspond to the Notion. The species is realised in existing individuals, but these are transitory ; the species is the Universal for itself. In the case of the finite, existence does not correspond to the Notion. On the other hand, in the case of the Infinite, which is determined within itself, the reality must correspond to the Notion ; this is the Idea, the unity of subject and object. Kant criticised

this proof, and the objections he urged against it were as
follows. If God is defined as the Substance of all realities, then Being does not belong to Him, for Being is no
reality. It makes no difference to the Notion or conception whether it exists or does not exist, it remains the
same. Already in Anselm's day this objection was urged
by a monk who said, " The fact of my forming an idea of
anything does not therefore imply that the thing exists."
Kant maintains that a hundred thalers really remain the
same whether I merely form an idea of them or actually
possess them ; consequently Being is not a reality, or real
predicate, since nothing is added by it to the Notion. It
may be granted that Being is not any determinate content ; all the same, nothing certainly should be added to
the Notion. (We may remark in passing that to speak
of every wretched form of existence as a notion is to go
on quite wrong lines.) On the contrary, it should be rid
of the defect attaching to it in that it is merely something subjective, and is not the Idea. The Notion which
is only something subjective, and is divorced from Being,
is a nullity. In the form of the proof as given by
Anselm, the infinitude consists in the very fact that it
is not one-sided, something purely subjective to which
Being does not attach. The Understanding keeps Being
and the Notion strictly apart, and considers each as self-
identical. But even according to the ordinary idea the
Notion apart from Being is considered one-sided and untrue, and so, too, Being in which there is no Notion is
looked on as notionless Being, Being which is inconceivable. This antithesis which is found in finitude cannot
have any place in connection with the Infinite or God.

But it is the following circumstance which makes the
proof unsatisfactory. That most perfect and most real
existence is in fact a presupposition measured by which
Being for itself and the Notion for itself are one-sided.
Descartes and Spinoza defined God as the cause of Himself. Notion and existence form an identity ; in other

words, God as Notion cannot be conceived of without Being. What is unsatisfactory in this view is that we have here a presupposition, and this means that the Notion measured by this standard of hypothetical necessity must be something subjective.

The finite and subjective, however, is not finite only as measured by the standard supplied by that presupposition. It is finite in itself, and is consequently the antithesis of itself. It is the unsolved contradiction. Being is supposed to be distinct from the Notion. We may imagine we can regard this latter as strictly subjective, as finite; but the essential characteristic of Being is in the Notion itself. This finitude of subjectivity is done away with in the Notion itself, and the unity of Being and the Notion is not a presupposition relatively to the latter, and by which it is measured. Being in its immediacy is contingent, and we have seen that its truth is necessity. The Notion necessarily involves Being, and this is simple reference to self, the absence of mediation. If we consider the Notion, we find it to be that in which all difference is absorbed, and in which all determinations are merely ideal. This ideality is mediation or difference, which has been absorbed and removed, perfect clearness, pure transparency, being at home with self. The freedom of the Notion is just absolute reference to self, identity which is also immediacy, unity without mediation. The Notion thus has Being in itself potentially. Its very meaning is that it does away with its one-sidedness. The idea that Being can be separated from the Notion is a mere fancy. When Kant says that it is impossible to extract reality from the Notion, he is thinking of the Notion as something finite. But the finite is just what annuls itself; and if we were to think of the Notion in this way as divorced from Being, we should just have that very reference to self which Being essentially is.

The Notion, however, has not Being in itself potentially

only. It is not seen to be there merely *by us;* but, on the contrary, the Notion is actual Being, Being for itself also. It abolishes its subjectivity, and objectifies itself. Man realises his ends; that is, what was, to begin with, merely ideal loses its one-sidedness, and is consequently made into something which has Being. The Notion shows itself eternally in that activity whereby Being is posited as identical with itself. In perception, feeling, &c., we have outward objects before us; but we take them up into ourselves, and thus the objects are ideal in us. The Notion is thus the continuous act whereby it abolishes its difference. When we regard closely the nature of the Notion, we see that this identity with Being is no longer a presupposition, but a result. The course of procedure is as follows: the Notion makes itself objective, turns itself into reality, and is thus the truth, the unity of subject and object. God is an immortal living Being, says Plato, whose body and soul are united in one. Those who separate the two sides do not get beyond what is finite and untrue.

The standpoint which we here occupy is the Christian one. We have here the Notion of God in its entire freedom. This Notion is identical with Being. Being is the poorest of all abstractions; but the Notion is not so poor as not to contain this determination in it. We have not to deal with Being in the poverty of abstraction, in immediacy in its bad form, but with Being as the Being of God, as absolutely concrete Being, distinguished from God. The consciousness of finite Spirit is concrete Being, the material for the realisation of the Notion of God. Here it is not a question of any addition of Being to the Notion, or merely of a unity of the Notion and Being — such expressions are awkward and misleading. The unity is rather to be conceived of as an absolute process, as the living movement of God, and this means that the two sides are distinguished from each other, while the process is thought of as that absolute, con-

tinuous act of eternal self-production. Here we have
the concrete and popular idea of God as Spirit. The
Notion of Spirit is the Notion which has Being in-
and-for-itself, that is to say, knowledge. This infinite
Notion is negative reference to self. When thus posited
it is judgment, the act of distinguishing, self-differentiation. But what is thus differentiated, and which at first
appears as something outward, devoid of Spirit, outside
of God, is really identical with the Notion. The development of this Idea is the absolute truth. In the Christian
religion it is known that God has revealed Himself, and
it is the very nature of God to reveal Himself, and to
reveal is to differentiate. What is revealed is just that
God is the revealed God.

Religion must be something for all men ; for those
who have so purified their thought that they know what
exists in the pure element of thought, and who have
arrived at a philosophical knowledge of what God is, as
well as for such as have not got beyond feeling and
ordinary ideas.

Man is not merely pure thought. On the contrary,
thought manifests itself as perception or picture-thought,
or in the form of ordinary ideas. The absolute truth
which is revealed to Man must therefore exist for him
as a being who forms general ideas and sensuous images,
who has feelings and sensations. This is the mark by
which religion in general is distinguished from philosophy.
Philosophy *thinks* what otherwise exists only for the
ordinary idea and sensuous perception. Man who thus
forms general ideas, is in his character as Man a thinking being also, and the substance of religion comes to
him as a being who thinks. It is only a thinking being
that can have a religion, and to think is also to form
ideas, though the former act alone is the free form of
truth. The Understanding thinks too, but it does not
get beyond identity; for it the Notion is Notion, and
Being is Being. These two one-sided categories always

keep this one-sided form, so far as it is concerned. In their true nature, on the other hand, these finite forms are no longer held to be inherently identical on the ground that they *are*, but rather they are considered to be merely moments of a totality.

Those who find fault with philosophy for thinking religion, for stating religion in terms of thought, don't know what they want. Hatred and vanity here come directly into play under the outward guise of humility. True humility consists in having the spirit absorbed in the truth, in losing ourselves in what is most inward, in having within us the object, and the object only. Thus anything subjective which may still be present in feeling, disappears. We have to consider the Idea from the purely speculative point of view, and to justify its claims as against the Understanding, and against it as being hostile to all content of religion whatsoever. This content is called a mystery, because it is something hidden from the Understanding; for the latter does not get the length of the process which this unity is, and thus it is that everything speculative, everything philosophical, is for the Understanding a mystery.

INDEX

VOL. III.

THE END